A WOMAN'S WORK IS NEVER DONE

By the same author

One Family, Two Empires:
The Spanish Hapsburgs, The Hapsburgs in Europe
(published by H. B. J. Press)

edited

Science in Contemporary China
(published by Stanford University Press)

The Country Housewife and Lady's Director
(published by Prospect Books)

A WOMAN'S WORK IS NEVER DONE

A history of housework in
the British Isles 1650–1950
by Caroline Davidson

Chatto & Windus · London · 1982

Published by Chatto & Windus Ltd
40 William IV Street, London WC2N 4DF

Clarke, Irwin & Co. Ltd, Toronto

BRITISH LIBRARY CATALOGUING IN PUBLICATION DATA

Davidson, Caroline
    A woman's work is never done.
    1. Housewives – Great Britain – History
    2. Home economics – Great Britain –
    3. History
    I. Title
    648'.0941   TX323

ISBN 0 7011 3901 3

The author acknowledges permission to reproduce
copyright material as follows:
Extracts from *A Kind of Magic* by Mollie Harris, Chatto & Windus;
Lark Rise to Candleford by Flora Thompson, Oxford University Press.

Phototypeset by Western Printing Services, Bristol
Printed in Great Britain by
Butler & Tanner, Frome, Somerset

Contents

for Clive Cookson,
my beloved husband

Acknowledgements

During the six years I have spent working on this book I have received a great deal of help and encouragement from my family and a large number of friends. I thank them all, from the bottom of my heart.

In England I am particularly grateful to Jennifer Stead for her wonderful letters on Yorkshire scouring habits, Honor Godfrey for interesting me in the design of domestic appliances, Betty Palmer for improving my prose, Elizabeth David for scrutinizing my cooking chapter, Peter Thornton for teaching me to look at pictures properly, and Christine Adams for assistance in searching for them. My parents, Alan and Jane Davidson, and my aunt, Rosemary Davidson, deserve special awards for their patient support, editorial and otherwise, but I cannot possibly enumerate all the ways in which they have helped me over the years. I would also like to thank all those who kindly put me up while I worked in nearby libraries and museums. Graham Nicholson, Joanna Innes and Peter and Judith Judd were especially generous with accommodation in Cambridge, as was my sister Pamela in Oxford. Finally, my thanks go to the Phoenix Trust for contributing to the cost of the illustrations and to Hugo Brunner, who could not have been a more inspiring editor.

In America I am indebted to many members of the Library of Congress for outstanding bibliographical advice. I also received valuable assistance from Frank Sommer at Winterthur and John Davis and his colleagues at Colonial Williamsburg. Thomas Laqueur, John Edwards, and Karen Offen made useful criticisms of specific chapters. But the person who helped me most on this side of the Atlantic was Marybeth Jones who typed successive drafts of the book, commenting perceptively on each.

Washington, D C
July 1981

INTRODUCTION

The majority of women throughout the history of the world have spent their lives doing housework. No other occupation can boast nearly half the population as its work force; and no other form of labour can claim such an immediate impact on people's way of life. For these reasons alone, the history of housework is clearly an extremely important subject. But it also offers fascinating insights into a society's values and cultural characteristics and an invaluable perspective from which to view its economic and industrial development.

Yet despite all this, the history of housework is not a recognized field of scholarly enquiry. It has been almost entirely ignored – not only by historians, but by economists, anthropologists and sociologists too. By contrast, most other aspects of women's history have attracted attention. A great deal is now known about such topics as women's education, their participation in the labour market, fertility, political and legal rights, economic status, social roles etc. etc. There are also numerous biographies of women whose lives are deemed exceptional for one reason or another. There is no clear explanation for this curiously lop-sided approach to women's history. One can point to the low status of housework, the difficulties of categorizing it economically, and people's inclination to concentrate on the unusual rather than the hum-drum happenings of everyday life, but this does not wholly account for the imbalance.

What is housework? The answer might well seem obvious. But when I was half-way through writing this book, a sudden impulse sent me to the *Shorter Oxford English Dictionary* to look the word up. To my consternation, there was no separate entry for housework. I looked under 'house' and found a three-word definition that read 'cleaning, cooking etc.'. Somewhat perturbed, I went to the multi-volume supplement of the *Oxford English Dictionary*. Surely here there would be sufficient space to define the work that has kept women busy throughout history? But no. Housework was still one of many words with the prefix 'house', although the definition had been expanded to 'the work required to keep a house clean and in order'.

In fact housework means a great deal more than cooking and cleaning and keeping a house in order; it includes every activity required to maintain a home and meet the physical needs of its members (usually a family). The union of the two words 'house' and 'work' implies that these activities are conducted within the home. But this is not always the case: as we shall see, housework can also be done out of doors, some distance away.

Apart from preparing food, housework does not consist of a fixed body of activities common to all peoples at all times; its scope varies from one culture and time to another. It does not, however, include child care, a distinct occupation, or cottage industries carried on within the home. Nor should it be confused with housekeeping, the term for *managing* household affairs.

This book is concerned with the history of housework in the British Isles between 1650 and 1950. The geographical area and period covered are carefully chosen to show the effects of rapid industrialization and urbanization on housework and domestic life in general. Britain is particularly interesting from this point of view because it was the first country in the world to experience a fully-fledged industrial revolution.

The changes which took place during these three centuries were truly remarkable. In 1650 the British Isles were sparsely populated. There were less than five million inhabitants in England and Wales. Over three quarters of them lived in the countryside, in villages and hamlets, and they earned their livelihood mainly from the land.[1] There were some small towns, but only one major city, London. Manufacturing industry and mining were conducted on a small scale. Transport and communications, except by sea, were very poor. Most people were born, married and buried within the same county and communities were largely self-sufficient.

A century later, the population of England and Wales had grown to just over six million. London, with 675,000 inhabitants, was the major centre for economic and intellectual life, accounting for 11 per cent of the total population and 46 per cent of city dwellers, but at least 50 other towns now had populations of over 5,000.[2] Some areas in the north and midlands of England were showing incipient signs of industrialization. The coal, iron and textile industries were soon to be transformed by steam power and other unprecedented developments in technology.

In 1850 Britain was preparing to hold the Great Exhibition, which celebrated its stature as the industrialized giant of the world. The sooty fingerprints of industry smudged the landscape of the midlands and north of England. Canals, roads, and railway lines criss-crossed the country.[3] According to the census of 1851, the population of England and Wales now stood at 17.9 million and was roughly balanced between rural and urban areas.

By 1950 the classical phase of the Industrial Revolution was more or less complete. The population of England and Wales had swollen to 43 million and most people (about three-quarters in the 1930s) lived in towns and cities.[4] Only one in 20 persons earned their living by agriculture.[5]

There is an abundance of printed materials shedding light on domestic life during these three centuries. To write this book, I have not had to decipher the hand-writing of obscure manuscripts or confine myself to predictable sources of information such as diaries, memoirs, autobiographies, and novels, valuable as these are. Nor have I had to pay undue attention to cook books, housekeeping manuals and women's magazines, which tend to reflect domestic ideals rather than domestic reality. Instead, I have immersed myself, with considerable profit, in two literary genres that became extraordinarily popular in the eighteenth and nineteenth centuries: the travelogue and the local history book. These are not only charmingly written (often by adventurous eccentrics and observant clergymen), but invariably packed full of pertinent information. I have also made use of account books and inventories of household possessions, which survive in large numbers, from rich and poor alike. For insights into the lives and attitudes of agricultural labourers and industrial artisans up till the early nineteenth century I have read the chap-books and penny histories that they read themselves, as well as the works by which philanthropists hoped to raise their standard of living; but for working-class life in the later period, I have relied more on parliamentary reports and socialist tracts.

In tracing the technological changes that have affected housework, I started off by looking at patents, but soon found that mechanical treatises, industrial histories and scientific/technical journals were rather more enlightening. Finally, as a balance to all these written sources of information I have searched for pictures of people engaged in domestic activities. But in contrast to other European countries, notably Holland and France, British artists did not often draw or paint household scenes. Depictions of domestic life are generally to be found in prints, book illustrations and advertisements, all of which, significantly, are printed art forms.

The title of *A Woman's Work is Never Done* comes from a seventeenth-century ballad that was rewritten over the centuries to take account of intervening changes in the nature and scope of housework. (See Appendix for one of three different versions.) The book itself consists of a series of linked but self-contained essays on the history of housework between 1650 and 1950.

To begin with, there is an account of the spread of piped water supplies to people's houses, which was the single most important change in housework during the three centuries. The spread of gas and electricity supplies, being better known and less significant, is treated more briefly.

There follows the history of cooking, heating, lighting, cleaning and laundry. These, along with fetching water, were the most important household tasks during the three centuries. As will be seen, they all changed fundamentally, but only water carrying and lighting disappeared completely.

Other aspects of housework might have been included but were not. For example, the production of food for home consumption was excluded on the grounds that it was extremely difficult (if not impossible) to distinguish it from farming and animal husbandry. A women with more than two cows would send most of the butter and cheese she made to market. If she kept poultry, as many rural women did, she would sell eggs and chickens as a side line. Much the same applies to pig-keeping. After slaughtering a pig, a household often gave some of its meat away to neighbours in payment for past favours or sold it. The processing and preserving of raw foodstuffs are also rather difficult to categorize as housework, even though this work took place in or near the home. In the first place, such activities as the grinding of corn in a quern, the storage of grains and root vegetables, the preserving of fruit and the salting of meat, have more to

1 *'The tythe pig', coloured engraving, c. 1760. A country parson has come to claim his tythes, but the farmer and his wife, who have ten children to support, would clearly prefer to hand over their latest born rather than the young suckling pig the parson has his eye on. Pigs and poultry were kept near the house. While poultry-keeping was women's work, the care of pigs fell to the whole family.*

2 *'Rustic Courtship', detail from a coloured etching by Thomas Rowlandson, 1785. It was very common for women to spin out of doors because the light was better and they could chat to passers-by.*

do with running a farm than a house; and in the second, men were just as deeply involved in them as women. Indeed before the 1780s, when the practice of brewing beer at home began to die out, it was as common to find a man at the wort tub as a woman.

Textile production has also been omitted for good reasons: it was only undertaken by a minority of women in the remoter parts of Britain; it had largely died out by the early nineteenth century; and it frequently constituted a cottage industry. Mending clothes and sewing, on the other hand, were universal domestic chores. But as these dismal tasks hardly changed, even with the advent of the sewing machine in the late nineteenth century, they did not seem to merit a chapter of their own.

3 *Women knitting with four needles, photographed in 1876 by Arthur Munby, an eccentric civil servant.*
4 *An old woman sewing. From a manuscript sketch book kept by Caroline Elizabeth Hamilton in 1838. She lived in Dublin.*

The concluding section of the book discusses the following questions: the importance of domestic servants; the time women spent on housework and whether this diminished with the spread of the three utilities and time- and labour-saving appliances; the extent to which men and children helped with household tasks; what women thought about housework and why they exercised almost no control over the technology that changed it.

All historians have special interests and I must be frank about mine. Although this book concerns the domestic practices of all social classes between 1650 and 1950, I am more concerned with the domestic lives of the agricultural and industrial working-classes than those of their social betters and more interested in seventeenth- and eighteenth-century developments than those that occurred later. Readers should not be surprised, therefore, to find detailed descriptions of early water-raising techniques but few details about the manufacture of coal-gas. Nor should they be disconcerted to learn more about the homes of Irish peasants, Scottish Highlanders, Cornish tin miners, Midland artisans and impoverished Londoners than those of the aristocracy. But enough introductory remarks. It is important to start reading about why a woman's work is never done . . .

Chapter 1 WATER

Louis J. Jennings was on a walking tour in Surrey in 1876 when he met a thin, miserable looking woman near a little roadside spring. She was walking inside a hoop, with a pail of water in each hand. Jennings, astonished to see that the water was splashing all over her worn gown, suggested that she put a flat piece of wood on top of the water in each pail to prevent the slopping. To his surprise, the woman said she had never heard of such a thing. She then revealed that she had to fetch all the water needed for her husband, her three young children, and her pig from the spring, which was a quarter of a mile away from her cottage. When the spring dried up she had to go even further.[1]

Because Jennings was an American and anxious to learn about British ways, he described this sad encounter in some detail. There was, however, nothing unusual about the plight of the women he met. Obtaining and transporting water was an onerous and everyday task for most women until the late nineteenth and early twentieth centuries, when the supply of piped water to houses became normal. This task was not

5 *A girl carrying water with the aid of a hoop. From James Colston,* The Edinburgh and district water supply, *1890.*
6 *A well with windlass and rope. From William Gray,* Social contrasts portrayed in a series of 22 coloured litho-graphic plates from pen and ink sketches, *1865.*

always acknowledged as 'housework'. Yet it was a major household chore in its own right; and one of great importance for other activities such as cooking, washing-up, laundry, and cleaning. And it was nearly always women's work: men rarely fetched water unless they earned their living by doing so.

The amount of labour and time which a woman spent on obtaining water depended on several factors, one of which was the proximity and convenience of her nearest sources of supply. In the country, almost every cottage, farm and large house had a water butt at its side for catching water from the roof. This rainwater was particularly good for cooking, washing, and cleaning because of its softness and comparative purity, but there was rarely enough of it. According to calculations made in 1900, the average amount of rain falling on the roof of a medium-sized cottage was 4,000 gallons a year, of which only 3,000 gallons were collected. This was barely enough to supply drinking and cooking water for a small family.[2] And during a dry season the butt would quickly become empty. Some people solved the problem by digging deep ponds outside their houses to collect rainwater on a larger scale. Pehr Kalm, a Swedish naturalist who visited England in 1748, described how the inhabitants around Little Gaddesden and St Albans in Hertfordshire used water from such ponds 'for want of any other for cooking food, washing dishes, linen etc.'.[3]

But most families procured additional water supplies from springs, streams, rivers and wells. Public wells were more common than private ones. In the hamlet of Juniper Hill on the Oxfordshire-Northamptonshire border, for example, only three out of 30 cottages had private wells at the end of the nineteenth century: 'The less fortunate tenants obtained their water from a well on a vacant plot on the outskirts of the hamlet, from which the cottage had disappeared.'[4]

Where the well water was near the surface, it was reached by lowering a pail on the end of a pole. But in most places it lay deeper and had to be raised to the surface with a windlass* and rope, or winch† and chain. Primitive kinds of pump, which raised water up to 32 feet, were normally only found in villages, typically on the village green or in the main street, or in the yards of large country houses.

In chalky districts where water lay at great depths (mainly in southern England), water was occasionally raised by animal power. In the 1740s the Duke of Bridgewater employed a horse and engine for this purpose at his house, Ashridge Park, in Hertfordshire. The machine, which had been in existence since the late sixteenth century and raised water from a well 275 feet deep, consisted of a large wheel with a thick axletree 'around which there went a long rope, which had a large bucket, fastened to each end', so that 'when the one pail went up with the water, the other went empty down'. The horse walked inside the great wheel driving it round, and thus lifting the buckets up and down.[5] A similar system existed at Saddlescombe, a sheep farm on the Sussex Downs.

* A device for hauling or hoisting which has a horizontal drum (turned by a handle) on which a rope attached to the load is wound.
† An alternative word for windlass.

7 *'Dying for love, or Captain Careless shot flying by a girl of fifteen who unexpectedly popped her head out of a casement', coloured etching by Thomas Rowlandson, 1810. The village pump was a great place for gossiping and eavesdropping. Note the variety of vessels used for transporting water.*

The well house, which supplied 11 households with drinking water in the 1860s, was 'a square building open on one side with a huge broad wheel in which donkey, pony or man stepped on and on like a squirrel in a cage, bringing up from 150 feet below the pure water . . .'.[6]

Despite the variety of potential water sources in the country, many women had to travel long distances to fetch it. B. Seebohm Rowntree and May Kendall, who visited 42 agricultural labourers' houses in different parts of England in 1912, found that the nearest well was sometimes a quarter of a mile (440 yards) away.[7] Similarly, a Royal Commission which investigated rural housing in Scotland reported in 1917 that water was commonly carried 150 yards, and sometimes as far as 400 yards.[8] A more detailed survey of three rural parishes in Scotland published in 1937 showed that almost half the households lacked piped supplies; that their distance from water ranged from 25 to 1,000 yards; and that a quarter of a mile was not unusual.[9]

Houses without piped supplies nearly always lacked sanitary conveniences too. This meant that women bore an additional transport burden: without sinks and drains, they

8 *A donkey wheel, photographed at the end of the nineteenth century.*

had to remove all dirty water and 'slops' from their homes, either by throwing them out the window or by carrying them outside. Even in the houses of the gentry, where sanitation was slightly more advanced, servants spent their mornings and evenings carrying water to individual basins and baths and later discreetly removing it again.

Obtaining water in towns and cities was sometimes easier than in the country. For a start, mechanical means of raising well water such as pumps and horse engines were far more common, and there was nearly always an alternative to the laborious and time-consuming windlass and rope. For instance, when Celia Fiennes visited Beverley in Yorkshire in 1697, she found that the town's wells had a pulley and weight system for letting down and drawing up buckets of water, which she said was an 'Imitation of Holland, they being supply'd with water soe'.[10] Secondly, there was almost invariably some form of organized public water supply. The simplest system was to bring water from a lake or reservoir lying above the town to public fountains in the centre by means of conduits. More complicated systems involved raising river water to an elevated service reservoir, whence it was distributed by pipes to private houses and public outlets. It was quite common for towns to have several different systems in operation at the same time, all supplementing the simpler sources of supply such as rainwater butts,

9 *A woman going to fetch water from a stream at the back of* The Queen's Head and
Artichoke, *Regent's Park, London. From Jacob Larwood and John Camden Hotten* Old
London Illustrated, *c. 1884.*

private wells, rivers and streams.

Thus most urban women had several sources of water at their disposal and few had to
carry water over long distances. On the other hand, when demand outstripped supplies,
they had to put up with water shortages and waste time queuing up for it. Some people
managed to extract enjoyment from this tiresome situation. The inhabitants of eight-
eenth- and early nineteenth-century Edinburgh, who waited for water at the public wells
between 6 pm and 3 am each day, filled the weary hours 'with as much scandal as could
be talked, or with as much inspiration as the use of tobacco or snuff could instil into
them'. But this jollity did not stop the outbreak of serious rows between the professional
water carriers (known as 'caddies') and the servant girls despatched from private
households. And the shrill cry of 'Wha's next?' was always to be heard far above the
babble of tongues.[11] Others were less cheerful about queuing. As the *Belfast News Letter*
reported in 1801: 'We often see a crowd of females [at the main fountain off Linnenhall
Street] quite in despair, and after waiting an hour, they either go away without being
supplied, or walk some distance out of town, to obtain somewhere else this indispensable commodity.'[12]

Walking out of town was only possible, of course, if the town was small or one lived near the edge of it. The inhabitants of large cities had no choice but to wait. In Exeter it was a common sight in the 1820s to see 20 or 30 people queuing for up to four hours at a public conduit.[13] And the majority of Gateshead's 38,000 inhabitants in 1845 had to wait from one to three hours at the city's wells before they could obtain a few gallons.[14] Water conveyed to public stand-pipes (vertical pipes) did not necessarily eliminate the shortages. As Mr Joseph Quick, engineer to the Southwark Water Company in London, reported in 1844: 'I have seen as many as from 20 to 50 persons with pails waiting round one or two stand-pipes.' He added that there was inevitably 'quarrelling for the turn; the strongest pushing forward, and the pails, after they are filled, being upset'.[15]

Until the early nineteenth century urban water shortages were usually temporary. A spell of wet weather would end them; or effective measures to produce new supplies might be taken. A town council might decide to construct a new conduit or erect additional pumps; a private waterworks company might undertake to supply a new part of the town. But during the nineteenth century, towns and cities expanded so fast that it was impossible, in most places, to keep up with the ever-increasing demand for water. By 1845, when the *Second Report of the Commissioners for Inquiring into the State of Large Towns and Populous Districts* was published, the problem had become overwhelming. The Commissioners visited 51 towns, 'the seats of all the chief manufactures of the kingdom, together with the four principal seaports (after London)', and found that only six of them had a good water supply, 13 being indifferent and 32 very bad indeed.[16]

The majority of towns categorized as bad or indifferent suffered from intermittent piped water supplies. As the Commissioners explained: 'The system of supplying water usually adopted by companies, is to turn it on to the several districts of the town at certain periods of the day, generally two or three hours three times a week.' The wealthier people, with supplies piped directly to their houses, did not suffer unduly because they had large cisterns or water butts in which they could store water until the flow resumed; but the poorer classes did not and were 'obliged to retain the water in such vessels as they happen to possess'. Being unable to store large quantities they had to ensure that they were around when water was available at the public outlets, or else do without. Not surprisingly, the Commissioners found that a high proportion of assault cases arose from quarrels and brawls that broke out while people waited for water.[17]

It is extremely difficult to estimate how much water the average woman brought home each day if she did not have a piped supply in her house; for this depended not only on the amount of effort and time it took to obtain water and the distance it had to be transported, but on other variables too, such as the size and needs of her household, her personal inclination, and the amount she was physically capable of bearing at a time. The latter, incidentally, is not easy to determine because of the marked regional differences that existed in water-carrying techniques. In Wales, for example, women carried water in pitchers balanced on their heads. As Catherine Hutton noted while at

10 *Women and boys queuing for water from a stand-pipe in Fryingpan Alley, Clerkenwell, London. From* The Builder, *June 1862.*

Aberystwyth in 1787, 'I have seen a hundred times a woman carrying a pitcher of water on her head, a child or a loaf in [her] wrapper, and knitting as she walked along'.[18] These pitchers were clearly very large indeed: Edward Daniel Clarke, who visited Wales in 1791, marvelled at the ability of Welsh women to 'carry great weights upon their heads, and balance their milk pails, buckets of water, etc. . . . without taking any hold of them'.[19]

In the north of England and in Scotland women generally carried water on their heads in 'skeels'. These were wooden tubs or buckets wider at the base than the top with one stave prolonged upwards to form a handle, and they contained anything from 3 to $6\frac{1}{2}$ gallons. To carry them more comfortably women padded their heads with a circular roll of straw or wool, called a 'weeze'.[20] But some preferred to carry water by hand, in a stoup. This was a circular wooden receptacle, about 24 inches high, girded round by four iron hoops, with a wooden handle. A woman carrying more than one stoup usually made use of a wooden hoop or 'girr' round her body, which helped to balance her load and avoid spills.[21] In the south of England, by contrast, most women carried water by hand in small vessels such as pitchers, cans, barrels, buckets, pails, tins, casks, pots, etc.

Women usually transported water alone. But occasionally they joined forces. In Orkney, two women would carry water in a 'sae'. A local joiner, John Firth (1838–1922), described this as 'a water-tub, with lugs formed by two opposite staves longer than the others, and having large holes in them through which a long, round stick, called the sae tree, was passed when the sae was carried to and from the well'. It was no light task, he said, 'even for two well-built women to swing a heavy sae with ten gallons of water shoulder high, and, barefooted, to carry this home over broken road and heathery brae'.[22]

These variations in water transport methods show that there was no standard load. However, it seems clear that adult women rarely carried less than 1 gallon or more than 6 at a time, and that 3 gallons was probably the average. These estimates are consistent, incidentally, with the water loads borne by women in developing countries during the 1970s which averaged 3 to $3\frac{1}{2}$ gallons per journey.[23]

This 3 gallon figure is useful in that it provides a basis for hypothetical calculations illustrating the relationship between water consumption and the effort expended in procuring supplies. For example, if a woman transported 3 gallons at a time and was providing water for three persons, individual consumption would be 3 gallons if she went on three water-procuring expeditions a day, 4 gallons if she went on four trips, and so on. If she was supplying a family of six with the nineteenth century sanitary reformers' ideal of 12 gallons per head she would have to make 24 journeys a day.

It is also helpful to bear the figure in mind when considering the estimates of water consumption made by nineteenth and twentieth century water-supply engineers, government investigators, and medical authorities. The famous water engineer, Thomas Hawksley, for example, calculated that the average consumption in the city

11 *A woman lifting a bucketful of water from a spring. The water pot by her side has an improvized rope handle. This idealized picture of fetching water on a summer's evening comes from the 1879 edition of Mary Russell Mitford's best-selling book* Our Village.

of Nottingham was 7 gallons per head per day (ghd — a pleasantly arcane abbreviation which will be used in the rest of this chapter) prior to the introduction of domestic piped water supplies in 1830–1. (He thought the 7 gallons required three journeys a day, each taking about 10 minutes.)[24] But he was probably optimistic; a series of investigations conducted in 1850 in three Scottish towns with constant supplies available from public stand-pipes revealed much lower rates of consumption.[25] In Paisley the majority of the population did not obtain more than 1.4 ghd for domestic purposes. In the area of Glasgow north of the River Clyde, where the buildings were particularly tall, consumption fell to the nadir of 0.82 ghd. And in Stirling the working classes seldom used more than 2 ghd, although the middle classes, who washed their clothes at home, consumed up to 12 ghd.

Similarly low estimates were made of rural consumption. Mr R. Rawlinson, a member of the House of Commons Select Committee on Public Health in 1875, testified that rural water supplies rarely exceeded 3 or 4 ghd.[26] And in 1919, John Thresh, medical officer of health for Essex, wrote that most cottagers did not use much more than a gallon a day.[27]

It seems that consumption was not determined by the quantity of water available at a supply point, unless there was an acute shortage. Economic considerations were far more important. In 1850, for example, the General Board of Health advocated consumption of 6–7 ghd, or 60 gallons per house per day for the labouring classes, explaining that this would be a great increase on their current consumption which often only consisted of one pail or large jugful a day. But, it calculated, if a labourer's wife *did* supply her family with 50 gallons a day and lived on the third or fourth floor of a building:

This would be upwards of 20 pailsful per diem, or 140 pails per week to be fetched from the stand-pipe below. The weight of the water alone to be carried per diem would be 500 lbs, or, per week, 3,500 lbs . . .

The Board pointed out that it would probably require two days' labour to fetch this amount of water and a further two days to get rid of it again as 'few of the tenements occupied by the labouring classes, or indeed of the upper rooms of houses occupied by the higher or middle class, have any waste or "return pipes"'. Thus any woman who actually fetched 50 gallons of water a day would utterly exhaust herself. And just as importantly, she would also be depriving herself of wages that she might otherwise earn in a paid job.[28]

Another curb on consumption was the high cost of buying water from professional water-carriers. In 1844, for example, Londoners living in Southwark paid carriers 1 shilling a week for water deliveries, at a time when average weekly earnings were $7\frac{1}{2}$ shillings for women, 18 for labourers, and 32 for mechanics.[29] The poor invariably paid more for water bought from carriers than the better-off did for water piped to their homes. As Parliamentary returns showed in 1834, the London waterworks companies

12 *Water-carts in suburban London, as shown in an unidentified newspaper cutting of 1875. These respectable houses did not have piped water supplies.*

13 *A professional water-seller with halter and buckets. From* The cryes of London drawne after the life *by Pierce Tempest, 1711.*

received three quarters of a farthing for piping 36 gallons of water, whereas water-carriers charged 8 pence for delivering 36 gallons from wells and 4 pence for the same amount of river water.[30] And in some cities where water was very short, people were charged for water even when they fetched it themselves. In Newcastle-upon-Tyne, the poor bought 7 million gallons of water a year from 'sale-pants' in the 1840s, for which they were charged 1 farthing for a 5-gallon skeel, more than four times the price of the same quantity of water piped to houses in the city.[31]

It would seem from all this that the vast majority of city dwellers without piped supplies cannot have consumed more than 5 ghd and that most of them got by on considerably less, say 3 ghd. Agricultural labourers probably averaged 1–2 ghd, because water often had to be carried further in the country and, in the absence of urban pollution, there was less washing and cleaning to do. The minority of households that

14 *In towns and cities without decent water supplies, the well-to-do sometimes installed pumps in their kitchens. They were usually next to the sink, as in this sketch by Caroline Elizabeth Hamilton of the kitchen at Northumberland Place, Harrogate in 1839. The servant is busy plucking birds.*

lacked piped supplies but employed several servants obviously had more water at their disposal, but their consumption rarely exceeded 12 ghd. These estimates are comparable to the figures for known water consumption in developing countries. In 1970, for example, the World Health Organization surveyed non-piped domestic water supplies in 91 nations and found that 1½ ghd was about the minimum necessary to sustain life, that 6 ghd was the average for people obtaining their supplies from public hydrants, and that in most countries consumption was below 12 ghd.[32] In a highly industrialized country such as the United States water consumption averaged 72 ghd.[33]

But to return to Britain. The subject of water consumption before the spread of piped domestic supplies is important not only for the light it sheds on the onerous household chore of obtaining water, but also for the insights it provides into many other aspects of the history of housework. For example, once it is clear that the majority of urban and rural households only fetched very small amounts of water, it becomes obvious that a great deal of housework must have taken place outside the house. As kitchens had no running water it was easier to prepare food for cooking by the side of a well or a stream. When eight-year-old Janet Greenfield went into service at a small Sunderland farm in 1814, one of her first tasks was to take the potatoes down to the burn to wash and scrape them.[34] In the same way, it was far more practical for women to take their laundry to the nearest well, stream, river, or public washing place where they had ready access to unlimited water, than to do it at home. Thus, the spread of piped water was very significant in changing the locus of several household activities and in encouraging women to stay at home.

Similarly, it becomes evident that the shortage of water affected the scope of housework and the frequency with which it was done. Cleaning (at least with water) tended to be kept to the minimum. Cooking had to be kept simple and, if necessary, virtually abandoned. When the Fenland rivers, drains and dykes dried up in the summer (a frequent occurrence during the late nineteenth and early twentieth centuries), the pot would disappear from its hook over the fire. The only sign of culinary activity was 'a man or a woman in the bottom o' the dyke, waiting for the water to seep into a tablespoon to be put into a kettle for the one cup o' tea o' the day'.[35] And laundry had to be postponed indefinitely. When Clifton Johnson visited the Lake District in the 1890s, he met a farmer's wife who had just finished a seven weeks wash: 'Until the rains of a few days before there had been no water in their well for all that time'.[36]

The spread of domestic piped water supplies was undoubtedly the most far-reaching change in housework in Britain between 1650 and 1950. As soon as women had as much water as they needed, at the turn of the tap, water consumption rose dramatically. By 1878 it was 12 ghd in Norwich, 14 in Sheffield and Nottingham, 15 in Liverpool, 26 in London, 34 in Edinburgh and 50 in Glasgow, where water-closets were particularly numerous.[37] It was to increase much further during the course of the next century, as households gradually acquired the sanitary conveniences made possible by piped water supplies. By 1951, 52 per cent of households in England and Wales had a kitchen sink, water-closet and fixed bath; although 45 per cent still lacked a bathtub, 21 per cent a water-closet, and 12 per cent a kitchen sink.[38]

The effects on housework of these increases in water consumption were revolutionary. Women no longer had to carry great weights of water over long distances, queue up for it, do without or plan ahead; and cooking, washing-up, cleaning, and laundry all became much simpler operations. Furthermore, because piped water was generally pure, it could be drunk safely straight from the tap; it was no longer necessary, if one wanted to survive, to drink beer or tea, both of which were made with boiled water.

How did this liberation take place? Given the immense importance of domestic piped water supplies one might expect the seventeenth, eighteenth, and nineteenth centuries to have been marked with unremitting efforts to perfect the technology, legislation and financial arrangements required for their spread. And one might expect women to have been at the forefront of efforts to introduce or improve piped supplies. But in fact this was not so. Progress was slow and uneven and it usually occurred for reasons completely unrelated to domestic convenience or the specific needs of women. And there is no evidence that women ever contributed to the development of piped water supplies in any way, or even advocated their spread. To illustrate this, and to explain how Britons came to acquire water in their houses, it is convenient to divide the period 1650–1950 into three phases, and illuminating to treat each at some length. For the history of water supplies provides a striking illustration of the way in which women failed to control or direct changes in their working lives, and also of the incidental fashion in which the conduct of housework has been transformed.

The first phase (1650–1750)

At the start of this phase, as we have already seen, domestic water supplies were extremely primitive. The majority of the population depended on collecting rainwater and fetching water from wells, springs, streams and rivers. There was almost no sophisticated technology. A few country estates, which were fortunate enough to be located below a spring or reservoir, obtained their supplies by means of simple brick or stone conduits. For example, at Lord Lemster's country seat at Easton in Northamptonshire, water was conveyed in oak pipes from a spring 2,000 yards away.[39] However, conduits were subject to many drawbacks such as 'the continual Grief of seeing the Conduit-Pipes broke by the Malice of Country Fellows, who take Delight in anything that will mortify a Gentleman', the apprehension of 'having your water cut off and diverted' (which frequently led to tedious law suits), and the geological surprise of finding that 'the Vein of Earth and Bed of Clay should change its Situation' and the spring disappear.[40]

A number of towns also had conduits. But their efforts at organized supply stopped there. London was the only city in the British Isles with a variety of waterworks. According to Samuel Sorbière, a Frenchman who visited England around 1660, some people got their water from water conduits, while others were supplied 'with great Difficulty, and in less Quantity than could be wished' by the Somerset-House wooden waterworks on the River Thames.[41] This seems to have consisted of a pump worked by a water wheel at full tide and by horses at low tide. There was also another machine dating back to 1582 which raised water from the Thames at London Bridge.[42] London had piped supplies in the sense that some areas had wooden pipes distributing water to convenient public points. But because the pipes cracked, leaked and required frequent repairs, and because the only alternative, lead piping, was very expensive, these public piped supplies were minimal and only a small proportion of rich households had private connections. The primitive nature of the capital's water supplies were shown up in lurid light by the Great Fire of London, which broke out in September 1666. The fire raged unchecked for four days, consuming 13,200 houses, 88 churches, 52 companies' halls, four bridges, four prisons, three city gates, and numerous civic buildings such as the

Guildhall, Royal Exchange and Customs House. Had adequate water supplies been available, much of this mediaeval London might have been saved.

However, although domestic water supplies were so rudimentary and the consequent risk of conflagration so great, there was surprisingly little pressure to improve them. The majority of the population had no conception of any other state of affairs and in any case lacked the necessary technical and financial means to bring about change. The rich and the educated were in a slightly different position. They knew about the excellent water supplies of classical antiquity and they had money. But they had no real incentive to improve their domestic water supplies, for they could afford to install pumps and to employ as many servants and water-carriers as they needed.

Nevertheless, several members of the aristocracy and gentry became very interested in water power and waterworks between 1650 and 1750. According to Sorbière, this interest could be traced to the Civil War and Cromwell's Protectorate, when the nobles, lacking the distractions of court life, 'apply'd themselves to their Studies: Some turning their Heads to Chymistry, others to Mechanism, Mathematicks, or Natural Philosophy'. They 'Built Elaboratories, made Machines, opened Mines, and made use of an Hundred Sorts of Artists, to find out some new Invention or other'.[43] Following the Restoration in 1660, and the resumption of court life, these varied scientific activities continued to flourish. Charles I himself was most interested in science; and the Royal Society, founded in 1661 with his full support, provided a useful forum where men (there were no women members) could exchange ideas and publish their findings. The Society's *Philosophical Transactions* were soon filled with papers on *hydrology*, the science of the properties and laws of water, *hydraulics*, the science of conveying liquids through pipes and using them as a source of motive power, and *hydrostatics*, the branch of mechanics concerned with the pressure and equilibrium of liquids at rest.

To a certain extent this new-found interest in water was academic. But it also had its practical aspects. Many members of the aristocracy had invested in coal mines and the profitable glass and salt industries fuelled by them. They were therefore very concerned with the problems involved in raising water from considerable depths; for without adequate drainage the coal seams could not be mined at all. Existing types of pump worked by water-wheels and horses were expensive and inefficient. Furthermore, they could not raise water in one 'sink' or shaft from below 240 feet, without doing it in several stages, a costly and often impracticable process.[44] By 1708, when *The Compleat Collier*, the first book devoted to coal mining in Britain appeared, most new pits were being sunk to depths of 300–400 feet. The invention of an effective machine to drain mines had become the greatest engineering problem of the age. As the author of *The Compleat Collier* commented: 'were it not for Water, a Collery . . . might be termed a Golden Mine to Purpose, for Dry Colleries would save several Thousands per ann. which is expended in drawing Water . . .'[45]

In addition, most of the nobility and gentry of the time wished to imitate in their own gardens the magnificent and elaborate fountains, *jets d'eau*, water spouts and cascades fashionable in Italy and France. To create these spectacular effects they needed to know how to find water, convey it to their gardens, store it in reservoirs, and distribute it at the appropriate pressure and in the correct quantities. Success depended on measuring the flow of running or spouting water accurately, understanding the pros and cons of different types of piping, and calculating the diameters necessary for the pipe bores. In other words, it was impossible to design garden waterworks without considerable skill and expertise in hydraulics.

These two very specific concerns – mining and landscape gardening – proved to be important for the development of domestic water supplies in Britain because they stimulated amateur scientists and inventors to conduct experiments on the raising and conveyance of water. Some of their experiments sounded impressive but did not come to anything. For example, Edward Somerset, Marquis of Worcester, devised a hydraulic machine that enabled one man to raise 'Four large Buckets full of water in an Instant, Forty Foot High, and that through a Pipe of about Eight Inches long'.[46] It impressed Sorbière and Cosimo de Medici when they saw it at Vauxhall outside London in the 1660s, but there is no evidence that it was developed commercially.[47]

Other inventors, however, succeeded not only in making important technological breakthroughs but also in promoting their work in influential circles. The diplomat Sir Samuel Morland, for example, perfected a pump which consisted of an improved piston and barrel coupled with a new 'cyclo-elliptical movement'.[48] The pump, which could be worked by men or water, was demonstrated at Woolwich Dockyard in 1673 to Charles I, his courtiers and principal naval officers and by 1675 it was in commercial production.

Morland's most expensive pump for a private house cost £25 and could force water out of a well 50 to 60 feet deep. One must have been installed in his London home, Vauxhall House, for according to Roger North, 'He had a cistern in his garret which supplied water to all parts of his house, as he thought fit to contrive it'. Among the many novelties and conceits in his house was a large fountain sprinkling glasses with little streams of water. It may have been these innovations that piqued Charles I's curiosity about the pump's domestic applications, for Morland conducted a series of water-raising experiments at Windsor Castle during the 1670s, 80s and 90s.

The most astounding of these were written up in the *London Gazette*. In July 1681, for instance, an enormous assembly that included the King, Queen, Prince of Orange, foreign ambassadors, 'Persons of Eminent Quality', English noblemen, and a 'train of near 1,000 persons' watched eight men force wine-stained water 'in a continuous stream, at the rate of above sixty Barrels an hour, from the Engine below at the Parkpale, up to the top of the Castle, and from thence into the Air above sixty Foot high, to the great admiration of Their Majesties and all the Beholders . . . who unanimously concluded that this was the boldest and most extraordinary Experiment that has ever been performed by Water in any part of the World'.

In 1698 Thomas Savery patented the first working engine for raising water 'by the

Impellent Force of Fire'. It did so through two combined forces: the weight of the earth's atmosphere (which raised water to a maximum height of 32 feet) and the force of steam under pressure (the steam being created by a controlled fire in the engine). Savery's invention was in fact the first steam engine. He thought it would be 'of great use and Advantage for Drayning Mines, Serveing Towns with Water, and for the Working of all sorts of Mills where they have not the Benefitt of Water nor Constant Windes'.[49]

By 1702 Savery had set up a workshop in London. He had also published a book about his engine in which he explained that:

It may be of great use for Palaces, for the Nobilities or Gentlemens Houses: For by a Cistern on the top of a House, you may with a greal deal of Ease, and little Charge, throw what Quantity of Water you have occasion for to the top of any house; which Water, in its fall, makes you what sorts of Fountains you please, and supplys any Room in the House.

He stressed that 'this command of water' would provide certain protection against fire and reduce the labour of brewing and washing.[50]

The engine was tried out, with success, in several houses. For example, the machine Savery set up for Mr Robert Balle of Campden House in 1712 was praised as being 'the truest proportion'd of any about London'. It cost about £50 and, fuelled by coal, was able to raise 104 gallons a minute to a height of 58 feet. Once started, the engine could keep going for four or five hours.[51]

However, according to John Theophilus Desaguliers, the great expert on water-works in the early eighteenth century, Savery's steam pump 'could not succeed for Mines, or supplying Towns, where the Water was raised very high and in great Quantities: for then the steam requir'd being boil'd up to such a Strength, as to be ready to tear all the Vessels to pieces'.[52]

Although Savery's engine suffered from so many defects that it never became a commercial success, it was an extraordinarily significant invention. Under the hands of engineers such as Desaguliers, Thomas Newcomen, John Calley, John Smeaton and James Watt, the steam engine was soon developed into a much more efficient and power-ful machine.[53] At first it could only drive a piston backwards and forwards and there-fore raise water, but by the 1770s it was capable of rotative motion too and thus could be used to power all sorts of machinery. This second capability, because it was so significant in transforming the nature and location of Britain's manufacturing industry, is normally treated as the more important. But the first, which made possible a revolutionary advance in the provision of domestic water supplies, was also of great moment.

In addition to stimulating far-reaching experiments such as those on the steam engine, aristocratic interest in hydraulics encouraged the emergence of water engineer-ing as a specialized industry. The first engineer to become famous throughout England was George Sorocold of Derby who provided several towns with piped water supplies, including Derby (1692), Norwich, Portsmouth and Great Yarmouth (1694), Leeds

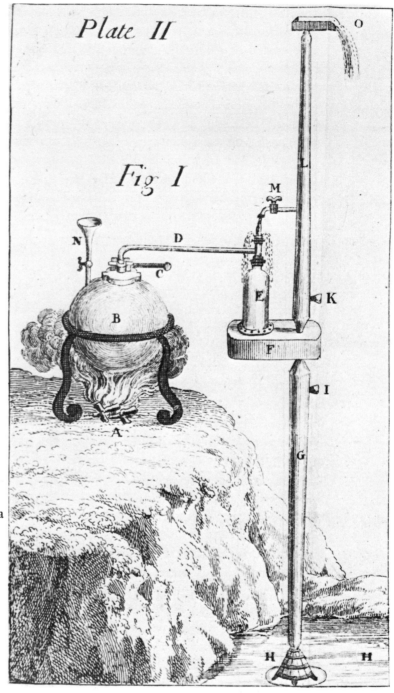

'A The *Fire*; B The *Boiler*; a Copper Vessel of a spherical Figure, in which *Water* is boiled and evaporated into *Steam*, which passes thorow C The *Regulator*, which opens to let it into D The *Steam-Pipe* (of Copper) thorow which it descends E The *Receiver*, which is a Vessel of Copper; that at first setting at Work is full of Air, which the *Steam* will discharge thorow F The *Engine-Tree*, and up the *Clack* at K (The *Plug* of the said *Clack*, to come at and repair the same if need be) and so the Air goes up. L *The Force-Pipe*. – After E is void of Air, which is to be found by its being hot all over, then stop the *Steam* at C, and thorow a little cold Water on E, and the *sucking Clack* will open at I (Which is the *Plug* of the said *Clack*) and fill E with Water, which will ascend thorow G The *Sucking-Pipe*, from H The *Pond*, *Well*, or *River*.' The operating instructions are, unfortunately, too long to reproduce here.

15 *Richard Bradley, the most famous horticultural writer of the early eighteenth century, provided this illustration of the Campden House steam engine of 1712 in his* New improvements of Planting and Gardening, both philosophical and practical, *1720.*

(1695), Sheffield (1697), London Bridge (1701), and Bridgenorth (1706). His skill, which was much admired by contemporaries, lay in designing sets of pumps worked by water-wheels which forced water up into elevated cisterns from which the water was piped into the town by gravity.[54] Thanks to his associate, John Hadley, the water-wheels rose and fell in accordance with the level of the water that was turning them.[55]

From the early eighteenth century a growing number of engine-makers had London workshops. Richard Bridges and William Vream, for example, were making models of water-raising engines in the 1710s.[56] In 1720 a Mr Fowke of Nightingale Lane in Wapping was manufacturing 'Pumps which may be work'd by one Man, for raising water out of any Well, upwards of 120 Feet deep, Sufficient for the Service of any private House or Family, and so constructed that by turning a Cock may supply a Cistern at the Top of the House, or a bathing Vessel in any Room'. His largest pump, which cost £45, could deliver 180 gallons of water a minute.[57]

By the 1720s there were so many water engineers in England that Desaguliers pronounced that there were 'perhaps more Quacks in this Art than any other except one'.[58] (The exception being medicine.) A French Huguenot by origin and a clergyman by profession, Desaguliers' career was devoted to science and engineering.[59] From 1713 he was established in London as a popular lecturer, tutor, and writer on hydrostatics, optics and mechanics. His reputation was such that in 1714 he was elected a fellow of the Royal Society and became chaplain to James Brydges, Duke of Chandos, one of the richest men in England. Brydges employed him to design and supervise the waterworks on his magnificent estate, Canons, in Middlesex. (The gardens were a showpiece and the house, unusually for its time, included three water-closets and a bathroom.) Desguliers was also involved in improving London's and Edinburgh's water supplies and he built water-raising engines in his garden to test, compare and improve them. In 1716–17 he effected improvements in Savery's fire engine, so that it could 'be more easily work'd, cost almost half less, and raise a third more water'. He also tested new kinds of pipes for their ability to withstand high water pressure and, with the help of two friends, invented a 'jack-in-box' contraption designed to discharge air pockets from lead and iron pipes. But his most important achievement may have been to raise standards in engineering by popularizing the subject in his lectures and books.[60]

The second phase (1750–1840)

During this second phase, the achievements of the previous century were consolidated and applied more widely; and there were three significant developments.

One was the adoption of the steam engine in urban waterworks. At first this was on a small scale. Most towns only erected steam engines if they had plenty of cheap coal available or if they had no choice in the matter.[61] But during the early 1800s the steam engine came into greater favour: its performance and manufacture had been greatly improved as a result of its application to manufacturing industry; coal was more widely distributed; and the growing urban demand for water-closets and bathrooms made it

16 *'Water', 1760. The print shows an aristocratic woman collecting water in a silver bowl from one of the fountains in her garden.*

desirable to raise piped water supplies to the tops of houses, which conventional pumps could not do.[62]

Another important development was the large-scale replacement of wooden piping with cast-iron, which began to occur in the 1780s. As William Matthews, a waterworks historian, pointed out in 1835, this was a prerequisite for introducing plentiful and constant urban water supplies. Wooden pipes suffered from several major disadvantages. They were generally made out of elm, a soft, porous timber particularly liable to fractures and decay. Thus they had to be repaired frequently and replaced completely every two to four years. In addition, it was impossible to make large wooden pipes capable of carrying large quantities of water. (The maximum bore was about 8 inches.) As a result streets were lined with row upon row of small pipes and when one of these sprang a leak, havoc ensued. Iron pipes, on the other hand, could be made in any size, rarely leaked, and had the strength to withstand considerable pressure.[63]

The idea of purifying polluted water by passing it through large-scale filtration works before distribution was the third important development. Glasgow embarked on an unsuccessful filtration project in 1806[64] and Chester started one in 1826.[65] But the sand and charcoal plant which James Simpson built for Chelsea Waterworks Company in 1829 was the first effective filtration system in Britain.[66]

These technological advances – steam engines, cast-iron pipes and filtration – were a necessary preliminary to the final phase in the evolution of domestic water supplies. But they could not, by themselves, solve the enormous water supply problems caused by rapid and unprecedented urban expansion in the first half of the nineteenth century.[67]

The third phase (1840–1950)
The most important factor in the eventual resolution of these problems was public concern over the excessively high rates of mortality prevailing in towns and cities, especially among the labouring classes. In this third phase, the needs of people (as opposed to the experiments of learned aristocrats, the requirements of collieries, the fashion for elaborate fountains, the growth of the iron industry, etc.) came to the forefront. But it was their health which commanded attention, rather than any labour-saving considerations. As Dr W. H. Duncan, physician to the Liverpool Infirmary, wrote in 1844:

It has long been known that where a number of individuals are gathered together within a narrow compass, as in towns, the mortality among them considerably exceeds that occurring among an equal amount of population scattered over an extended surface, as in country districts.

But, he went on to explain, it was not until 1838–9, when the Registration Act for England and Wales came into operation, that this phenomenon could be studied scientifically, on a large scale. During that year it was found that the annual mortality rate in towns was one in 38.16, whereas in country districts it was only one in 54.91. The average age of death in rural counties such as Rutland and Wiltshire was $26\frac{1}{2}$ years,

17 *A group of cottages in Preston with a cesspool running down the middle, illustrated in the 1844 report of the Commissioners appointed to investigate the state of large towns.*

while in such cities as Liverpool, Manchester, Leeds, and Bolton it was 19. Similarly the number of people dying at the age of 70 or over per 1,000 population was 202 in the country and 90 in the towns.[68]

These findings, which confirmed what had been obvious to some observers since the mid-eighteenth century, aroused considerable concern and triggered a series of government-sponsored inquiries into the causes and possible remedies. They all focused, rightly, on the quantity and quality of water supplies in towns and on their arrangements for sewage, drainage and cleansing. The first and most famous of these inquiries was Edwin Chadwick's *Report on the Sanitary Condition of the Labouring Population of Great Britain* which was submitted to Parliament in 1842. This showed that poor people lived in the most appallingly insanitary conditions. Chadwick was horrified: 'No previous investigations had led me to conceive the great extent to which the labouring classes are subjected to privations, not only of water for the purpose of ablution, house cleansing, and sewerage, but of wholesome water for drinking, and culinary purposes.'[69] He was in no doubt that immediate sanitary reform was imperative. He urged local administrative bodies to use their powers to improve water supplies and recommended that building regulations should, in future, make provision for them.

Chadwick's findings were more than confirmed by the reports issued in 1844 and 1845 by the Commissioners appointed 'to Inquire into the State of Large Towns and Populous Districts'.[70] They were also given an additional edge when the London doctor John Snow proved that the cholera epidemics of 1832 and 1848 were spread by polluted water containing their victims' excrement.[71] This was hardly a surprising discovery. In Jacob's Island, Bermondsey, an area of London where cholera mortality was very high in 1848, women could be seen all day long 'dipping water with pails attached by ropes to the backs of the houses, from a foul foetid ditch, its banks coated with a compound of mud and filth, and strewed with offal and carrion'. They used the water for all purposes, including cooking, even though 'filth and refuse of various kinds' were 'plentifully showered into it from the wooden privies of the wooden houses overhanging its current'.[72]

Although Chadwick and his followers succeeded in influencing informed public opinion, the necessary reforms were slow to follow. This was mainly because water supplies were not generally seen as a public service. Individuals, private companies, and town corporations provided water to make money. It was extraordinarily difficult to persuade them that they should cooperate with landlords in extending piped water supplies to the houses of the poor. Equally hard was the job of convincing water supply companies and municipal authorities that it was irresponsible not to invest large sums of money to filter their water and to provide constant rather than intermittent supplies. In London, for example, the filtration of domestic water supplies was not a legal requirement until 1852 and none of the metropolitan water companies was obliged to start providing constant supplies until 1871.

Such were the obstacles to reform that urban water supplies in Britain hardly improved in the two decades following Chadwick's report of 1842. As Alexander Patrick Stewart and Edward Jenkins reported in *The Medical and Legal Aspects of Sanitary Reform* (1866), the main and house drainage in most cities was still very unsatisfactory and the water supply of the poorer districts thoroughly defective. Limited, piecemeal sanitary legislation had not been effective and mortality rates were continuing to rise in many urban districts. The only solution which Stewart and Jenkins could see was to remove water supply from private hands and entrust it to 'public and responsible bodies, in the interest of the consumer'.[73]

This was in fact exactly what happened. From mid-century, an increasing number of town corporations raised large amounts of money to improve local amenities and in return derived substantial profits from them.[74] Most of them spent the bulk of their capital on obtaining pure water from distant springs, lakes and reservoirs. This was partly because local sources were insufficient, but mainly because they were so dangerously polluted.[75]

One of the first cities to invest heavily in new water supplies was Manchester, which by the early 1840s had become desperately short of clean water. In 1846, 49 per cent of its 46,577 households had no supplies at all other than from pumps and wells polluted by cesspools and sewers. The Corporation decided that the only solution was to buy the private water company and pass a bill through Parliament enabling it to levy an unlimited rate to finance the costs of obtaining a new supply from Longdendale and building several reservoirs. It did so successfully and by 1876 80 per cent of the city's 70,366 houses had internal water supplies and some 28 per cent had baths. In 1879 the Corporation passed another bill empowering it to raise the necessary money to obtain water from Thirlmere in the Lake District, via an aqueduct 96 miles long. After this major engineering feat had been completed in 1894, Manchester's water supplies were excellent.[76]

In the same way Glasgow's Town Council took over the city's rival water companies in 1853 and two years later obtained a Parliamentary bill giving it the power to obtain water from Loch Katrine in the Perthshire Highlands. The reservoir and 43-mile aqueduct completed in 1860 cost £920,000. There was considerable further expenditure in the following three decades but the Council still made a consistent profit by supplying water.[77]

Bradford was yet another successful example of municipal take-over. When the Corporation assumed control in 1854, the town's supply of water was very scanty. The larger houses were supplied by private wells or from a small reservoir. The rest of the town was supplied by carriers who obtained water from deep wells sunk at great expense by the proprietors. But soon Bradford was supplied by a 24-mile conduit leading from a series of large reservoirs in the valleys of the Rivers Aire and Wharfe. In the words of a proud local historian, Bradford's waterworks constituted 'one of the mightiest triumphs of this engineering age', its conduit surpassing 'the greatest of the famous aqueducts which supplied Imperial Rome with water'. Needless to add, the Corporation's income from water sales rose from £10,255 in 1856 to £85,000 in 1881.[78]

It was thus by abandoning laissez-faire policies and by considerable capital expenditure that the majority of towns and cities in Britain managed to solve their basic water supply problems by the early twentieth century. However, it took a long time for many of them to perfect their distribution systems. For instance, almost every street in Oxford had water laid on by 1912, but the taps were often outside the houses and had to be shared with neighbours. Frequently there was only one tap between 6–12 houses.[79] Later still, in 1934, an extensive survey of working-class London showed that it was the exception rather than the rule to have water at hand. In half the houses investigated, it had to be fetched 'from outside the tenement, often from a tap on the landing, sometimes from across a yard, at others up or down three flights of stairs'.[80]

Sanitary reformers only began to focus their attention on the countryside at the beginning of this century. This was long overdue. The Rivers Pollution Commission of 1868 had shown that water was drawn, all too often, from a shallow well contaminated by foul drainage from a nearby scullery, yard, privy, cesspool or pig sty. Or it would be taken from streams and rivers polluted by untreated sewage and industrial waste. The quantity of water might be abundant, the Commissioners noted, but 'it is hopelessly spoiled within a mile of the place where it rises pure, and long before the people wanting it'.[81] Rural water supplies had not improved since then. In one Oxfordshire parish, 92

18 *The Welsh women in this photograph of c. 1870 were lucky: they had a pump just outside their door. The woman on the left is knitting a stocking.*

per cent of the wells contained water unfit for human consumption in the 1920s.[82] Houses with taps inside them were few and far between: 62 per cent of rural houses in 19 English counties surveyed in 1913 lacked piped water supplies. (The percentage of houses with internal supplies varied considerably, from 6 per cent in Norfolk to 92 per cent in Durham.)[83]

The main obstacle to progress was financial: the cost of procuring and distributing water was frequently out of all proportion to the number of people who were to benefit. However, government loans helped to remove this difficulty. Following the passage of the Rural Water Supplies Act in 1934, for example, some 2,000 parishes in England and Wales were supplied with piped water within 10 years. By 1944 the government estimated that 70 per cent of the rural population in England and Wales and 67 per cent in Scotland had piped supplies.[84] But this may have been over-optimistic. An independent survey of Gloucestershire published in 1946 showed that although 62 per cent of the county's 292 parishes had piped supplies, these often only amounted to public taps or stand-pipes in the streets.[85] And the figures for England, Wales and Scotland certainly did not apply to Ireland, where conditions remained extremely primitive.[86] About 92 per cent of the houses in the rural parts of Ulster lacked piped water in 1947.[87]

By this point, however, rural households were in a small minority. The 1951 Census, the first to enquire about water and sanitation, concluded that 80 per cent of private households in England and Wales had exclusive use of their own piped water supplies.[88] The most fundamental revolution in the working lives of British women was thus almost complete. Soon the centuries-old sight of women bearing water – on their heads, by their hands, and from their shoulders – was to disappear altogether.

Chapter 2 GAS & ELECTRICITY

Gas and electricity were discovered centuries before their domestic potential was appreciated and exploited. In the case of gas, its widespread adoption in the home was a development of the 1880s and 90s. Yet the existence of natural gas, and its ability to burn and produce heat, was already well known in the seventeenth century. Thomas Shirley, for example, visited a natural gas spring near Wigan, a Lancashire coal-mining-town, in 1659. His *Description of a Well and Earth in Lancashire Taking Fire by a Candle approached to it* appeared in the *Philosophical Transactions* of the Royal Society for 1667. By the end of the century, this spring (or possibly others like it) had become a local curiosity and tourist attraction. The indefatigable Celia Fiennes, for instance, saw it while riding from Wigan to Warrington in 1698. In her diary she noted that her guide '. . . set ye water in ye well on fire and it burned blewish just like spirits and continued a good while . . .'.[1]

Coal-gas was also well known to many eighteenth-century scientists. Lord Dun-donald, for example, was distilling tar from coal at his estate, Culross Abbey, in about 1782, when he noticed that the vapour which arose during the distillation was inflammable. His son relates how 'by way of experiment' he fitted a gun barrel to the pipe leading from the condenser and 'on applying fire to the muzzle, a vivid light blazed forth'. Unfortunately, he dismissed the illuminating properties of gas as just 'a curious natural phenomenon' and persisted with his unsuccessful attempt to retrieve the family fortune by making tar.[2] The list of gentlemen who experimented with coal-gas in similar ways, but failed to recognize its value, is surprisingly long.[3]

The first person to demonstrate that gas made a brilliant and practical illuminant was William Murdoch. He lit his own house at Redruth in Cornwall with gas in 1792 (it was carried by pipe from an iron retort in his backyard through a hole in the window frame to a ceiling burner and portable lamp made out of tinned iron);[4] and in 1802 he illuminated Matthew Boulton and James Watt's famous Soho manufactory outside Birmingham, to celebrate the Peace of Amiens. According to William Matthews, an early gas enthusiast, the illuminations were extraordinarily splendid:

The whole front of that extensive range of buildings was ornamented with a great variety of devices, that admirably displayed many of the varied forms of which the gas-light was susceptible. This luminous spectacle was as novel as it was astounding; and Birmingham poured forth its numerous population to gaze at, and to admire, this wonderful display of the combined effects of science and art.[5]

After this, gas-lighting came into vogue. Murdoch and his colleague, Samuel Clegg,[6] were showered with commissions to light mills and other factories in the Midlands;

while a German entrepreneur called Frederick Albert Winsor vigorously promoted gas-lighting in London by lectures and demonstrations. In 1807 Winsor lit up part of Pall Mall, the first street in Britain to be illuminated by gas. By 1812, when the London Gaslight and Coke Company received its charter, the industry was born. Gas companies, with elaborate apparatus to make and purify gas and the authority to break up streets to lay mains and pipes, sprang up all over urban Britain. According to M. E. Falkus, the establishment of the new companies corresponded closely with booms in the British economy and occurred in three main bursts between 1818–25, 1831–7 and 1842–6. Most towns with populations over 10,000 had their own gas companies by the mid 1820s; and by 1846, there were relatively few towns of more than 2,500 inhabitants without one.[7] There was thus a considerably time lag between early discoveries of coal-gas and its manufacture in urban Britain.

The same was true of electricity, a term first coined in 1600 by William Gilbert. In the centuries that followed, the phenomenon was the subject of continuous investigation and speculation, both in Europe and North America. Most of the discoveries with domestic significance were, however, made in Britain. For example, Sir Humphrey Davy demonstrated in 1808 that electric lighting was feasible with his arc lamp (sparking between two electrodes); and Michael Faraday made his fundamental discovery of electro-magnetic induction, which demonstrated that electricity could be generated by mechanical means, in 1831. Yet incandescent carbon filament lamps – the forerunner of modern light bulbs – were not invented until the 1870s. Dynamos capable of generating electricity cheaply enough for commercial and domestic use made a similarly belated appearance.[8] So the first public supply companies were not established in London and provincial cities until the 1880s and 1890s respectively.[9]

Another striking aspect of the development of gas and electricity is that none of their first applications was domestic. Initially gas was used almost exclusively for lighting factories, business premises, public buildings and streets. Companies made little or no effort to promote it as a form of domestic illumination until the 1870s and 80s; and they did not devote much energy to developing gas for cooking and heating purposes until the 1880s and 90s. So too, with electricity. Until the simultaneous development of public and domestic lighting in the 1880s, its current had only been used to drive locomotives, plate silver and illuminate lighthouses. Gas and electricity companies fell into the business of supplying individual houses and promoting the use of appropriate domestic appliances only when there were very strong economic reasons to do so.

The gas industry, for instance, had the manufacturing capacity and means to distribute gas to domestic consumers by the mid-nineteenth century. Furthermore, with R. W. Bunsen's invention of the 'atmospheric' or 'aerated' burner (1855) which produced ideal conditions for combustion by mixing air with gas in the optimum proportion, the essential component of effective gas lights, fires and cookers was available. However, the gas industry did not turn to the domestic market until it was faced with a challenge and threat: electricity.

19 *A satirical print by Isaac Cruikshank, 1807. Winsor, the German gas promoter, is shown straddling a pipe between two cockspur street lights.*

When investors learned of the clean, bright light emanating from Swan and Edison's incandescent bulbs (houses were first lit with them in 1880), the price of gas shares slumped.[10] The industry was forced to respond vigorously and promptly, by making domestic gas-lighting more efficient and desirable and by promoting the use of gas for cooking and for space and water heating. The International Electric and Gas Exhibition mounted at London's Crystal Palace in 1882–3, despite the inclusion of electricity, was aimed mainly at publicising the domestic uses of gas and at raising the standard of gas appliances. Manufacturers from all over Britain were invited to send in their products. These were subjected to rigorous tests and the best were awarded prizes. Thus, for the first time, both the industry and the public could compare the relative efficiency of different types of appliance, as well as their cost.[11] The gas companies also set out to woo domestic consumers by other means. They adopted the sensible policy of hiring out appliances rather than attempting to sell them and in the 1890s they introduced prepayment or 'penny in the slot' meters which soon became the main way in which gas was sold for domestic purposes.[12] The manufacturers of gas appliances also set up local show-rooms where their products could be demonstrated and inspected.[13]

As a result of all this activity, as well as major technological improvements in gas-lighting during the 1890s, the industry expanded rapidly. Between 1882 and 1912, the number of statutory undertakings (i.e. those with powers from Parliament to make and supply gas in a defined area) rose from 400 to 826 and the volume of gas sold trebled.[14] The domestic market for gas rapidly outstripped the others. By 1939, the gas industry estimated that 65 per cent of its sales were domestic, compared to 20 per cent industrial, 10 per cent commercial, and 5 per cent street lighting.[15] About 75 per cent of the gas consumed in an average family was used for cooking.[16]

In much the same way, the electricity companies which were established after the Electric (Lighting) Act of 1882 were forced to become interested in promoting the other domestic uses of electricity besides lighting when they realized that this was the main way by which they could hope to generate electricity economically and reduce its high price. As the pioneering electrical engineer, Rookes E. B. Crompton, explained:

At a very early stage we engineers saw how necessary it was to use electrical energy for purposes other than lighting, so that the use of the plant could be extended from the few hours of darkness, when artificial lighting is required, to other parts of the day, and we began to seek for means to popularize other uses of electrical energy.[17]

Electric lighting in the 1880s was followed by demonstrations of electric heating, cooking, and ironing in the 1890s and by motor-driven appliances such as vacuum cleaners, washing machines, and refrigerators during the first decades of this century.

Because it was easier and more profitable to supply large concentrations of consumers, both utilities spread first in highly populated areas. This process was relatively quick in the case of gas, which was easy to manufacture and distribute: most towns and

20 *Margaret Fairclough cooking with electricity at her School of Cookery in Gloucester Road,
London. From* Black and White, *January 12, 1895. The journalist reporting on the 'school
with trained lightning' wrote that: 'The table was an ordinary one (to the casual observer) of
unpainted wood. Miss Fairclough stood behind it, rolling pastry, while in front, in a neat little
row, were six cooking utensils. All were of bright and shining copper and steel, from the kettle
to the fluted "griller," and they simply stood on the table, without any fire, or apparent signs of
heat. Yet there, on the griller, was a chop cooking gaily away, "with an independent air;" in
the kettle, water was boiling; on the "hot plate," scones were toasting; in a frying-pan,
potatoes were frying; while two little pots were occupied by stewing bird and simmering jam. I
touched the table. It was cold, and I found I could lay my gloves and handkerchief upon it
with impunity.' Miss Fairclough's electric ovens were reported to 'retain their warmth for
an almost incredible time after the electrical current has been removed'. Crompton & Co
supplied the electrical appliances, probably free of charge.*

cities had their own gas supplies by 1850, and when gas companies started to exploit the domestic market, the extension of supplies to new urban consumers was fairly simple. But the generation and distribution of large-scale public electricity supplies was much more complex because it required greater capital investment and an extraordinary amount of co-ordination and standardization between different companies and manufacturers.[18] The initial spread of electricity in Britain was thus very slow.

Although the superiority of electric to gas-lighting was generally acknowledged, most people simply could not afford it in the early days. At the beginning of the 1880s, an hour's electric lighting cost 0.65d; an equivalent gas-light cost 0.20d in London and 0.17d in the large provincial cities.[19] It was not until about 1911, when metal filament lamps had been perfected, that electric lighting became competitive for the first time.[20] However, by the end of the First World War, the use of electricity in the home was still confined to the rich. According to Leslie Hannah, only half a million houses in Britain, perhaps 6 per cent of the total, were wired for electricity.[21] By 1921 the proportion of wired households had doubled to 12 per cent,[22] but little real progress was to be made until the passing of the Electricity (Supply) Act of 1926. This set up a Central Electricity Board with power to standardize the generation of electricity (a great variety of different voltages and frequencies were in use), to rationalize the haphazard distribution of stations, and to create a national grid to connect different sources of supply and extend them to the countryside. The Act encouraged electricity companies to take positive steps to gain new customers, such as introducing assisted wiring schemes and simplified tariffs.[23]

The price of electricity fell steadily with the extension of supplies. The cost of installing a modest lighting system dropped from a maximum of £20 in 1919 to about £6 in the 1930s,[24] and between 1921 and 1939, the average price of a kWh of electricity consumed for lighting and other domestic purposes fell from 5.75d to 1.57d.[25] As electrical engineers and economists had predicted, the proportion of households with electric service jumped dramatically: from 18 per cent in 1926 to 32 per cent in 1931, 65 per cent in 1938, and 86 per cent in 1949.[26]

These figures, however, are a somewhat misleading indication of the extent to which British housewives were benefiting from electricity by 1950. Apart from lighting, most households only used electricity for two functions: ironing and occasional space heating. By 1948, 86 per cent of households had electric irons and 64 per cent electric fires. But only 40 per cent owned a vacuum cleaner, 19 per cent a cooker, and 15 per cent a water heater, while a mere 4 per cent had a washing machine and 2 per cent a refrigerator.[27] Compared to other countries, notably Germany and the United States, the British market for electrical domestic appliances was in its infancy; its was only to mature in the affluent decades that followed the Second World War.

Women's reactions to gas and electricity were totally different. In the case of gas, they were slow to appreciate its domestic benefits. They played no part in the industry's early history and made no effort to extend national supplies or to improve the quality and design of gas appliances. But from the start, a significant number of women realized that electricity was 'a new servant' capable of liberating them from much household drudgery and allowing them to make better use of their time. Some even thought that electricity made a better servant than the human kind. As Mrs Lancaster, whose book on the use of electricity in the home appeared in 1914, pointed out:

. . . it is always at hand; *always* willing to do its allotted task and do it perfectly *silently*, swiftly and without mess; never wants a day off, never answers back, is never laid up, never asks for a rise; in fact it is often willing to work for less money; never gives notice and does not mind working overtime; it has no prejudices and is prepared to undertake any duties for which it is adapted; it costs nothing when it is not actually doing useful work.[28]

One woman actually entered the nascent electrical industry in the 1870s. Pretending to be a man (she assumed the name of Charles Torr) she rose to become managing director of a large Birmingham firm called Winfield's which produced ornamental brass-work, chandeliers and fittings suitable for interior electric lighting. She joined a dining society of electrical engineers called the 'Dynamicables' where many of the problems facing the new industry were discussed. She obviously had the vision to see electricity's brilliant future, as well as a flair for business and exceptional talent for concealing her sex. For, in the early 1880s, she approached Rookes E. B. Crompton with a proposal that their two firms should go into partnership; Crompton's was to carry out lighting installations and Winfield's was to supply the capital and fitments. Her plans were extremely grand: she wanted to apply for a Parliamentary act to light Birmingham and to sell electrical goods world-wide. However, after the two firms had co-operated for several years, Winfield's ran into financial difficulties and Charles Torr committed suicide: only then did her colleagues learn her true sex.[29]

Another woman to contribute to the industry's development was Hertha Ayrton. A graduate in mathematics from Girton College, Cambridge, she became a student at Finsbury Technical College in the 1880s, where she attended lectures on electricity and magnetism given by her future husband, William Edward Ayrton. She devoted her career to doing research on electricity and in 1899 was elected the first woman member of the august Institution of Electrical Engineers. In 1900 she read a paper on arc lighting at the International Congress of Electricity in Paris and in 1906 the Royal Society of London rewarded her research efforts with a medal.[30]

The majority of female electrophiles lacked the necessary scientific knowledge, engineering expertise and capital resources to enter the electrical industry. They promoted electricity by more orthodox means; by begging their husbands to install private generators, showing off the wonders of electricity to their friends, applying pressure to government officials, and writing about it. For example, Crompton relates that after he had lit Lord and Lady Randolph Churchill's London home with electricity in the 1880s, 'Lady Randolph became most useful as an advertising agent'. She delighted in 'showing off to her friends in the fashionable world our various electrical

21 *Hertha Ayrton (1854–1923). Her education at Cambridge University was subsidized by George Eliot, the novelist. Few women were admitted to the Institution of Electrical Engineers after Hertha Ayrton in 1899. The second had to wait until 1916; and by 1938, when the Institution had 18,252 members, there were only 22 women.*

22 *Caroline Haslett (1895–1957) started off her remarkable career in 1913 by leaving home and joining the Suffragettes. During the First World War she worked as a clerk in the London office of a Scottish boiler factory, drawing up quotations and specifications. In 1919 she became the organizing secretary of the newly founded Women's Engineering Society, before switching her attention to the Electrical Association for Women in 1924. She was interested in the application of factory time and motion studies to the home and believed that electricity was a revolutionary social force, providing 'a means whereby the work of women could be dignified, demanding intelligence rather than physical labour'. She worked indefatiguably to improve women's working lives and to extend their influence in public life. But her success in the latter area was limited. For example, she was the only woman appointed to the British Electricity Authority when it was founded in 1947.*

appliances, among them a pear-shaped switch, christened the "Randolph" which enabled her ladyship to light up or switch off without leaving her bed'.[31]

When Caroline Haslett[32] became the first director of the Electrical Association for Women (E.A.W.)[33] in 1924, individual campaigns for the expansion of electricity supplies and the improvement of electrical appliances acquired a national character and

23 *An advertisement from* The Electrical Age for Women – the Official Journal of the Electrical Association for Women, *showing the full panoply of appliances available in 1927.*

organization. The E.A.W., following as it did in the footsteps of the Suffragettes, became a sophisticated political pressure group, exerting considerable influence on the electrical and building industries, as well as on the government itself. It promoted electricity by a variety of means. Its illustrated magazine, *The Electrical Age for Women*, contained numerous articles explaining the advantages of electricity in the home and monitored improvements in electrical appliances, while its books explained in detail (to mostly ignorant readers) what electricity was and how it worked.[34] The E.A.W., which was London-based, also developed numerous branch associations: there were over 80 by 1939.[35] These were usually chaired by titled ladies – a shrewd tactical move as they had the means to help subsidize E.A.W. activities and the social standing to have an impact on their communities, especially if they already served in local government. In addition, the E.A.W. opened showrooms and mounted special travelling exhibitions. It encouraged electric cooking classes at schools and colleges and it organized major campaigns to advertise the need for more electric outlets in homes and for rural electrification.

Some of the E.A.W.'s work was also devoted to helping the handful of women who succeeded in entering the electrical industry during the 1920s. Margaret Partridge, for example, established an electrical engineering firm in Devon which employed young women as apprentices and, in the small Suffolk town of Bungay, an electrical supply company was set up in 1926 with a majority of women shareholders. Both firms aimed to provide openings for women but found their efforts were hampered by legislation prohibiting female employment between 10 pm and 5 am. Caroline Haslett, who was a director of the Bungay company, and fully aware that electrical supply companies work round the clock, campaigned hard to change the law, which was partially repealed in 1934.[36]

Although the E.A.W. was masterminded by well-educated, well-married and well-connected ladies, it was very much concerned with the welfare of housewives less well off than themselves. Mrs Wilfred Ashley, the E.A.W.'s second president from 1928 to 1931 (she was married to the Minister of Transport), was typical:

I see electricity as the best friend of the middle-class woman, and of the poor woman. I want the people who have only one servant, or none, to have cheap power in their homes. I want them to have heating plugs in the right place, and plenty of them. Electricity should be the housewife's friend, at her command for whatever purpose she might want it.[37]

In 1934 the Association passed a resolution at its annual conference 'that the time has now come when electricity should be available at an economic rate to the homes of the working people'. Elsie E. Edwards accordingly compiled a report on electricity in working-class homes which was designed to show what working-class women thought about electricity and which appliances they most wanted in their homes; to identify the main barriers to their introduction; and to suggest how these might be overcome. On the basis of data collected from branch associations, she attempted to show that women

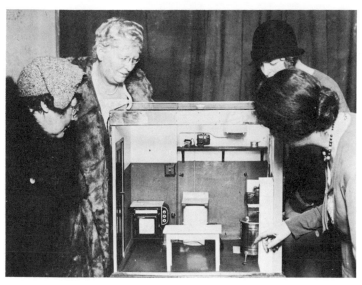

24 *E. A. W. members photographed in 1931 as they examined a model electric kitchen for working-class flats which featured a whistling kettle, cooker, bungalow fire, water heater and wash boiler.*

spent much less time on housework after their houses were fully electrified. She found, for example, that the average housewife in an unwired home spent just over 26¼ hours a week attending to lamps, cooking stoves, and fires, washing, ironing and cleaning; while in a house lit and powered by electricity her work load was reduced by 73 per cent to just over 7 hours. The chores of cleaning and filling paraffin lamps (which took 2.30 hours a week) and making fires (another 9.72 hours), simply disappeared with electricity and the time devoted to most other household chores was halved. The hours spent cleaning and lighting ranges dropped from 2.75 to 1.06; on ironing from 2.95 to 1.55; on cleaning from 8.26 to 4.12. The time spent on laundry dropped even more dramatically from 4.03 to 1.60 hours.[38] There could be no doubt about electricity's revolutionary effects on housework or the desirability of its introduction to all homes.

Enough has now been said, by way of background, about gas and electricity. By 1949, 79 per cent of British households had a gas supply, 86 per cent had electricity and 68 per cent had both utilities. Only three per cent lived in such remote areas that they had neither.[39] Before discussing their effects on housework in subsequent chapters, it is worth emphasizing that women were simply passive beneficiaries of two of the three utilities that transformed housework in the nineteenth and twentieth centuries – water and gas. They did not campaign for supplies or contribute to their development in any way. Electricity, by contrast, was a different story. The E.A.W. thus has a significance that overrides the practical importance of its work: it is the only example of women actually changing the conduct of housework through collective action during the three centuries covered in this book.

Chapter 3 COOKING

How did women cook the foods they had at their disposal? Fortunately, a great deal is known about the history of British foods and recipes, thanks to such masterly studies as C. Anne Wilson's *Food and Drink in Britain*[1] and the current fashion for reprinting old cookery books and investigating the origins and development of traditional British dishes,[2] so it is not necessary to go into those aspects of the subject here, fascinating though they are. Some excellent work has also been done on the evolution and design of cooking utensils (mostly by museum curators and antique collectors), so there is no need to cover that ground either.[3] Instead, this chapter is devoted to the technology of cooking, a subject which has, so far, aroused rather little curiosity. What were the methods women used to perform different culinary operations? Were they easy or difficult, satisfying or tedious? What triggered changes? Were there distinctive variations in culinary practice between different social classes and regions?

In answering these questions it is helpful to describe British cooking methods between 1650 and 1950 in terms of five evolutionary stages, though of course many of the stages overlapped. Stage One, for example, was universal in the seventeenth century, dominant in the eighteenth, common in the nineteenth and not unknown in the twentieth. It thus coexisted with all four later stages. However, the disadvantage of over-simplification seems to be outweighed by the desirability of identifying the main phases of development in a comprehensible and memorable way.

Stage one – The longest-lived
This first stage was characterized by three basic and quite distinct cooking operations: boiling, baking and spit-roasting.

Boiling was the most important of these operations: the normal, daily method of preparing food common to rich and poor alike, all over the British Isles. Food and water were boiled in an iron pot (or kettle) suspended over the fire – a wood or peat fire on an open hearth or a coal fire in an iron grate. These pots went by all sorts of names: in seventeenth-century Devon, for example, they were called 'crocks', 'cauldrons' and 'catherins',[4] in Bedfordshire they were 'kettles',[5] in Yorkshire just 'pots'.[6]

They were suspended from a wooden cross beam or iron bar high up in the chimney, by means of a rope, a wooden stick, an iron chain or an iron rod with a hook at the bottom. Wooden or rope devices for hanging pots were fairly common in the seventeenth century, but by the late eighteenth century they were almost invariably made out of iron. The alternatives were considered very primitive indeed. When the missionary John Lanne Buchanan visited the West Hebrides in the 1780s he found, to his surprise,

25 *The pot is suspended by an iron chain and hook in this Scottish farmhouse which has an unusual free-standing grate. Note the hens in the house, feeding from the earth floor and roosting in the rafters, and the bed in the corner near the fire. From Allan Ramsay,* The Gentle Shepherd, *1796. The aquatint illustration is by D. Allan and dated 'Edinburgh 1788'.*

that 'Instead of iron crooks they use a stick of four feet long, full of holes, with a pin to pass through to raise or lower their pots when placed above their fires. The pots are suspended from the roof, in the middle of the house, by a rope made of benty grass'.[7]

The pot was usually suspended in a stationary position over the fire. Gradually, however, ingenious ways of adjusting its height were introduced. From about 1730 it became usual to raise or lower the pot by the addition or removal of different sized pothooks (also called 'trammels', 'hangers', 'recking-crewkes', and 'crooks'). It also became possible to alter the angle and position of the pot over the fire by means of a swinging chimney crane. However, this sophisticated contraption, which was almost unheard of in the seventeenth century, and very rare until the middle of the eighteenth, never became very common.[8]

These developments in pot hanging methods enhanced the great advantage of boiling as a cooking method: its simplicity. It made use of existing heating arrangements and required no special effort, unless the fire had to be made up specially. It was also amazingly versatile. The same iron pot was capable of producing a simple meal, say of boiled potatoes to be eaten with buttermilk; or an elaborate, two course repast of meat, dumplings, potatoes and greens followed by suet pudding (the different ingredients being put into the pot in stages, separated if necessary by the use of nets).

Pot cooking was very easy indeed if only one thing was cooked at a time, as this model Irish peasant woman's description of making 'stirabout'* in 1813 suggests: 'I let the water boil before I stir in e'er a grain; and when once it boils fast, I put in handful after handful, till I think there is near enough, stirring it very well all the time; then I lift the pot a hook or two higher, and cover it up for a good share of half an hour, very seldom stirring it'.[9] Elaborate pot cooking, on the other hand, required rather more attention. Mollie Harris, who comes from an Oxfordshire farming family, remembers how her mother concocted wonderfully tasty and filling meals in the 1920s: 'In a great oval pot that was suspended over a good fire she cooked hunks of fat bacon along with potatoes and cabbage. The vegetables were put into string nets to keep them separate. When they cooked she would fish them out of the steaming saucepan with the aid of a fork. Then into the same water and along with the bacon she would drop a suet pudding, perhaps a roly-poly or a currant "spotted dick", and sometimes just a plain suet to be eaten with golden syrup on it as a special treat.'[10]

However, pot cooking did have disadvantages. It was hot, smoky, and susceptible to the occasional disaster. The *Ladies Dictionary* of 1694 warned readers against entering the kitchen because the heat of the fire made servants 'hot and fretful'. An interfering lady might find 'the Sawces waisted to nothing', and that the over-boiling pot had 'pist out the Fire'.[11] A good meal could also be spoiled by soot falling down the chimney, as a Norfolk boy called George Baldrey discovered around 1870: 'Sunday come, the pot was put on, and mother made five Norfolk swimmers and then slipped across to a neighbour telling me to look to the pot and keep it boiling because of the dumplings. I thought that

* *Stirabout*: porridge made by stirring oatmeal in boiling water or milk.

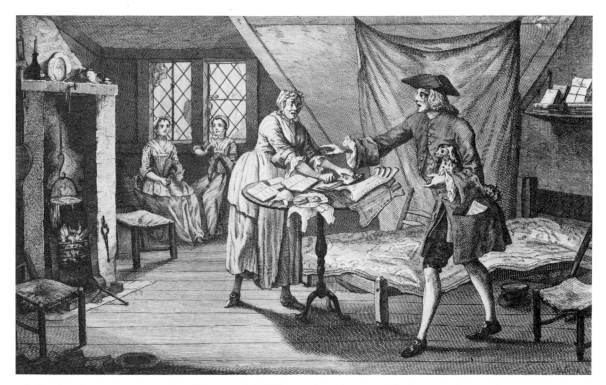

26 *In this dramatic engraving of c. 1750, Mr 'Rhymer', an impoverished poet, points to the fire where the pot containing his family's next meal is boiling over. He thus diverts his wife from throwing his latest manuscript into the fire. She, poor thing, is pregnant and worried about money and, when he returns to their garret home with a lap-dog under his arm (yet another mouth to feed), she flies into a rage. The two daughters are mending stockings.*

was a great job, tended the fire up and kept it going full gallop. Presently the lid lifted a bit with the steam and I peeps in and sees the sheep's head going round the pot with its mouth open, like old Nick after the sinners, and only one swimmer to be seen.' Thinking the sheep had swallowed the other dumplings and was about to consume the last, the boy rushed to find his mother. 'She came running and dang me if I hadn't been in such a mortal hurry I'd left the top of the pot off and in wallops a great whack of soot. Mother starts trying to fish that out and up come the swimmers from the bottom of the pot, Mother muttering, "This what comes of leavin' a silly young lout to watch the dinner".'[12]

In some aristocratic houses boiling also took place over a separate stewing stove built against a wall to the right or left of the fireplace. Richard Bradley, in his translation of R. Chomel's *Dictionnaire Oeconomique* (1725) described it as 'a sort of furnace where they dress pottages,* and where they prepare ragoes:† It's made of Brick Work, furnish'd with chaffing dishes above and an ash-pan underneath'.[13] Such stoves were very much a

* *Pottage*: a thick soup. † *Ragoe* (i.e. ragout): a stew of meat and vegetables.

27 'Change of Diet; a Ballad: being a Sequel to the Roast Beef of Old England', 1757. *There is a typical stewing-stove in the centre of this satirical broadside attacking the French and their foods ('frogs and ragout').*

French import and were generally employed in producing 'made dishes'. Partly for this reason and partly because they burned expensive charcoal and gave off a lot of unwholesome gas, they never became popular outside grand establishments.[14]

Baking was done in several ways, depending on the region and on the items to be baked. Oatcakes and bannocks, for example, which were widely eaten in the north of England and Scotland, were cooked on bakestones. In some households these were great slabs of stone or iron to the side of the main fireplace, with their own separate heating system. But in modest establishments bakestones were simply stones heated up in the main fireplace. These smaller bakestones were often works of art, carefully constructed to support the cake and with perforated ornamentation serving to vent the steam.[15] They only disappeared during the course of the nineteenth century, when they were superceded by round plates of iron called 'girdles', 'griddles', or 'yetlins' which were suspended or placed over the fire and which heated up much more quickly.

Baking was also done in an iron pot, particularly in Wales,[16] Ireland,[17] and English

28 *A Yorkshire woman making oat cakes in her cottage, c. 1814. She mixed the oatmeal and water in the large bowl. She then sifted some dry meal onto the flat board and poured on a few ladle-fulls of mixture. Once she had formed the cakes, by a circular horizontal movement of the board, she baked them for a few seconds on the bakestone to the left of the fireplace. After the cakes had cooled on the back of the inverted chair, they were hung on the bread creel suspended from the ceiling. From George Walker* The Costume of Yorkshire, *1885.*

counties such as Cornwall,[18] Cumberland, and Westmorland,[19] where the method continued in use well into the twentieth century. Sometimes the pot was hung over the fire; at other times it was detached from the pot hanger and converted into an oven by turning it upside down over a heated stone, or covering it with a lid, and burying it in burning fuel. All sorts of things were baked in this way, including bread, cakes, puddings, fish, and stews. In 1798, Eliza Melroe described its use in Cornwall and Ireland for making pies:

. . . the lid of the pot is first heated and put on the hearth, with the pot turned upside down upon it; this soon communicates a heat to the whole: – When the pye intended to be baked is put in, and embers, such as charcoal, cinders, turf, and wood-ashes are put round and over it in a smothered manner, so as to retain the heat: – In this state it may be left by families, whose employment is out of doors, and whose absence may be for four or six hours: during which time their pies are baking sufficiently, without hazard of burning or being over done.[20]

Although it was impossible to see how the food was cooking when it was concealed in a pot oven, women could monitor the progress of certain dishes by listening. In some

29 *Florrie and Bessie Howden in front of the communal bread oven at Mickley Colliery, near Prudhoe, Northumberland. The photograph was taken c. 1914.*
30 *Mrs Jane Davies and her daughter Mari photographed in front of their bread oven in a Merioneth farmhouse, 1948. The copper can just be seen to the right.*

places they even made use of crude amplification devices. In the parish of Mylor, Cornwall, for example, it was common practice in the early 1900s for them to 'use an iron rod applied to the kettle and the ear to ascertain by the sound thereby conveyed if the article covered over was boiling or not'.[21]

Portable earthenware ovens were also used for baking in some places. When Richard Pococke travelled through Devonshire in 1750 he noticed that the inhabitants baked their bread in pot ovens in the western part of the county but elsewhere made use of 'Cloume ovens, which are earthenware of several sizes . . . and being heated they stop 'em over with embers to keep in the heat'.[22]

Larger-scale baking took place in brick and stone ovens. These were to be found in most parts of England and the lowlands of Scotland. Their use implied ample fuel supplies and at least a week's worth of baking. Communal ovens, shared by the inhabitants of a small hamlet or village, were free-standing constructions, often in the open air. But the ovens used by individual households were generally built into a side wall or corner of the kitchen fireplace. Houses belonging to the landed gentry in the south tended to have bee-hive ovens built out from a wall. These appear in many of the frontispieces of seventeenth- and eighteenth-century cook books.[23] Whatever their type, however, these brick and stone ovens worked in the same way. They were heated

31 *'Dr Syntax turned nurse', 1820. The oven is built into the wall in this kitchen turned nursery. From William Combe,* The Tour of Dr Syntax, in search of the picturesque, *illustrated by Thomas Rowlandson, 1855.*

32 *A bee-hive oven, with a woman sticking a peel into it, 1670. Detail from the frontispiece of* The queen-like closet: or, Rich cabinet, stored with all manner of rare receipts for preserving, candying and cookery *by Hannah Woolley, 1684.*

with peat or faggots of wood or furze. When the ashes were red-hot, they were removed, the oven cleaned, and the weekly bake inserted with a wooden spade called a peel. No further fuel was added: the heat stored in the bricks or stones was sufficient to cook the lot. Large loaves were the first to go in and were placed at the back; the rest of the baking followed in relays according to the required cooking time. Large loaves of bread took two and a half hours to bake, cakes and pies from one and a half to two hours, batch cakes an hour and a half and buns 25 minutes, in an Essex oven heated by faggots in the 1890s.[24]

Considerable skill was needed to make the ovens work. In the first place they had to be heated properly. In the eastern Fens at the end of the nineteenth century, 'It took 13 cesses [pieces of turf] to heat the oven for baking. The cesses would be stood in a ring round the edge of the oven, with one or two broken up in the centre of the ring. When they were all burned to ashes, the woman would rake them out, and in would go her bread'.[25] Secondly, it was vital to seal the ovens adequately, or the heat would escape too rapidly. One black day in 1697, a Yorkshire farming family found 'The ewn for lack of dittin, has slacken'd all i'th' heet' and 'Puddings and pyes are naught fit to eat'.[26] (Their oven door had not been mortared up properly.)

It also took experience to know when the oven was heated through. One method was to observe changes in the colour of the brick or stone. This was used in the east Suffolk village of Blaxhall at the beginning of this century. 'The bricks would change in colour from black to red as they got hotter; and when a handful of flour, thrown lightly against

33 *Spit-roasting in front of an open hearth fire without a jack, 1670. Another detail from* The queen-like closet.

34 *Opposite: A sucking pig is being spit-roasted three notches away from the fire in this grand kitchen. There is a jack to the left of the mantelpiece and a cauldron suspended from a relatively crude pot hook. Frontispiece to* The Complete English Cook; or Prudent Housewife *by Catherine Brooks, 1762.*

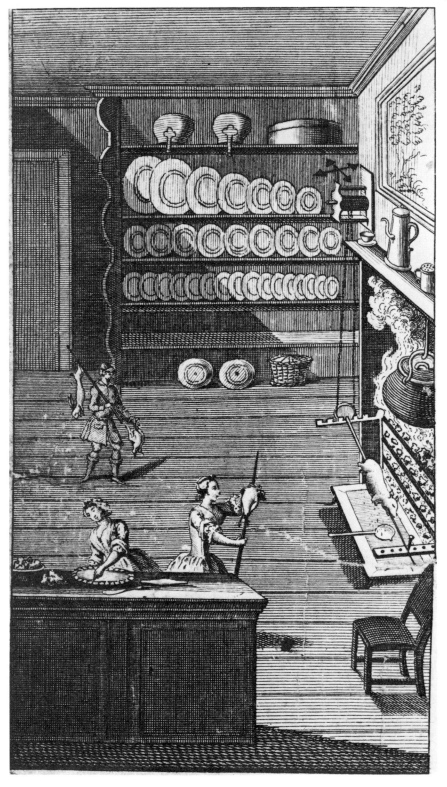

53

I do rule the the roast _ and certainly can
get a sop in the pan when ever I please _ but
my Spouse is a sad plague to me

the side of the oven, burned with a blaze of sparks, the housewife knew that her oven was hot enough for baking.'[27] In nineteenth-century Warwickshire a large white or light coloured stone was built into the wall opposite the oven door. This served as a rude thermometer by changing colour as the oven heated. Eventually it glowed at 'white' heat – 'a marked object against its blacker neighbours'.[28] In Buckinghamshire, the stone was built into the side or top of the oven and called 'a wise man'.[29]

Spit-roasting, the third basic cooking method, was already well established in the seventeenth century. The bird or hunk of meat was held horizontally in front of the fire by means of a spit. The spit was supported either on hooked firedogs, by the grate bars, or very occasionally on separate stands placed in front of the fire. The fat fell into a rectangular, four-legged dripping pan below. This method of cooking meat seems to have been more popular than the alternatives: the grid-iron, a horizontal iron frame supported on short legs used for broiling meat or fish over the fire, or the much superior vertical broiling-iron. This prototype of the Dutch oven was described by Gervase Markham in 1623 as 'a plate Iron made with hookes and pricks, on which you may hang the meate, and set it close before the fire, and so the plate heating the meate behind, as the fire doth before, it will both the sooner, and with more neatness be readic'.[30] References to these instruments do occur in seventeenth-century inventories and household accounts, but they are far less common than spits. Indeed it is hard to find an inventory – no matter how humble – which does not boast at least one spit, 'broche', 'peake', of 'flesh pike'.

Many different methods were used to keep the spit turning. At the beginning of the period it was usually turned by hand, a tedious job, often assigned to children. John Macdonald, the eighteenth century's most distinguished footman, tells how he was 'taken into a gentleman's house to turn the spit' as a boy in the 1740s.[31] In a few large country houses the spits were turned by water.[32] But more frequently, animals were employed to tread a small wooden wheel in a box attached to the spits. According to Venterus Mandey and J. Moxon, writing in the 1690s, '. . . the animals which are commonly made use of for the turning of spits, are Dogs, but Geese are better, for they will bear their Labour longer, so that if there be need they will continue their Labour 12 Hours'.[33] The trouble with dogs was that they were too intelligent. As Thomas Somerville learned during his youth in mid-eighteenth-century Scotland, the dogs 'used to hide themselves or run away when they observed indications that there was to be a roast for dinner'.[34]

The mechanical devices most frequently used to solve the problem of spit-turning were the wind-up or weight jack and the smoke jack. The former was operated by winding up a weight which, in its controlled descent, imparted a turning motion to the

35 *Opposite: 'Coplinda Lindhursta the cook' is spit-roasting a joint of meat on the hooks of a grate in this satirical etching by William Heath, 1829.*

36 *While Mrs Suds and Mrs Mangle have a heart-to-heart about rising prices, a goose is roasting in front of the fire, suspended by a poor man's spit. The print was published in 1801 during the inflationary era of the French Revolutionary Wars.*

spit. The latter required a really vigorous fire, for it depended on the force of the ascending hot air, visible as smoke, to rotate a fan which in turn caused the spit to turn.

The origin of the first device is somewhat obscure. However, it seems almost certain that the smoke jack reached Britain from Italy in the second half of the sixteenth century[35] and was adopted in some large households. John Evelyn, writing to John Aubrey in 1675, described a smoke jack which had been installed in a kitchen chimney at Wooton in Surrey about a century earlier. He said that 'it makes very little Noise, needs no Winding up, and, for that, preferable to the more noisy Inventions'.[36] This suggests that the most common form of jack in the seventeenth century was the wind-up type.

Contemporary inventories and household accounts confirm this impression and also show that jacks were still rare and only found in the houses of the gentry.

The wind-up jack was certainly the most common kind in the eighteenth century. R. Campbell, author of *The London Tradesman* (1747), said that their manufacture constituted the London jacksmiths' main business[37] and in 1748 Pehr Kalm commented that there were wind-up meat jacks turning spits 'in every house in England'. He commented that they constituted 'a very useful invention, which lightens labour amongst a people who eat so much meat'.[38] By the end of the eighteenth century no household of any pretension was without a jack.

Not until the beginning of the nineteenth century did it become common practice to speed up the roasting process by placing the meat in front of a wooden screen lined with tin which faced the fire and reflected its heat. This was followed by a smaller tin machine, often called a roaster, which the anonymous lady author of *The new London cookery and complete domestic guide* (1827) recommended as 'much more convenient and effectual; it just occupies the width of the fire bars, not the whole grate, and has within itself a dripping pan, and a place for a roasting jack; also a door at the back to open for basting and salting the meat'.[39]

The jack's history in the nineteenth century is rather more difficult to disentangle. Many different types were patented; but it is hard to know what proportion of these were manufactured and which of them proved most successful. Thomas Webster in his *Encyclopaedia of Domestic Economy* (1844) describes five kinds: the familiar wind-up and smoke jacks, the new spring* and bottle† jacks (usually used in conjunction with the roaster described above) and the poor man's spit, a weighted piece of worsted string.‡[40] He does not discuss their relative popularity of distribution over the country, and cookery writers tend to be vague about what kind of jack they envisage in their readers' kitchens. However, it is clear that by the early nineteenth century few people turned meat by hand – except in remote, poverty-stricken areas such as Ireland, where jacks were a novelty in the 1840s, even among landowners.[41]

Stage two – The 'open' range

The first phase in the evolution of cooking methods was certainly the most widespread and long-lasting. None of the next stages was so important. The second – the 'open' range developed in the mid-eighteenth century – never affected the whole population and was soon overtaken by technological developments. It was marked by the transition from a wood or coal fire in a simple iron grate to a more elaborate iron 'range'. Movable iron stands called 'trivets' or 'crans' were attached to the grate's upper bar to support a

---

* *Spring jack*: this consisted of a spring in a box which activated a wheel and endless chain so as to turn a horizontal spit.

† *Bottle jack*: this consisted of a spring enclosed in a brass cylinder which turned a horizontal spit with hooks at the end. It required winding up every time it was used.

‡ The *poor man's spit* required a slight twist every five minutes.

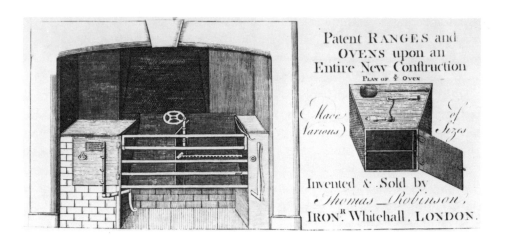

By His Majesty's *Royal Letters Patent.*

PERPETUAL OVENS in KITCHEN RANGES, upon an entire new Construction, heated without the Affistance of any Flew, or additional Fire. Replete with every Advantage and calculated for univerfal Benefit, being capable of every Ufe and Purpofe that can poffibly be required, without the leaft Expence or Trouble.

The RANGE has alfo many new and excellent Improvements, deriving great Advantage and Utility from the Oven being connected with it.

Recommended to Houfe-keepers of every Degree and Denomination, as the moft compact, moft ufeful, and leaft expenfive Invention of the Kind ever made public.

Great Variety may be feen fuited to any Size Chimney (with One in ufe,) and a fuller Defcription given.

EXPLANATION.

THE Range is made to wind up with one Cheek only (the Side of the Oven forming the other); upon the Cheek is fixed a fwinging Trivet, which turns on or off the Fire. The Top Bar falls down occafionally to a Level with the fecond Bar, and the top Part of the Cheek lets down in the fame Manner alfo, when required for a fmall Fire; the lowest Bar but one from the Bottom takes out, for the more fpeedy raking the Fire out at Night; and a fliding Spit Rack is fixed at each End. The Hob, Front, and Side in which the Pinion is placed, are of Caft-Iron; on the other Side is fixed the Oven, covered over with a Plate of Iron, which forms an excellent Hob, and will contain fufficient Heat to keep any Thing warm; within the Oven is a movable Shelf with a Regulator.

DIRECTIONS for FIXING.

THE Range is to be fet as in the ufual Way, leaving Room enough for the moving Cheek to work eafy, and alfo in the Side and Back of the Chimney for the Winding Rack and fliding Spit Racks to move without Obftruction.

The Oven muft be fixed on a folid Pier of Brick Work, and filled up quite clofe, particularly at the Side and Back; Lime mixed to a proper Confiftency, fhould be grouted in, to prevent the leaft Cavity. The Top of the Oven muft alfo be enclofed, and the Iron Plate on the Top raifed to a Level with the Arm of the Range, the Whole cemented clofe as poffible to retain the Heat.

You muft obferve to place the Range and Oven fo that the ufual Size Fire may be in the Middle of the Chimney.

N. B. Old Ranges altered according to the Patent, and Ovens annexed to them.

37 *An advertisement for Thomas Robinson's 'open' range which he patented in 1780.*

tea kettle or other small utensil. The size of the fire could be altered or adjusted by contracting the sides or 'cheeks' of the grate or by folding down its front bars. Thus, for boiling a pot or kettle over the fire the grate would be kept small, but for more ambitious operations, such as meat roasting, it would be 'built up'.

By the 1860s open ranges usually included side boilers for heating water and ovens for baking, heated by conduction or by a system or primitive flues.[42] These additional fixtures were innovations from the north of England, the centre of Britain's burgeoning iron industry. According to John Holland, cheap cast iron ovens came first: 'It was about the year 1770 that these conveniences began to be furnished by the founders of the north of England, and to be set with grates as we now see them . . .' He added that cast iron boilers 'occupying the side of the ordinary fire range, opposite to the oven, and covered with a lid serving as a hob' followed 10 or 12 years later, 'the heated water being either drawn off by means of a tap at the side, or ladled out at the top'.[43]

The fully developed open range was the outcome of two separate but related developments. The fundamental one was the great expansion in coal mining that occurred in the eighteenth century. Thomas Newcomen's 'fire' engine, on sale from

38 *The late seventeenth-century hearth at Frog's Hall, Biddendon, Kent, photographed by Edwin Smith c. 1950, when still in use. In districts near the Sussex Weald, a traditional iron-founding centre using charcoal, farm and cottage hearths were usually equipped with a thick, cast-iron plate, supported by bricks on each side. A wood fire burned on the plate, heating the pot suspended above: the space below was used for baking and keeping food hot.*

1712, enabled the exploitation of water-logged, deep-lying seams which had been the despair of seventeenth-century colliers. Using canals for distribution, mined coal not only replaced wood and peat in more and more urban areas during the course of the eighteenth century, but also spread inland.

The second development was of a different order. Coal not only changed cooking methods by forcing the introduction of grates, but also had a profound effect on the iron industry. Until the middle of the eighteenth century, cast iron was made with charcoal: this fuel was in short supply and the cast iron made with it was too hard and brittle. The discovery of a system of making good quality iron, using charred coal (coke) as fuel, transformed the situation. Cast iron production increased rapidly; and the boom was sustained by the application of steam power to the various manufacturing processes at the end of the century. Already the dramatic rise in iron production was having an impact; cast iron grates, ovens and boilers were flooding on to the market. By 1830, when John Holland was writing, these were commonplace. He described the iron oven as 'an economical fixture' within the means of the poorest persons. 'To find a dwelling house, however small, without an oven beside the fire, would be an exceedingly novel occurrence now-a-days.'[44]

Stage three – The 'combination' and 'closed' ranges, iron monsters
The transition from the 'open' range which evolved in the eighteenth century to the 'closed' range of the nineteenth century constitutes the third evolutionary stage. Here the open fire was covered over by a hot plate, ending the need for a suspended pot: a coal-guzzling iron monster had been born. The closed range began to be manufactured commercially in the 1810s. Its spread was mainly confined to the south of England and to the Midlands. Ovens and boilers, sometimes two or three per side, were heated by complicated arrangements of flues, their temperature controlled by a register and dampers. The front of the range usually had movable panels which could be shifted either to shut off the fire or to expose the flames to view. This type of 'combination' range or 'kitchener' as it was often called, was especially popular.[45] Britons have always loved an open fire and been fond of roasting their meat in front of it. Many ranges, however, were truly 'closed' in that the fire was completely encased in iron.

Maintenance of the closed range was extremely arduous. It was necessary to get up very early to clean the flues and light the monster. It also required regular polishing and black-leading to look presentable. Jane Coates, who married a railway policeman in 1912, described her daily cleaning routine as follows:

1. Remove fender and fire-irons.
2. Rake out all ashes and cinders; first throw in some damp tea leaves to keep down the dust.
3. Sift the cinders.
4. Clean the flues.
5. Remove all grease from the stove with newspaper.
6. Polish the steels with bathbrick and paraffin.

IMPROVED PATENT KITCHEN RANGE,

WITH Oven, Boiler, Hot Plate, and Hot Closets; calculated to Bake, Boil, Roast, Steam, Stew, and heat Flat Irons, by a small Fire, with a continued Supply of Ten Gallons of boiling Water; the Consumption of Fuel about one half the usual Quantity, and a *certain* Cure for a Smoky Chimney; warranted to answer (if not, to be returned), never having failed in a single instance. It embraces every useful improvement, and is so systematically arranged as to be rendered suitable from a small to the most extensive Establishment: it also combines Economy, Cleanliness, and Simplicity in every Description of Cookery. The Vessels are used without the least Soil, and, of course, far more durable than those used over common Fires. Daily in Use for Public Inspection from 10 till 4.

The Manufactory for the undermentioned Articles.

All Kinds of Kitchen Ranges, upon the most approved Principles, embracing the late Improvements in Steam Boilers, Ovens, Roasters, Hot Plate, Steam-Closets, &c.

Cast Iron, Bronzed, Japanned, and bright Steel Sarcophagus, Register; and Half-Register Stoves, for Drawing-rooms, Parlours, Libraries, &c. on new and improved Principles, with a Safeguard. which draws out to prevent Accidents, or the Fire to retire into the Chimney.

Patent Warm-Air Stoves, and Stoves with descending Flues, for Halls, Churches, &c.

Portable Kitchens of various sizes convenient for Fishing, Sailing, and Shooting Parties; also for Camps, or to be used in the open Air; which will Bake, Roast, Boil, and Steam by one Fire.

Fire-proof Boxes, for Deeds, Papers, &c.

Bells and Alarums hung upon the most approved Principles, by the best London Workmen.

Patent, Secret, and curious Locks, of all Sorts.

A curious Padlock, without a Key, only to be opened by the Person who locked it.

Spring Guns, for Gardens, Plantations, &c.

Ditto, for Dwelling-houses, Hot-houses, &c.

Patent Humane Man Trap, to secure Depredators without injuring them.

Small Portable Fire and Garden Engines.

A Portable Shower Bath, enclosed in a Wood Frame, with Curtains and Water Receiver.

Steel Wheat-Mill, to grind Corn and dress the Flour at one Operation.

Best London-made Tea and Coffee Urns, of the most fashionable Patterns; also Cutlery, Japanned, Plated Articles, &c.

Patentee of the Spring Roasting Jack, to go without Weights or Pullies, which acts Vertically and Horizontally at the same time. The Works being all enclosed, are secured from Dirt and Injury, and, from its extreme simple Construction, not liable to be out of Order.

Every Article requisite for Furnishing Houses, connected with the above Branches, to be had at the Manufactory of

HENRY MARRIOTT,

NO. 64, FLEET STREET, ⸪

Furnishing Ironmonger, &c to the Hon. Corporation of the City of London.

Printed by J. Warwick, 7, Nevil's Court, Fetter Lane, London.

39 *Advertisement for a 'closed' range, 1813. The fire is visible, though covered by a hot plate.*

40 & 41 *The wealthy often cooked over small grates from choice. In these satirical aquatints by Thomas Gillray, 1791, the King and Queen are preparing a midnight snack in their private chambers. He is toasting muffins and boiling a kettle for tea and she is cooking sprats on a gridiron.*

7. Blacklead the iron parts and polish.
8. Wash the hearthstone and polish it.[46]

However, from the cook's point of view, the closed range had advantages – so long as it actually worked! It permitted a large number of varied cooking operations to take place simultaneously and it was less hot and sweaty than the open range. Unfortunately a large proportion of ranges didn't function properly and were more trouble than they were worth. All too often the ovens and boilers didn't heat satisfactorily. The reasons for this common failure were a mixture of scientific ignorance, shoddy workmanship and avarice on the part of ironmongers. The principles of heat as applied to cooking had been explained elegantly by the American philanthropist Count Rumford at the end of the eighteenth century[47] and reiterated by his chief British disciples, John Claudius Loudon, Thomas Webster and Frederick Edwards at frequent intervals thereafter. These principles established the waste and inefficiency of making cooking apparatus out of iron. The metal absorbed too much heat from the fire and radiated it into the room. This may have made the kitchen a snug place in which to work, but the heat was not being used for cooking purposes and was anyway unwelcome during the summer.

Stoves built largely of brickwork, as Rumford recommended, did not suffer from these faults. However, manufacturers had their own interests to consider. Many of them did take up Count Rumford's idea[48] of cooking meat in a roaster, an iron oven heated by a furnace below, because this created a new demand for iron. But they blithely ignored those other parts of his teaching which did not suit their own convenience. In fact it was a frequent nineteenth-century practice to advertise under the name 'Rumford' ranges which were a travesty of what he had actually recommended.[49] The amount of iron used in the construction of ranges rose steadily. Indeed, the marketing skills of the manufacturers largely explain why the 'combination' and 'closed' ranges ever came to compete with the open type in the nineteenth century.

The importance of the closed range should not be exaggerated. It was always a comparatively expensive apparatus to buy and maintain and, on the whole, its use was confined to prosperous households with servants. Most people in Britain cooked by simpler methods. For example, agricultural labourers living in a Hertfordshire village boiled most of their food over an open grate and baked their bread in a communal bakehouse until side-oven grates were put into their cottages in the 1870s.[50] And the multitude of Londoners living in tenements in the 1890s generally did their cooking by balancing a kettle, saucepan or frying pan over a fire in a small open grate.[51] Furthermore, it seems that the closed range never caught on in the north of England. In the 1920s, for instance, the open range was to be found in the majority of houses in Lancashire, Yorkshire, Durham, Cumberland and Northumberland.[52]

Stage four – Gas

Cooking by gas is now so common that it is difficult to appreciate what a radical technological change it constituted when it was first introduced on a wide scale in the 1880s. In the first place, the gas stove or cooker consumed a new, centrally distributed fuel: coal-gas. Secondly, the gas stove was used only for cooking; unlike the open fire and the range, it did not heat rooms and provide hot water as well. Cooking by gas was also remarkably easy. No longer was it necessary to carry coal around, clean up the mess which it made, rise early to light the stove, and tend it during the day.

These and other advantages were naturally brought to public attention at the time. A. Pearson, an Oxford ironmonger and gas engineer, provided a typical list of them in a promotional booklet which he published in 1889. The gas range, he wrote, 'is always ready at hand to be called into full service at a moment's notice, will burn for any length of time without attention and can be extinguished in an instant'. He stressed the bliss of perfect temperature control. 'The heat can be regulated at will to the greatest nicety, so that fast boiling or the gentlest simmering can be secured by the adjustment of a tap, while any degree of temperature can be maintained as long as desired.'[53] Marie Jenny Sugg, author of the first gas cookery book, *The Art of Cooking by Gas* (1890), claimed that '. . . those who adopt gas in the kitchen will find themselves freed from all that trouble, dirt and uncertainty in working which attend a coal kitchener'.[54]

It is interesting to note that gas cooking first took place in the seventeenth century. The Reverend John Clayton wrote to Robert Boyle in 1687 about a visit he had made to a

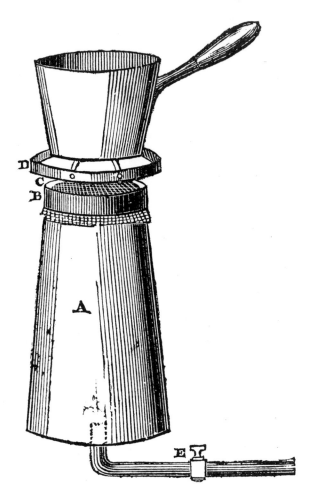

42 *John Robison's gas cooking device, as shown in* The Mechanic's Magazine, *1831. A, a conical tube of thin sheet iron. B, a hoop of the same material, by which a piece of wire-gauze, C, is secured over the mouth of A; the joints of A and B should be hard soldered, and the hoop should fit over the wire-gauze so tight as to prevent any gas escaping from A except through the gauze. A, a bracket or shelf, made of hoop iron and wire, to support any vessel which is to be heated. E, a gas-pipe and stop-cock; the jet or nozzle of the pipe to enter two or three inches within the cone.*

natural gas spring near Wigan in Lancashire, commenting that the flame was 'so fierce that several strangers have boiled Eggs over it'. He added: 'The people thereabouts indeed confirm that about 30 years ago it would have boiled a piece of beef . . .'[55]

However, although many scientists were interested in coal-gas during the eighteenth century, none seems to have pursued the idea of cooking by gas. Count Rumford, for instance, never mentions the possibility in all his voluminous writings about cooking methods. Similarly, William Murdoch, the gas pioneer of the 1790s, was only interested in manufacturing coal-gas for lighting purposes.[56] This lack of interest persisted until

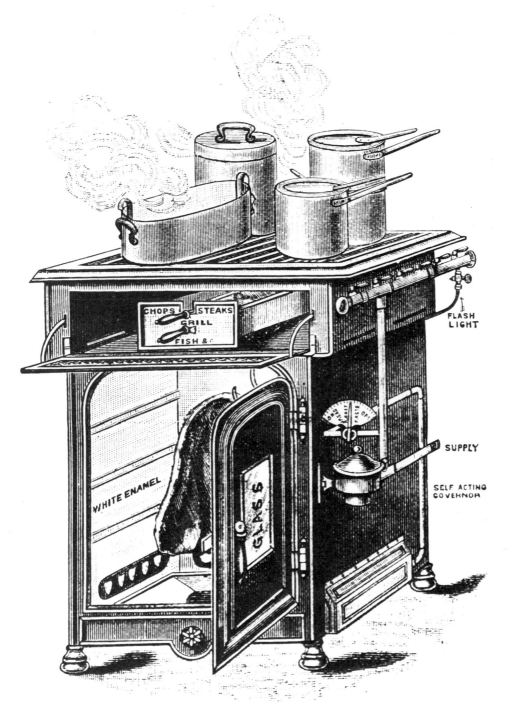

43 *The 'Charing Cross Kitchener', as shown in Marie Jenny Sugg's* The Art of
Cooking by Gas, *1890. The Sugg family owned one of the most successful gas-appliance
companies in the late nineteenth and early twentieth centuries. By looking inside the oven,
one can see that the tradition of roasting meat in mid-air* over *a dripping pan died hard:
it is only comparatively recently that people have taken to roasting their meat* in *the
dripping pan.*

the 1820s, when cities and large towns in Britain began to acquire public supplies of piped gas.

According to the gas engineer Samuel Clegg, the first piece of apparatus specifically designed for gas cooking was made by men at the Aetna Iron Works near Liverpool in 1824. It 'consisted of a gun-barrel turned backwards and forwards, and pierced with numerous small holes. When anything had to be fried the gridiron was kept in a horizontal position; when anything had to be roasted it was turned in a vertical position, and a plate of tin was placed behind the meat, as a reflector, or hastener . . .'.[57]

This crude contraption was clearly not a commercial proposition. John Robison's invention at the end of the 1820s of a gas burner for heating water and other liquids in the butler's pantry was far more sophisticated in design. In 1831, it was the first gas cooking device to be described in *The Mechanic's Magazine*.[58] Robison, an Edinburgh man who was one of the founders of the Scottish Society of Arts, explained that: 'Several of my friends have had apparatus of this kind put up in their houses for general culinary purposes . . . and . . . are enabled to apply it to almost every operation of the kitchen, excepting roasting and baking.' But he made no attempt to patent or manufacture it.

It seems that the first man to try to make money out of a gas cooking apparatus was James Sharp. Appointed fitter and assistant manager of Northampton Gas Works in 1822, he started designing gas cookers in 1826. By 1828 he had a satisfactory model installed in his own home. In 1830 he started to publicise its virtues by giving lectures and demonstrations in Northampton – a practice he continued when he moved to Southampton in 1837. It was around this date that Sharp began to sell his gas cookers.[59]

Despite the publication of experimental designs for gas cookers in trade journals and popular magazines from the 1830s, and a burst of patenting activity in the 1840s and 1850s, gas cooking enthusiasts were rare. John Claudius Loudon was one of the first important writers on domestic economy to advocate gas cooking. He maintained that it was both economical and efficient, and he provided a full account of Robert Hicks' gas cooking apparatus in *An encyclopaedia of cottage, farm and villa architecture and furniture* (1833).[60] But there is little evidence to suggest that his advice was taken by the philanthropists whom he hoped to influence. The famous chef Alexis Soyer was a more flamboyant and better known enthusiast. He converted the London kitchens of the Reform Club to gas in 1841 and stage-managed impressive public demonstrations of gas cookery. But he too failed to sway public opinion in its favour.[61]

In the end gas cooking only became a success in the 1880s and 1890s because gas companies felt threatened by the new competition posed by electricity. Galvanized by the realization that electricity would eventually replace gas-lighting, they were impelled to increase and diversify their gas sales; and to promote gas cooking was one of the most obvious and simple solutions.

A substantial number of firms manufacturing gas cooking apparatus were already established.[62] The cooker's standard form – bunsen burners on top, with a grill in the middle and an oven below – was fixed and many of the refinements that we associate with the modern gas stove were patented and awaiting commercial exploitation. For example, glass oven doors were patented in 1855, and vitreous enamel panels, which made cleaning a wipedown process, in 1869.[63] The Smoke Abatement Committee, which tested a large number of gas cookers in 1882, found that manufacturers were producing excellent 'stoves of every size and capacity, from the small griller, suitable for cooking a simple chop, to the large roaster, adapted to the requirements of the most extensive establishments'. Compared to previous gas exhibitions, 'a considerable advance had been achieved, in style and finish no less than in completeness and adaptation to the varying necessities of the kitchen'.[64]

From the late 1880s, manufacturers of gas cooking apparatus were able to take advantage of 'penny-in-the-slot' meters which extended gas sales to modest homes unable to manage quarterly bills. They also adopted the policy of hiring out gas cookers at a modest rental[65] to people lacking the money (or confidence) to buy their own and to the large proportion of the population living in rented accommodation. The Newcastle-upon-Tyne and Gateshead Gas Company was typical in increasing its number of 'hired-out' gas cookers from 95 to 1884 to 1,035 in 1890, 3,297 in 1910 and 16,110 in 1920.[66]

Vigorous propaganda, in the form of exhibitions and cookery lectures, systematic advertising, good showrooms and canvassing, was needed to overcome widespread suspicion about gas cooking. Many people feared it might be poisonous. Thus, when Ellen Youl, a working-class housewife who lived in Northampton at the end of the nineteenth century, acquired a gas cooker and showed it proudly to her husband, he was horrified. He thought the gas contained poison and refused to eat anything cooked by it. Ellen, however, would not get rid of her new labour-saving contrivance. She cooked his dinner every day in the gas stove, transferring it to the open fire a few minutes before he returned from work. This farce went on until the day he died.[67]

Others believed that food cooked by gas would taste or smell of it. According to the Philosophical Society of Glasgow, which held an exhibition of gas cooking apparatus in 1880, 'a strong prejudice against this use of coal-gas' arose 'from the peculiar and unsavoury gas flavour imparted to the food by the earlier stoves' which had defective burners and badly ventilated ovens.[68] These suspicions only faded during the 1890s when properly ventilated, well constructed gas cookers became common. By 1900 most models had removable enamelled fittings and linings, grills, and well insulated ovens with an adequate number of shelf runners. Later improvements included: plate racks, splash backs and spillage trays (1910–14), and thermostats (1923). The latter innovation enabled cooks, for the first time, to control oven temperatures numerically (eg. 350°F.) rather than in general terms (eg. 'a slack oven').[69]

As soon as efficient models were available, gas cooking spread very rapidly, especially in urban areas. In 1898 one in four households with gas supplies had a gas cooker. In 1901 the proportion was one in three: the total number of gas stoves had almost doubled in three years.[70] By 1939 it was estimated that there were between eight and nine million gas cookers in Britain and that three quarters of all families had one.[71] The progress of gas cooking in the countryside was only limited by the availability of gas supplies. For example, 81 per cent of Londoners cooked by gas in 1942,[72] but only 3 per cent of people living in rural Gloucestershire did so in 1946.[73]

The open fire often coexisted with the gas cooker in working-class homes. For example, most cooking was conducted over an open fire in the Salford slums during the first quarter of this century, although single gas rings had already come into general use there.[74] The same was true of London in the early 1930s: most of the poorer households lacked any sort of range and cooked over an open fire or gas ring.[75]

In middle- and upper-class households there was a similar period when gas cookers were used side by side with the 'closed' range. Lady Troubridge had such a transitional arrangement in her London house before the First World War. Not only did she have 'a range that gorged coal', and 'keep a kitchen-maid almost solely that she might set the ruinous monster going in the morning', but she also put in a gas ring. 'This was only supposed to be lit in moments of emergency, but I never entered the kitchen at any time, morning, noon or night, without seeing the yellow ring of light full blaze and a kettle merrily singing upon it.'[76]

Stage five – Electricity

The fifth and last evolutionary stage, electric cooking, followed swiftly after gas. In 1890 the General Electric Company started to sell 'electric rapid cooking apparatus', which boiled a pint of water in 12 minutes.[77] In 1891 an exhibition at the Crystal Palace publicized electric cooking.[78] Three years later, in 1894, the City of London Electric Lighting Company held an 'all-electric' banquet for 120 guests and started to sell and hire out electric ovens.[79] The pioneering electrical engineer Rookes E. B. Crompton fitted Margaret Fairclough's School of Electric Cookery in Gloucester Road, London, the same year.[80] By the early 1900s there were several companies manufacturing electric cooking apparatus.

But after this initial flurry of activity electric cooking made slow progress. It was handicapped by the slow spread of electricity supplies in Britain, especially in rural areas. The high price of electricity compared to its rivals, coal and gas, was also crucial: many families could afford to run an electric kettle and toaster but baulked at the thought of an electric cooker. Because of these distribution and cost factors, electrical manufacturers were slow to produce efficient and inexpensive cooking equipment. Until the 1920s they tended to convert gas cookers to electricity by replacing gas burners with electric heating elements. These were slow to heat up and liable to burn out. In 1914, for example, it took 15 to 20 minutes to boil two pints of water, and up to 35 minutes to preheat an oven.[81]

Electric cooking only began to gain popularity in the late 1920s. This was partly due to improvements in the design of electric cookers and a fall in their price. Manufacturers

44 *A woman making toast with an electric toaster, photographed in the 1920s.*

had evolved longer lasting, more efficient heating elements and introduced complete vitreous enamel finishes, as well as automatic temperature control; and by 1935 the average electric cooker cost almost half what it had in 1925.[82] But the growing acceptability of electric cooking also reflected the work of the Electrical Association for Women. In 1927, for example, the E.A.W. investigated 11 different models of electric cookers and made various recommendations for their improvement. (They were to be 36 inches high, have more runners for oven shelves, a larger grill with a three-heat switch, and removable enamel linings with rounded corners.)[83] A new offensive was launched in 1931: the promotion of saucepans with perfectly flat, machine-turned bases designed to make complete contact with the hotplate or electric ring. Experiments showed that it took $16\frac{1}{2}$ minutes to boil two pints of cold water in a buckled aluminium pan, but only $9\frac{1}{2}$ minutes in one with a perfect bottom.[84]

E.A.W. members even led 'cooker campaigns'. These involved persuading local electricity companies and housing authorities to promote electric cookery by reducing

Principal Features of
The "Belling" No. 6S Cooker

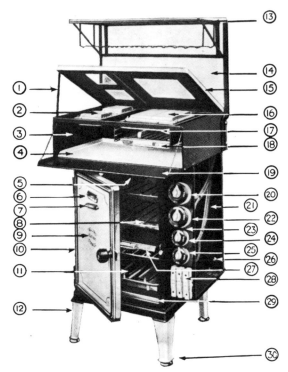

"BELLING" Electric Cookers—the products of a firm with fifteen years of specialised manufacturing experience—have been designed to give long and satisfying service.

They are very easy to use and extremely simple in construction, as will be seen from the illustration.

Every cook will appreciate the many carefully thought out conveniences which are provided and perfect results in cooking are assured from the start.

1. Support for hob when open.
2. Two small boilers for simmering and other purposes. Plug-in type and protected against spilt liquids.
3. Capacious plate-warmer.
4. Removable enamel crown-plate.
5. Three-heat top element of oven. Plug-in type.
6. Ventilator.
7. Thermometer.
8. Large oven lined with rustless steel.
9. White enamel door panel.
10. Nickel-plated door frame.
11. Three-heat bottom element of oven. Plug-in type.
12. White enamelled legs.
13. Large plate rack.
14. Enamelled back-plate.
15. Specially enamelled hob.
16. Combined boiler-griller element. Plug-in type and protected against spilt liquids.
17. Deflector plate.
18. Removable grill-pan and grid.
19. Door to griller and plate-warmer.
20. Three-heat switch for Boiler-griller.
21. Three-core asbestos covered connections.
22. Three-heat switch for two small boilers.
23. Switches at angle for easy reading.
24. Three-heat switch for top oven element.
25. Three-heat switch for bottom oven element.
26. Entry for main cables.
27. Drip tin.
28. Fuses.
29. Oven corners rounded for easy cleaning.
30. Feet adjustable for uneven floors and rounded to prevent damage to linoleum.

45 *Advertisement from the Belling Electric Homes catalogue of 1927–8.*

hire and tariff charges. When Councillor Mrs Gregory began her campaign in West Ham in 1933, she found that there were 22,000 gas cooking appliances in the town, but only 836 electric cookers. The introduction of a 'one penny a unit, cooker included' deal led to the installation of a further 2,630 electric cookers by mid-1934.[85]

However, despite the E.A.W.'s valiant efforts and a growing vogue among local authorities for 'all-electric' housing schemes, electric cooking assumed little national importance before 1950. Only 6 per cent of families in Britain had an electric cooker in 1936[86] and only 18.6 per cent in 1948.[87] Thereafter – but that is another story – the figure rose rapidly to 30 per cent (1961) and 46 per cent (1980).[88]

Concurrently with these main evolutionary stages in British cooking technology, a small proportion of the population lived in such abject poverty that their cooking methods were even more primitive than those characteristic of Stage One. For example, James Ray, a soldier who fought Scottish Highlanders in 1745 and 1746, found that his adversaries would 'boil a quarter of flesh, whether mutton, veal, goat, or deer, in the paunch of the beast'. The animal's skin was apparently turned inside out, cleaned and fixed to a hoop which was hung over a fire.[89]

Similarly, Edward Burt, who also visited Scotland in the mid-eighteenth century, relates how 'the custom of boiling the beef in the hide' prevailed among the islands, where 'the meaner sort of people' apparently lacked any sort of metal or earthen cooking vessels. Their other cooking method was to put water in a block of wood 'made hollow by the help of the dirk* and burning' and to heat it with red hot stones until it came to the boil.[90] Shetland housewives also used stones to make the local drink, *bland*, at this time. According to a gentleman who lived on the island for five years, 'When the woman had done churning, the butter being taken off, she has two or three large round stones, ready hot in the fire, which she takes out and puts in the churn'. This caused the curds to sink to the bottom, leaving the thin *bland* on top which was drunk warm from the churn.[91] Women living in remote parts of Scotland continued to heat liquids in this way in the late nineteenth century. Arthur Mitchell, author of a thought-provoking book entitled *The past in the present: what is civilization?* (1880), wrote that: 'Even when there are iron vessels in the home, the fluid is sometimes by preference placed in a vessel of earthenware, and heated by plunging into it a hot stone – one or two stones being kept constantly in the fire to be ready for this use.'[92] The custom also persisted in County Donegal, Ireland, during the 1880s; when the smooth-surfaced stones were not in use, they were stored in a little niche in the wall near the fire.[93]

Several minor technological developments should also be mentioned, such as oil cooking stoves. These became available in the second half of the nineteenth century, following the discovery of large-scale petroleum deposits in North America and the widespread adoption of paraffin lamps.[94] They were bought mainly by rural households

* *Dirk*: a kind of dagger characteristic of the Highlands.

lacking access to coal, gas and electricity supplies, mostly in Scotland, Wales and the southwest of England. Nobody pretended that oil cooking stoves were particularly satisfactory. They were economical, but they posed a fire hazard and suffered from several other disadvantages. Without constant vigilance, for example, the wicks smoked and gave off an unpleasant smell. The ovens were generally unreliable for precise culinary operations such as cake and pastry making. Thus it was hardly surprising that oil cooking stoves were never a great success. Of the 3 per cent of families lacking both gas and electricity supplies in 1948, 60 per cent chose coal as their cooking fuel and only 23.5 per cent oil.[95]

And what about the Aga? Now an institution in many British farm and country houses and fashionable in prosperous urban homes, this ever-ready, heat accumulating stove was invented in 1929 by the Swedish physicist Nils Gustaf Dalén. The original Aga, which burned coke or anthracite and only required attention once a day, was exported to Britain almost immediately. In August 1931 it was first advertised in *Good Housekeeping* as combining 'the merits of a coal range with the ease and cleanliness of electricity'. The advertisements that followed in the 1940s laid constant stress on the Aga's unprecedented fuel economy. But they neglected to mention that its creator was not only blind but also a Nobel prize winner,[96] and perhaps the most distinguished person to direct his attention to improving European cooking methods since Count Rumford in the eighteenth century.

In surveying the many changes that occurred in cooking technology between 1650 and 1950, two stand out as being especially significant. The first of these was the adoption of the enclosed, multi-purpose cooking range (Stage Three). For the first time in British history, cooks had a purpose-built apparatus at their disposal; they no longer had to make do with mediaeval cooking arrangements improvised around a fireplace which had also to serve several other functions. The second significant change was the switch from solid to non-solid (and 'clean') fuels, at Stages Four and Five. The effects of these developments was not only to make much more sophisticated cooking possible, but also to remove much of the drudgery from preparing meals.

Chapter 4 HEATING

Until recently, the open fire was the focal point of domestic life in the British Isles. In addition to providing heat and a cheerful blaze, it was in constant use for a variety of other functions, including cooking, water heating, lighting and rubbish disposal.

The hearth was a potent symbol of the family, of hospitality, and of life itself. In the majority of households where only one fire burned at a time,* in the main living room, the hearth was treated like an altar. The women of the household, who bore the main responsibility for maintaining the fire, kept the hearth spotlessly clean and lavished great care on its appearance.† Late nineteenth- and early twentieth-century photographs of fire-places nearly always reveal a shiny black range or grate, a whitened hearthstone, a gleaming fender, and a freshly starched 'chimney cloth' hanging from the mantel, with a display of treasured possessions above. The hearth was similarly revered in households where there was sufficient money and service to permit several fires: not only were the fireplaces kept in pristine condition, but considerable sums of money were expended on grand chimney-pieces, handsome grates, and elaborate hearth furniture.

A great variety of fuels was burned in Britain between 1650 and 1950. These included the fuels of the poor such as cattle dung, furze, heather, broom, and sticks from hedgerows and copses, as well as the main fuels – wood, peat, and coal. All these fuels were burned both on their own and in combinations with each other, as several types were normally available in any given place. The inhabitants of late seventeenth-century Staffordshire, for instance, burned peat and three kinds of local coal.[3] The islanders of Eriskay, who eked out a miserable existence off the west coast of Scotland, braced themselves against the biting Atlantic winds with fires of cow dung, barley straw and dried seaweed in the early 1700s. (Bread baked by seaweed had more relish 'than that done otherwise', they said.)[4] The wealthier citizens of County Meath, Ireland, burned coal in their parlours and bedrooms in the early nineteenth century, peat in their kitchens, and furze in their bread ovens. The poor made do with straw and wood from hedgerows.[5] A similarly diverse pattern of fuel consumption existed in Devon at that time. The main fuels were peat and wood, but coal was imported from Wales, Somerset and Newcastle, and those who could afford no better burned wood collected from

* Few families in Britain could afford to heat more than one room even at the end of our period.[1]
† Women were extremely superstitious about the cleanliness of their fireplaces. John O'Donoghue, who was born in a small Irish cottage in 1900, remembers that he often saw his 'grandmother sweep the fireplace immediately before going to bed, moreover during wild and stormy weather when, she said, the dead might be coming in for shelter. If they found the place untidy, she added, they might talk about it among the neighbouring pookies because the dead have endless time for gossip'.[2]

46 *The fire as a focal point for domestic social life. In this aquatint of* c. 1820, *Dr Syntax is reading aloud before an open hearth fire to an assembled company. He is sitting on a settle to protect his back from draughts. From William Combe,* The Tour of Dr Syntax, in search of the picturesque, *illustrated by Thomas Rowlandson, 1855.*

hedgerows and copses, supplemented with large quantities of cow and horse dung.[6] During the 1860s, farmers on the Sussex downs burned wood and their farm cottagers a mixture of wood and gorse;[7] while in Hertfordshire, villagers supplemented their scarce coal supplies with wood and furze.[8]

Such examples could be multiplied indefinitely: coal did not become the main domestic fuel in Britain until about 1840, long after its establishment as the nation's dominant industrial fuel. To understand the many variables in the work people put into heating their homes, as well as the different forms this took, it is necessary to treat each of the different types of fuel they burned.

The fuels of the poor

The poor burned an astonishing variety of substances in an effort to keep warm and cook their food. More or less anything that women and children could gather was fuel for the fire. On islands and along the coast they collected and dried seaweed. In inland areas, they made for wastelands where, depending on the local vegetation, they could cut shrubs such as heather, broom, furze and gorse.

When the shrubs grew tall and bushy, men sometimes did the cutting. In nineteenth-century Cornwall, for example, they would cut a year's supply of furze in early summer from thickets up to 10 feet high. To protect themselves from being cut and scratched,

47 & 48 *George Cruikshank makes use of the fire as a symbol of family life in these two glyphographs of 1847. In the one above, a happy family eats dinner before a cheerful coal fire. But the end of their bliss is in sight! The paterfamilias is offering his wife a drop of alcohol. In the picture below, the husband has become a drunkard, lost his job, and the family's clothes are being pawned to pay for the next bottle. Very significantly, there is no fire in the grate.*

they wore thick leather gloves and thigh-length leggings. According to Alfred Kenneth Hamilton Jenkin, 'A "tash" or armful of the furze was seized with one hand, and the stems severed with a hook, just above the ground. Each tash, as it was cut, was laid aside and afterwards made up into faggots, the latter consisting of four tashes bound round with thin green branches'. A skilful labourer prepared about 50 faggots a day, one thousand being the usual winter supply for a substantial farm. As soon as the faggots of furze were dry, they were built into ricks outside people's houses. When needed for burning, about seven or eight faggots were taken indoors at a time and carefully placed in the 'ookener' so that the sticks were out of sight, leaving only the yellow blossoms facing onto the room.[9]

In addition to shrubs, women and children also collected straw and stubble for use as fuel, and any kind of unwanted plant.[10] In 1813, John Christian Curwen observed that women and children were pulling up weeds and drying them for firing at Ardbracken in Ireland. 'They are glad to collect stubble or anything else that may create a momentary warmth' he said.[11] Similarly Humphrey O'Sullivan, an Irish draper, recorded that women round the small town of Callan were cutting thistles for firing in 1828; he saw 'a bundle or load of them on a poor woman as big as a pig's sty'.[12] In some areas, the poor burned waste products from local industries. For example, Richard Bradley, an observant early eighteenth-century writer on agriculture and husbandry, noted that the people of Lincolnshire, after pressing oil out of cole seed, burned 'the Cakes for heating of Ovens, and other Uses'.[13]

The most common fuel burned by the poor, however, was cow or horse dung. In *A York-shire dialogue . . . Being a miscellaneous discourse, or hotch-potch of several country affaires* (1697), a mother tells her daughter, Tibb, to 'clawt some cassons out o' th' hurne', meaning that she was to pull some dried cow dung (cassons) out of a hole behind the chimney. As the family were tenant-farmers who fattened cows for meat, it was only necessary for Tibb or her mother to walk next door to the barn or into the nearest field to collect some more.[14] When Celia Fiennes passed by Peterborough in Cambridgeshire in 1698, she 'saw upon the walls of the ordinary peoples houses and walls of their out houses the cow dung plaister'd up to drie in cakes which they use for fireing'. She commented that although cow's dung was 'a very offensive fewell', 'the country people use little else in these parts.'[15] Animal dung was also reported to be the 'principal firing' among the impoverished inhabitants of north Wales in 1743.[16] Little else was burned in Cornwall and Devon at the end of the eighteenth century: when Edward Daniel Clarke was travelling through them in the summer of 1791, his heart was touched by the sight of 'an old woman hobbling after our horses in hopes of a little fuel from their excrement'.[17]

With improvements in the distribution of coal in the late eighteenth and early nineteenth centuries, the burning of animal dung became less common. Not surprisingly, contemporaries considered this a mark of progress. As one writer from Louth, Lincolnshire, put it in 1795: 'It is hoped, that the introduction of coal will induce the inhabitants to desist from their ancient practice, not yet entirely disused, of using the dung of their cattle for fuel.'[18] However, the practice was not to die out entirely. Cornish women and children were to be seen collecting 'glaws' from pasture fields during summer evenings in the late nineteenth century,[19] and in the Aran Islands off the west coast of Ireland, cow's dung was still being collected, dried, and burned in the 1930s. Peat imported from Connemara was expensive and scarce; and so, to eke it out, the islanders made use of their cow's dung, kindled with brambles. The cow pats were collected in creels and put on walls to dry.[20]

Despite its acrid smell, which few people liked, animal dung was an excellent fuel. It was free, easy to collect and, so long as there were animals around, constantly re-plenished. Furthermore, it was simple to dry, could be burned in an open hearth, and gave out a great deal of heat. The calorific value of dung (4.0) is greater than that of wood (3.5), identical to that of peat, and over half that of bituminous coal (6.9).[21]

Wood

Overall, wood was the single most important domestic fuel in England and Wales in the second half of the seventeenth century. According to Gregory King, writing in 1696, 15 per cent of the land area was covered with woods, coppices, forests, parks and commons.[22] These provided abundant supplies of firewood, although good quality timber, such as was needed for ship-building, was in short supply.[23] The only place without local sources of firewood was Britain's largest population centre, London, which had been supplied with 'sea coal' from Newcastle since the middle ages.

Wood continued to be the predominant fuel in England and Wales during the eighteenth century.[24] Landowners recognized that Britain's forests and woods had become seriously depleted and saw that it was to their economic and aesthetic advantage to maintain their woodlands and to plant new trees, often in magnificent parks that provided a scenic setting for their country houses. Their efforts, however, were largely cancelled out by the combination of population growth and enclosures, and firewood became increasingly scarce and expensive in many parts of England during the late 1700s. Sir Frederick Morton Eden, in his epic study *The State of the Poor* (1797), found that agricultural labourers in the south had barely enough fuel for a single fire. Their cooking was reduced to the boiling of a kettleful of water for tea twice a day. Their Sunday roast was generally cooked at the baker's, as was the bread they ate during the rest of the week. They had never tasted and enjoyed the hot, nourishing dishes eaten by their counterparts in the north, such as hasty-pudding, crowdie, frumenty, and peasekail.[25]

This serious shortage of firewood was alleviated by the spread of coal supplies: thanks to improved river navigation, canals, and railways, coal was readily available in most parts of Britain by 1840. The importance of wood as a domestic fuel declined rapidly after this, except for the very poor and landowners with woodlands on their estates.

By the 1920s, only 5 per cent of Britain was covered with woodland[26]; after Portugal, it was the least wooded country in Europe.[27] But a ready market for faggots and billets of

WEALTH and RESPECTABILITY

Pray M*r*. *Firebrand* let me take this small bundle of faggots to my poor Daughter *Lucky Thousands* who has 7 unlucky babes just perishing for *Want* of a bit of *Fire* — Hm! he does not mind *Fire*, *Water*, the *Devil*, or *Death*, and you are now going to eat your *Lion* with *Dolly Sago* while poor *Wh-All* is gone for a *Yard* of new buckram to ----------

My Master *Baron De Clare* has ordered me to take *Young* and *Old* before *Justice Done*. that take his wood to boil their tea kettle ---------- begone *Nic* shall be with you to morrow and I must to the *Cock and Breeches* go. —

49 *Not all landowners were willing to have the poor collect faggots of wood from their property free of charge, as this print of 1805 shows.*

wood still flourished in cities[28] and open hearth fireplaces with andirons supporting logs of wood survived in a surprisingly large number of cottage and village homes, where they were faithfully recorded by artists at the beginning of the century.[29]

Although firewood could be bought from lumber yards or from travelling wood-sellers,[30] most families gathered the bulk of their supplies locally. A typical labourer's family living in Berkshire at the end of the eighteenth century, obtained most of its fuel for nothing by collecting beech from the local woods, but also spent a pound a year on additional supplies.[31]

All members of a family helped to collect wood.[32] If possible, they chose the heaviest, densest kinds, such as oak, beech, ash, hazel, birch and elm, which gave off more heat than softer woods like fir, pine, larch, linden, willow and poplar. They also looked for wood from mature healthy trees rather than those that were young or decayed. Many people, however, only had the right to collect inferior woods from commonlands. In the nineteenth century, for example, wood-burners could lop only hornbeams in Epping Forest and could cut only furze on Wimbledon Common.[33] George Sturt describes how Surrey village women were to be seen on the roads in the early 1900s, 'bringing home on their backs faggots of dead wood, or sacks of fir cones, picked up in the fir woods a mile away or more'. They carried prodigious loads too. Sturt said he had 'often met women bent nearly double under them, toiling painfully along, with hats or bonnets pushed awry and skirts draggling. Occasionally, tiny urchins, too small to be left at home, would be clinging to their mothers' frocks.'[34]

Some men got wood as a perquisite of their job. It was traditional for shipwrights, for instance, to have all waste pieces of wood under 3 feet in length. Their women were allowed to come to the shipyards to gather this 'offal timber' in their aprons: they did so with such energy that one commissioner working at Chatham in the late eighteenth century feared that 'two whole ships under repair would be carried away by the women in their laps'.[35] It was also common for agricultural labourers and estate workers to get free wood. In some places they had to collect it themselves; in others, the farmer or landowner would send a cart round to their cottages.

Once home, it was usually the man's job to chop the wood into logs and stack them on the woodpile to dry out for about a year before burning. As every wood-burning family knew, the dryer the wood, the easier it was to kindle and the more heat it emitted. It was very hard indeed to make a fire with unseasoned wood, which contained about one-third water, as opposed to one-sixth when dry. Dorothy Wordsworth describes a visit to a Highland house in 1803 in which a woman was trying desperately to get a fire going: 'there was little sign of it, save the smoke, for a long time, she having no fuel but green wood, and no bellows but her breath.'[36]

Wood fires were much more labour-intensive than those made with peat or coal[37] because the wood had to be replenished at frequent intervals. But on the other hand, they had two advantages: they did not create much dirt and their ashes could be used for making lye (see Cleaning and Laundry chapters).

50 *'Fire', an engraving published in 1799.*

51 *The Kitchen at Old Soar Farmhouse, Kent. The woman is using bellows to light the logs of wood supported by the andirons on the open hearth. Note the faggots of wood behind her, stacked up against the copper, and the 'chimney cloth' hung across the fireplace. From Peter Hampson Ditchfield,* The Cottages and the Village Life of Rural England, *1912. Drawing by A. R. Quinton.*

Peat

Peat was the national fuel of Ireland: supplies were virtually unlimited, as one-seventh of the island was covered with peat bogs.[38] The only rival fuel was coal; but Ireland's native deposits were paltry and the bulk (98 per cent in 1920) had to be imported from England and Scotland.[39] From Ireland's eastern ports coal travelled inland by rail, but it was not distributed to large areas in the west and northwest, which were too remote and unpopulated to merit the investment. Thus, at least 62 per cent of Ireland's farmsteads were still totally dependent on burning peat in 1920.[40] Elsewhere, peat and coal consumption was pretty evenly balanced by this point, but even in small country towns with coal supplies, most households burned a combination of coal and peat in their grates.

Peat was also burned in many parts of England, the principal deposits being in Northumberland, Cumberland, Lancashire, Yorkshire, Cheshire, Somerset, Cornwall, Devon, and in the fenlands of Lincoln, Norfolk and Cambridge.[41] In addition,

52 *An Irish family seated round a peat fire. From the sketchbook kept by Caroline Elizabeth Hamilton in 1838.*

there were large deposits in the remoter parts of Scotland, mainly in the north and west.[42] It was a popular domestic fuel, even in coal-producing districts. William Tighe, in his 1801 study of Kilkenny, one of Ireland's few coal fields, pointed out that small farmers and cottagers preferred to burn peat rather than coal 'because in their habitations, fires are not always burning, and seldom, except in very cold weather, do they consume more than is necessary for preparing their food; for which purpose a fire is easily and quickly made from turf [i.e. peat], which kindles sooner than coals'.[43] The same was true in England during the 1840s. According to John Holland, an expert on the coal industry, peat was burned 'either in admixture with coal itself, or as a cheaper substitute' even in those counties with unlimited reserves of coal. 'Considerable quantities of peat firing are expended in Northumberland and Yorkshire', he said.[44]

There are no statistics for peat consumption in England and Scotland during either the nineteenth or twentieth centuries: the full extent of reserves in these parts of Britain has never been known and peat, like firewood, has never been a major article of commerce. However, it is clear that significant quantities of peat continued to be burned in parts of England and Scotland during this century. Peat was the main fuel of agricultural labourers living in the Norfolk Fens in the 1900s and 1910s, for example,[45] and farmers in the Yorkshire hills and dales were still cutting themselves an annual supply of about 50 rooks (i.e. 16 wagon loads) in the 1940s.[46] Even crofters in the north and west of Scotland found it worthwhile to cut peat; coal might be marginally cheaper, but they did not have any other pressing work to do during the peat-harvesting season.[47]

The main housework involved in having a peat fire consisted of obtaining and preparing the fuel. This was usually a family enterprise in which all members participated. In some places neighbouring households even worked together as teams. In mid-nineteenth-century Ireland, for example, it was common to find four or more families joining forces during the peat-cutting season, which lasted from March to July. The work was divided into six distinct operations, with a strict allocation of labour between the sexes.[48]

The men were in charge of cutting the peat. The strongest sliced it into blocks with the aid of a 'wing slane', a tool resembling a narrow garden spade, except that it had a 'lug' or 'wing' sticking out at a right angle on one side, to enable two sides of a block to be cut at once. (A block weighed anything from 7 to 20 pounds, depending on its water content, and measured approximately 2 feet long and 6 inches square.)[49] A second man lifted the 'turf', as the block of cut peat was called, and deposited it on a barrow. When the barrow was full, a third man wheeled it to the 'spread field' where he dumped the turves in a heap. Meanwhile a fourth man paved and levelled the peat bank, preparing the cutter's way. By co-operating in this fashion, the men could obtain a 'dark' of peat in a day. This was an indeterminate amount of peat, but most small cottagers with only one fire reckoned that they got through two to four 'darks' a year.[50]

The second operation was always done by women and children. It consisted of spreading and scattering the turf over the 'spread field' to dry: its water content had to fall from 90 per cent to 25 per cent before it could be burned. A woman working full-time could spread about three 'darks' a day.

A week later, it was time for the third operation of 'footing'. The women and children made small piles of peat by collecting about six turves at a time and placing them on end in a circle in such a way that they met in a point at the top. A woman could usually foot a dark a day.

After another 10 days had gone by, the women and children returned to do the 'rickling' which consisted of making larger piles of turf. This was followed by 'clamping'; here the men stacked the turf in piles about 12 feet long, 6 feet high, and 4 feet wide. Turf from these clamps was usually transported home in horse-drawn carts, but in some districts the women carried it home in ricks on their backs. Fortunately, home was rarely more than a mile away and dried peat weighed a great deal less than that freshly cut. (A small, well-dried specimen might weigh three-quarters of a pound, a larger one 2 pounds.)[51] Once home, the men restacked the turf and covered it with thatch as protection from the rain.

In some parts of Ireland, notably County Kildare, the peat was cut with a short-

53 *Two women gathering peat to take home on wheel-barrows, from a postcard dated 1903. The scene may well be a moor in Somerset.*

handled spade without a side piece called a 'breast slane'. In other localities, the peat was too saturated with water to be cut with a slane at all. In this case it had to be dredged from the peat bog in a sack[52] or gathered by hand. It was carried to a dry place and trampled upon (by both sexes) until it acquired a dough-like consistency. It was then moulded into shape 'like loaves for the oven', again by both men and women, until it was ready for footing, refooting and clamping. In the opinion of Humphrey O'Sullivan, the Irish draper from Callan, the best turf of all was 'peat pulp which has been kneaded by human feet . . . and then made into brickettes by women's hands';[53] but most people found this inferior to turf cut by the slane.

There were many variations in the domestic routine of peat-gathering in Britain. In late seventeenth-century Staffordshire, for example, turf was cut from the moorlands 'with an instrument call'd a push-plow, being a sort of spade, shod somewhat in the form of an arrow, with a wing at one side'. It had a wooden cross piece below the handle to which the cutters fastened a pillow. By setting this against their thigh and thrusting forward, they could 'commonly dispatch a large turf at two cuts'. They piled the dried peat in mounds 10 to 12 feet high that resembled hay-stacks.[54] In mid-nineteenth-century Orkney (where neighbouring families always assisted each other in cutting peat), the men used 'pone-spades' for splaying the surface of the peat bogs and 'tuskars' for cutting the turf. The women's job was to throw the wet sods onto the edge of the peat bank: there was quite a knack in getting them to land on their ends in neat tiers ready for drying.[55] In Cornwall at this time, farmers and farm labourers cut bog turf from the

54 *An Irish girl with a creel on her back for collecting peat, photographed by Rose Shaw, probably in County Tyrone, c. 1915.*

moorlands with a heavy iron digger called a 'piggal'. An average farm consumed about a thousand 'squares' a year, which would take a man about a day and a half to cut. The dried peat was built into ricks beside the furze and the two fuels were burned together.[56]

The form and size of peat blocks likewise differed from place to place, depending on the peat's quality and the local climate. Professor Purcell, writing in 1920, found that on Dartmoor, in Devonshire, peat blocks were cut 2 feet long, 9 inches wide and from $1\frac{1}{2}$ to 3 inches thick. The block was 3 inches thick in early summer when drying conditions were at their best; later on in the season, the thickness was reduced to encourage quicker drying. On Bodmin Moor in Cornwall, where the peat was very fibrous, the blocks resembled large bars of soap; they were 4 inches square and up to 3 feet 6 inches long. In the Midlands and in Somerset, square peat blocks were favoured, measuring 10 by 10 by 3.[57]

Methods of transporting peat also varied in different localities. Celia Fiennes noted that Scottish women were using horse-drawn carriages, each containing four wheel-barrowfuls, in the 1690s.[58] Kenneth Macaulay, an eighteenth-century missionary to the island of St Kilda, found that women and children carried turf in wicker baskets or hampers which were lined with rags and carefully preserved by skin coverings.[59] Hely Dutton, writing about County Clare in 1808, said the carriage home was 'generally performed by placing two small baskets on a horse's back'. But when a family lived near a bog or by rocky or soft ground, the different members carried it on their backs. 'It is astonishing what a weight some of these little creatures will carry' he commented.[60] In

85

55 *Woman and child by a peat fire, photographed by Rose Shaw, probably in County Tyrone, c. 1915. A harnen stand for drying oat cakes is hanging on the cottage wall.*

the Shetland Islands, a century later, the women and children carried peats on the backs of ponies.[61]

Peat fires were very easy to handle. They were quickly laid (all you had to do was put a few peats on an open hearth) and easily kindled. Dorothy Wordsworth describes how a Scottish peasant woman she met in 1803 simply 'heaped up some dry peats and heather, and, blowing it with her breath, in a short time raised a blaze that scorched us into comfortable feelings'.[62]

Peat fires did not require nearly as much attention as wood (although they consumed faster than coal), and had the advantage of being very clean. They were also good for cooking. Peat could be heaped round a cooking pot to make an excellent oven; or the embers used for baking. Edward Burt relates that Scottish Highlanders roasted whole fowls in the embers of their peat fires in the mid-eighteenth century.[63] Because peat supplies were abundant, the fuel was often burned lavishly. In Westmorland, for example, peat fires were kept going for half a century at a time, without ever being extinguished.[64] There was no such record-breaking in Ireland, but large fires were generally kept alight throughout the year, and families consumed up to 40 tons of peat annually.[65]

The only disadvantage of peat was its characteristic, pervasive smell, which was especially pronounced in small huts with nothing but holes in the roof to let the smoke escape. 'It makes one smell as if smoaked like bacon' Celia Fiennes complained in 1698.[66] But women who were accustomed to peat loved its smell and disliked that of other fuels. The inhabitants of County Down, Ireland, so much preferred peat to coal that they would go 10 miles to fetch it in the early 1800s, although the latter was available on the spot. 'The coal smoke is so disgusting to the females, who have been used to turf, that nothing can reconcile them to it, and the men kindly give way to their feelings' a clergyman recorded in 1802.[67]

Coal

As the map shows, Britain's main coal fields were in the Midlands, the north-east of England, Scotland, Cumberland, and South Wales. Coal consumption outside these immediate areas depended on the availability of good, cheap transport. During the 1600s and most of the 1700s, the only effective means of transporting coal was by sea and river.[68] It was neither economical nor practical to carry it overland on pack-horses, ponies, or oxen for more than a few miles, 15 being the absolute limit.[69] For this reason, the coal fields situated on the north-east coast of England dominated the market until the late eighteenth century.[70] From Newcastle and Sunderland, coal was shipped down the east coast to ports such as Hull (whence it was boated up the River Ouse as far as York), and King's Lynn (whence it travelled inland along the Great Ouse), down to London, the largest coal market of all.

However, as soon as water ceased to flow, coal traffic came to an abrupt halt. Pehr Kalm, who was travelling in England in 1748, found that coal was the only fuel burned in London and the principal fuel in villages near the metropolis, although the local people had to spin it out with sticks cut from hedgerows. But, he said, 'about 14 English miles from London, and in places to which they had not any flowing water to carry boats loaded with coals, for the most part bare wood was used, either from the trees they had cut down in repairing hedges, or from dug-up tree roots, or fuel of some other kind, as brackens, furze, etc . . .'.[71]

Coal transport improved in England from the 1760s as canals were built to extend and connect existing navigable waterways. Of the 165 Canal Acts passed between 1758 and 1801, 90 were specifically for carrying coal.[72] However, the extent of the canal network was really quite limited (see map on p. 88) and most of the coal carried by canals was for industrial use. During the whole of the eighteenth century, Britain's coal production probably only increased from 3 to 10 million tons.[73]

The real breakthrough in coal production and transport came in the nineteenth century. Many new mines were sunk between 1820 and 1840 and the opening of the Liverpool and Manchester Railway in 1830 marked the beginning of the railway age. Within decades, lines criss-crossed all populated parts of Britain (again see map on p. 88). By 1848 there were already 4,982 miles of track, by 1867 some 12,319, and by 1926 (the all-time peak) 20,405.[74] The growth of track mileage allowed unprecedented amounts of coal to be moved and marketed,[75] much of it to new places. As might be

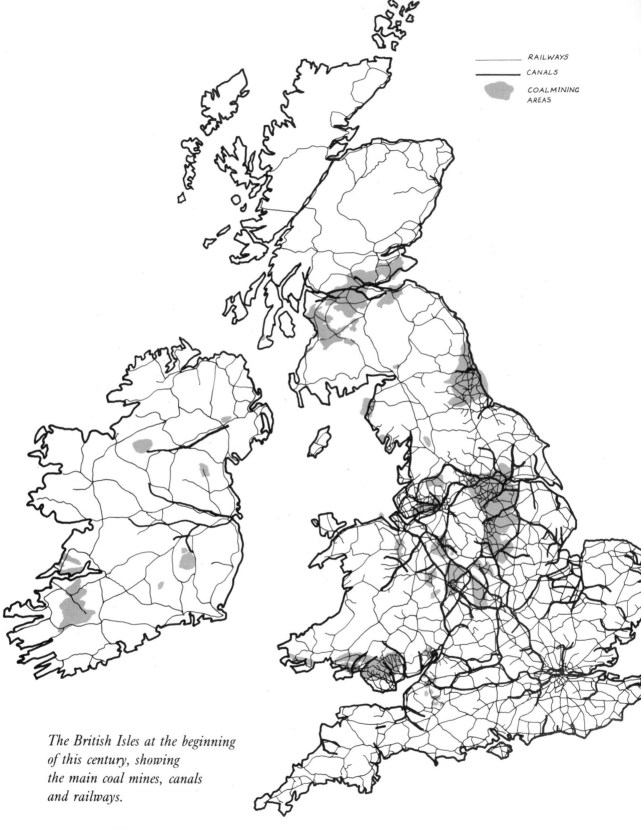

*The British Isles at the beginning
of this century, showing
the main coal mines, canals
and railways.*

88 – HEATING

Mr. Muirhead
Haseley Court
Tetsworth.
Oxon

39, LOMBARD STREET, LONDON, E.C.,

Oct. 21st 1876

SIR,

Below we beg to hand current rates for Coal, delivered free on rail, carriage paid, to _Siddington_ Station.

All orders we may be favoured with will receive our best attention.

Yours obediently,

REDHEAD, SON, & CO.

TERMS:—PROMPT NETT CASH ON DELIVERY.

HOUSE COALS.

In Ordering please quote Number.	QUALITY.	CHIEFLY USED FOR.	Price per Ton.
1	Best Coals	Drawing Room, &c....	22/10
2	Silkstone	Ditto	20/9
3	Best Brights	General House use ...	19/11
4	Kitchen ,, ...	Cooking, Kitcheners, Laundry, &c..........	18/1
5	Nuts (selected) ...	Ditto and Bakers ...	18/4
6	Bakers' Coal	Bakers use	16/11
7	Gas Coke (in truck loads of 4 to 5 Chaldrons)	Laundry and Cooking purposes, &c.	
16	Mixed Coal (nuts and small)	Laundry, Conservatory, Greenhouses, &c.................	13/11

STEAM AND MANUFACTURING COALS.

In Ordering please quote Number.	QUALITY.	CHIEFLY USED FOR.	Price per Ton.
8	Main Hards (hand picked)	Mills, Factories, Breweries, &c.	17/11
9	Hard Steam	Ditto and Steam Cultivating Traction Engines, &c..........	16/11
10	Hartleys	Ditto, ditto, Brick-burning, &c..........	15/11
11	Smokeless Merthyr, Aberdare, Welsh Steam	Factories, &c., where great heating power is required, together with absence of smoke	
12	Welsh Anthracite Malting Coal ...	Malting, Hop Drying, Gunpowder Makers, &c.	
13	Culm	Lime-burning, &c. ...	
14	Smithy Coal.........	Smiths' use	13/11
15	Foundry Hard Coke	Ironfounders, Maltsters, &c.	
16	Mixed Coal (nuts and small)	Steam, Brickmakers, Ballast-burning, &c.	13/11

N.B.—Special quotations forwarded for any particular Coal or Cannel required by Manufacturers, Gas Works, Iron Founders, Blast Furnaces, &c., and prices given for all description of House, Gas, Steam, Manufacturing, Cannel Coals, &c., *f.o.b.* Ship or Steamer, or delivered at English or Foreign Ports.

56 *Coal prices, 1876.*

57 *A weaver's cottage in the island of Islay, off the west coast of Scotland, 1772. It has a central fire-place with no more than a hole in the roof to let the smoke escape. The pot-hook is suspended from the rafter with rope. From Thomas Pennant* A tour in Scotland, and voyage to the Hebrides, *1774.*

expected, the cost of transporting coal plummeted: by the 1860s, for example, it was at least 70 per cent cheaper to move coal by rail than by canal.[76] Coal had become the most important domestic fuel in Britain. By 1869, 18 million tons of coal were burned in domestic grates; by 1922, the figure was 38 million, and an additional 16.5 million tons of coal were used to make gas, some of which was used for domestic heating too.[77]

There were various reasons why the spread of coal to domestic fireplaces lagged behind its adoption in factories. Taste and convenience played their part, as we have already seen. There were also important economic considerations. It was often cheaper to consume local fuels, if these were available, than to import coal. Another major obstacle was the expense and trouble of making fire-places suitable for coal. It simply was not possible to burn coal on an open hearth with a primitive chimney above, as one

58 *'The Comforts of matrimony — A smoky house & scolding wife'*, a print published in 1790.

could with wood and peat. Coal had to be burned in an iron grate below a properly constructed chimney that drew up all its smoke, rather than allowing it into the room. As James Anderson put it: 'If it is necessary in other parts of the world to exclude smoke merely for the sake of personal gratification, it becomes doubly so in Great Britain, where pit-coal is the most common sort of fewel, the smoke of which is not only disagreeable, but absolutely noxious.'[78] For people living in huts or hovels with no more than a hole in the roof to let smoke escape,[79] building a chimney and buying a grate were out of the question.[80] For others, it was a costly and difficult undertaking. Very few masons, let alone architects, understood the principles of chimney construction and only a small proportion of professional chimney 'doctors' knew how to help their clients when sooty smoke started to billow out of their fireplaces.

The problems involved in converting old chimneys and the inconvenience of having ones that smoked should not be underestimated. The eighteenth and nineteenth centuries saw a profusion of publications about smoking chimneys and how to cure them.[81] Furthermore, people were constantly writing about the subject in diaries and letters. 'Philip Syer alter'd the Fire place in the Paintry because it Smoaked' wrote Nicholas Blundell of Little Crosby, Lancashire in his diurnal in March 1708.[82] Could Sanderson Miller remember 'the pattern given by Mr Price of Foxly for the remedy he found for his smokey chimneys', enquired Mrs Hood in October 1765. She seemed to remember that the remedy was 'a square piece of tin, fitted to the top of the chimney, two sides being raised to resist the wind', but she wasn't sure.[83] 'The chimney in the inner drawing-room smokes when the fire is first lighted, which is very provoking and must not be suffered as it will spoil everything' Henry Temple, 2nd Viscount Palmerston wrote to his wife in 1795. (He had bought a new grate, which was higher than the old one, and intended to set it further back in the fireplace in an attempt to stop the smoking.)[84]

Because the coal industry was well organized, with its own distribution and marketing mechanics, the fuel was usually delivered directly to consumers' cellars or coal holes.[85] Men like Nicholas Blundell, who fetched their own coal, were in a tiny minority. 'I sent my own Teames to the cole pit' Blundell recorded in March 1704; and again in March 1707, 'I sent my carts to the Cole Pit, they brought home about 20 Baskets.'[86] By the nineteenth and twentieth centuries the only people who did not have coal delivered to them were the very poor. They could not afford the coal itself, let alone the delivery bill, and tried to collect what they could from beaches, spoil heaps and wharves and some even dragged canals for barge droppings.[87] 'I had to . . . walk two miles to a pit bank to pick coals, and carry it in a basket on my head' remembered a shoemaker's daughter who grew up in Wales in the 1860s.[88]

For the great majority of people the work created by a coal fire began at home. A classic description of how Britons prepared one is provided by Henri de Valbourg Misson, a Frenchman who visited England in 1698. First, he said, 'they put into the chimney certain iron stoves about a half a foot high, with a plate of iron behind and beneath'. They then filled this grate, which had bars in front and at the sides, with coal 'and in the middle they put a handful of small-coal, which they set fire to with a bit of Linnen or Paper'. As soon as this small coal began to burn, 'they make use of the bellows, and in less than two minutes the other coal takes fire'. It was necessary to 'blow a little longer after this, 'till the fire is a little spread about and then you hang up the Bellows . . . As it burns out you must throw on more coals, and thus with a little pains you have a fire all day long'.[89]

The effort required to keep up a good fire depended on what kind of coal was being burned. Different types varied remarkably in their readiness to take fire and stay alight, as well as in the amount of flame and heat they produced, their smokiness, the duration of their burning, and the quantity of ash and residue they left behind.

Some kinds of coal were far more troublesome than others. For example, the caking or bituminous coal brought from Northumberland and Durham, which constituted London's main supply during most of our period, fused into a hard mass. Unless they were broken up with a poker, the fire lacked oxygen and went out. Misson found that 'as the coal grows hotter it dissolves, becomes glutinous and sticks together; to keep it up and revive it, you now and then give it a stir with a long piece of iron made on purpose'.[90] 'Open burning' coals, on the other hand, did not behave in this way and therefore required much less attention. However, they produced far more ash than caking coals; removing this each morning added to the labour of laying a fire.

Anthracite, a non-bituminous kind of coal burned in Wales and in Kilkenny, Ireland, but not elsewhere, was a particularly practical type of coal for household use. It was extremely clean, produced almost no smoke, and burned for a long time with the minimum of attention. No praise was sufficient 'in commendation of the excellence of this species of fuel . . . for culinary purposes, the malt-house, and the laundry', wrote Mr Fenton in 1796. Once an anthracite fire was made up in the morning, it was known 'to endure a whole day, without renovation', he said. It was never extinguished 'for at bed-time it is plaistered over with what is called a *stumming* of the same, on which it feeds, and being only stirred up the morning, is, in a moment equal to any exigency that may arise; so that the business of the kitchen, the parlour, the study, or the counting-house may go on at any hour without the smallest impediment or delay, which all other fuel is liable to occasion'.[91]

Strong praise indeed. However, anthracite did have a major disadvantage; it was extremely difficult to ignite, without the help of bituminous coal or 'culm balls', a home-made fuel fabricated out of anthracite dust and mud or clay. According to a Society of Gentlemen formed in 1718 to promote the burning of culm balls in London (a lost cause), they were easily made by a servant; the method was to grind the coal in a malt-mill in the coal cellar and mix the resulting dust with 'black Owsy Mud' from the River Thames in a proportion of one to three.[92] Edward Daniel Clarke, who toured Wales in 1791, found that culm balls were made out of coal dust, mixed with an almost equal quantity of loam or clay; water was added until the mixture had the consistency of

59 *Servants making culm balls in the cellar of a grand house and the result of their labours: a handsome pyramid burning in a fire-place upstairs. From the Society of Gentleman's promotional essay, 1718.*

strong mortar and could be rolled into oval balls. When dry, they were carried to the fire in a pail and placed at regular intervals along the upper bar of the grate. As soon as they had heated through, they burned freely and gave off a great deal of heat. But to Clarke's English nose, the smell was 'of too sulphureous a nature to be borne long . . .'[93] In some households culm balls were burned on their own. Apparently, they could be put into the grate while still wet in the form of a pyramid, and, as soon as they were lit, made 'a most brilliant appearance'. If skilfully made, they lasted for 10 to 12 hours without being replenished.[94]

None of the numerous descriptions of making culm balls specifies which members of the family mixed the balls or how frequently they were made. This gap in the evidence is especially surprising because culm balls were still being burned after the First World War.[95] According to A. Leonard Summers, writing in 1919, the Welsh were then mixing anything from three-fourths to five-sixths' anthracite dust with one part clay; they sometimes added lime as well, to produce a brighter fire. After treading the mixture with their feet, they formed balls the size of an orange, either by hand or with an old tablespoon or metal mould.[96]

Compared to other fuels, coal was extremely dirty. A substantial amount of house-work generated by coal fires consisted in cleaning. No matter how careful women were, they spilled dusty lumps when carrying new supplies to the fireplace, just as they dropped ash when removing it. All these messes had to be cleared up at once; otherwise they blackened the floor and were trekked round the rest of the house. In addition, chimneys had to be cleaned regularly. Henry Mayhew, an expert on mid-nineteenth-century London, found that chimneys in large prosperous houses, where many fires were burned, had to be swept at least once every three months; such households yielded an average of 6 bushels of soot a year. Moderate-sized houses belonging to middle-class families had their chimneys swept almost as frequently, producing an annual average of 5 bushels of soot. Working-class homes, which had far fewer fires, only had to be cleaned once or twice a year; their average yield was 2 bushels of soot.[97]

Chimney cleaning was a nightmare, even though it was done by professional sweeps (men dominated the trade but there were some women). For there was no effective way of trapping all the soot brushed down the chimney into the fireplace. Innumerable black, greasy particles floated into the room and settled on all available surfaces and once the sweep had gone, women were left with the awesome task of removing them.

Chimney sweeping was even more hateful in cities where small boys were employed to clean chimneys by climbing up them. In London, for example, housewives and maids were often faced with the sight of thin, blackened little ragamuffins being sent up chimney stacks against their will. All too frequently their health and physique was ruined by this inhuman work and many got stuck and died before they could be rescued.[98] Thus until the use of boy sweeps was outlawed in 1840, a visit from the chimney sweep and his young assistants could be an utterly traumatic experience. Chimney sweeping was, however, unavoidable. Unless chimneys were swept regularly they posed a fire hazard and if the operation was put off, soot simply fell down the chimney of its own accord. This, of course, was a particularly frustrating experience for any woman who had just finished whitening the hearth below.[99]

Apart from the changes in the relative importance of different fuels, the history of domestic heating in Britain was curiously static. It is true that there was a continual evolution in the design of coal-burning grates from the mid-eighteenth century,[100] but this had little noticeable effect on housework. There were also innovations that made it easier to light a fire.

The 1820s and 30s, for example, saw the invention of various types of friction match. These produced fire and light virtually instantaneously, at a single stroke.[101] Before these became available, the usual way of lighting a fire was to strike steel against flint repeatedly, until a spark lit some tinder.* This was then used to light brimstone matches,† before being quickly snuffed out and saved for use on the next occasion.

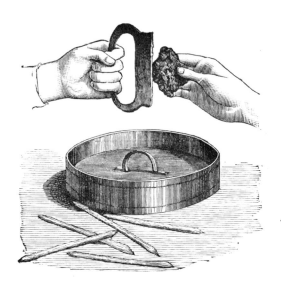

60 *Flint, steel, tinderbox and matches. From William Smith,* Morley: ancient and modern, *1886.*

Because it took at least three minutes to obtain a light with tinder and flint, and up to half an hour when the tinder was damp, friction matches were a most welcome convenience.[102] As George Croal, an octogenarian from Edinburgh, recollected in 1894: 'It was no small matter on a dark wintry morning to grope first for the necessary apparatus, and then to apply them to obtain the desired result. Working in the dark is a critical operation, and the knuckles had often a painful experience in the endeavour to procure the desired spark.'[103] Needless to say, people often became very impatient when it took time to ignite the tinder and their frustration fired many a domestic row.[104]

* The most common tinder was burned linen or cotton rag, but soft paper saturated with a solution of saltpetre, called 'touchstone', was also used.
† Juniper sticks or deal spills dipped in sulphur: these were homemade or bought from gypsies.

61 *Wheel bellows beside a cottage hearth in County Armagh, Ireland. From Emyr Estyn Evans,* Irish heritage. The landscape, the people and their work, *1942.*

Wheel bellows were another innovation that made fire-lighting easier. However, these mechanical contrivances, which produced a powerful draught below the fire,[105] thus kindling the fuel more quickly, seem to have been adopted only in Ireland. The job of operating them, incidentally, usually fell to the younger members of the household. Farmhouse children around Kilkenny, for example, were reported to be in charge of working chain-operated bellows to light coal fires in the early 1800s. They tried to start the fire as quickly as possible and to keep it alight for the absolute minimum time, so that potatoes could be boiled in 15 minutes flat.[106] Apparently, children particularly loved to ignite peat with wheel bellows, for as soon as the fuel was thoroughly aerated, it glowed like gold.[107]

Apart from designing coal-grates, inventing instantaneous matches, and devising mechanical bellows, Britain's record for innovation in domestic heating was very poor.

The subject aroused little interest, either scientific or practical. It was left to foreigners to supply information about the nature of heat and the best ways of warming houses.

Thus, in 1715, John Theophilus Desaguliers, the French Huguenot mentioned earlier in connection with water supplies, translated a major French book about how to prevent chimneys from smoking.[108] Desaguliers was probably also the first person in Britain to carry out scientific experiments on the best methods of constructing fireplaces for burning peat and coal.[109] In the same way, it was Benjamin Franklin, the celebrated American scientist and politician, who first denounced large open fireplaces as hopelessly inefficient. Not only did the draught carrying the smoke up the chimney draw off five-sixths of the fire's heat, but rooms could never be evenly heated through. Anybody trying to warm himself by a fire would find himself scorched in front, while his back remained stone cold. The only solution, in Franklin's view, was for people to buy his 'newly invented Pennsylvanian stove grate', a semi-enclosed iron stove with a small flue going up the chimney.[110] However, although his stove was on sale in London from the 1750s, it never became popular.[111]

By far the most important foreigner to try and reform domestic heating in Britain was Franklin's fellow American, Count Rumford. In a series of elegant essays composed in the 1790s and early 1800s, that were read and disseminated by the *cognoscenti* throughout the next century, Rumford explained all the basic principles of effective heating. He showed exactly what the proper shape and structure of a chimney fireplace should be if it was not to smoke. 'The great fault of all the open fireplaces, or chimneys, for burning wood or coals, in an open fire, now in common use, is, that they are much too large; or, rather, it is the throat of the chimney, or the lower part of the open canal, in the neighbourhood of the mantel and immediately over a fire, which is too large', he wrote in 1796, explaining in one deft sentence what had baffled people for centuries.[112]

His other revelation was that a fire gave out most of its heat by radiation. From this it followed that the fuel should heat the backs and sides of a shallow grate, and that the fireplace should be constructed out of a good radiating material, such as firestone or firebrick (NOT iron). It was also to be plastered and whitewashed to reflect heat.[113] This suggests that all the women who religiously whitened their hearthstones each morning understood the effects of what they were doing, if not their cause.

The only Briton to do important original research into domestic heating was a woman scientist, Dr Margaret Fishendon. In the 1910s and 20s she conducted a series of experiments that provided answers to all sorts of questions that had previously been mysteries. She showed, for example, that poking a fire did not make any difference to the amount of heat radiated into a room. The addition of 'fuel-saving' compounds sprinkled over coal likewise had no effect. She also made it possible to compare the relative cost of different kinds of heating, at a time when the supremacy of the open coal fire was just beginning to be undermined by the spread of new forms of trouble-free, automatic heating.[114]

Before discussing these, it should be stressed that just as most Britons were not

62 *A typical late nineteenth-century gas fire. It could be lit and extinguished at will and therefore eliminated heating as a household task. However, only a small proportion of households had gas heating before 1950.*

particularly concerned with fuel economy, so too they lacked interest in removing heating from the domain of housework. Whenever a more efficient heating method than an open fire became available, it was invariably spurned. In the eighteenth and nineteenth centuries, for example, close-stoves made almost no headway in Britain, despite their incontestable advantages and considerable popularity on the continent.[115] The introduction of hot water central heating was resisted too. By 1875, this highly efficient, safe, clean, and labour-saving method of heating was only employed in green-houses, zoos, churches, museums, and exhibition halls.[116] Gas heating, which was viable from the 1880s, was also slow to be adopted,[117] and the acceptance of electric heating proceeded at even more of a snail's pace.

Thus heating was still a major part of housework in most British homes during the first half of this century. 'The great majority of houses in this country are equipped for warming purposes with nothing but open fires for burning solid fuel', said Arthur Henry Barker in 1920.[118] As lecturer in heating and ventilation at London University, he was in as good a position to tell as anybody. By the outbreak of the Second World War, the situation had hardly changed. The Political and Economic Planning Group estimated that coal, coke, and anthracite constituted 75 per cent of the fuel used for domestic purposes in Britain, gas $18\frac{1}{2}$ per cent and electricity a mere $2\frac{1}{2}$ per cent.[119]

Why were people so slow to rationalize their heating arrangements? A great deal can be explained in terms of cost. A large proportion of the population lived in rented accommodation and could not afford to introduce time- and labour-saving methods of heating into their houses, especially as the latter were always more expensive than open coal fires. Margaret Fishendon, for instance, found that gas heating was up to five times more expensive than coal in the early 1920s.[120] The low status of housewives and domestic servants can also be blamed. After all, if women were at home doing housework, they might as well attend to the heating as well.

However, the fundamental explanation lies in the British addiction to the sight of an open fire with flickering flames. 'We like to see our fires, and the consequence is that we are never able to feel them' was the resigned comment of a heating reformer after the Royal Society of Arts announced that it could not recommend *any* of the 204 stove grates submitted to it for testing and examination in 1872.[121]

Such was the power of this addiction that even Mary Wollstonecraft, one of Britain's most remarkable feminists, was a victim. During her travels in Scandinavia at the end of the eighteenth century, she became acquainted with the wood-burning close-stoves prevalent there. She noted that they only needed fueling twice a day, were very economical, and gave out a great deal of heat. But, instead of advocating their introduction into British households as a way of liberating women, she said that she could not bear them. Indeed, she complained that the Scandinavian close-stoves were suffocating. 'I like a fire, a wood one in preference', she stated, 'and I am convinced that the current of air which it attracts renders this the best mode of warming rooms'.[122]

Chapter 5 *LIGHTING*

Now that electric lighting is almost universally available in Britain, at the flick of a switch, it takes an imaginative step back into the dark to appreciate how much time and effort our ancestors had to spend on providing themselves with artificial illumination. For, although most of them took advantage of natural daylight by rising with the sun, few wanted to go to bed at dusk. This was the time of day when they liked to cluster round the fire at home, to eat, talk and relax.

Except in mid-summer, all households had to have some form of artificial lighting in the evenings. Those who economized by relying solely on the flickering rays of their fires, were considered mean and contemptible, as can be seen in many of the popular jokes circulated in chap-books. According to one story, Leper the Tailor stayed overnight at a farm run by a miserly Scotswoman. He was horrified to see her preparing his bed in the dark, by laying some straw and bed-clothes on the ground. But thanks to the feeble flickers of firelight, he suddenly saw his opportunity for revenge: the woman had unwittingly made his bed on top of a sleeping calf! Leper ordered his bed to come to him by the fireside and the calf rose, with the bedding on top of it. The whole household was thrown into confusion and the farmer's wife was suitably humiliated.[1]

In the same way, a penny-pinching farmer in Northumberland who refused to allow his family and servants to eat their supper by candlelight, learned his lesson from Lothian Tom, another chap-book hero. Tom carefully positioned himself next to the farmer one evening, plunged his spoon into the heart of a piping hot dish of crowdy,* and clapped a spoonful into his master's mouth. The farmer burned his tongue badly, accepted Tom's protestations of innocence, and declared that a candle would henceforth illuminate the dining-table.[2]

Many people needed artificial light during the day-time as well as in the evening because they lived in poorly lit houses. This was especially true during the seventeenth and early eighteenth centuries when the window glass industry was in its infancy. In 1696, there were just 18 'glass-houses' in England and Wales making window glass, most of them in London and Bristol.[3] Only the rich could afford to live in light and airy houses. The peasantry, for the most part, lived in windowless hovels, with only a hole in the roof, slits in the wall, and a doorway for ventilation and illumination.[4] Although the use of window glass was to rise steadily (a window tax levied from 1696 to 1851 brought the Treasury much revenue), windows remained a luxury until the end of the eighteenth century.[5] Most people simply could not afford to have very large ones or many of them, and had to compensate for this by introducing light in other ways. (The old

* *Crowdy*: meal and water stirred together so as to form a thick gruel.

63 *Irish farmers talking by firelight, c. 1840. The candle holder suspended from the ceiling and the combined rushlight and candle holder in the foreground are both empty to save money. From William Carleton,* Traits and Stories of the Irish Peasantry, *1843.*

country cottages that survive today, with their pretty mullioned windows, are not representative of the homes of poor farm workers two or three hundred years ago. Very few of them still exist, and those that do have had windows added.)

The provision of light, unlike many other aspects of housework discussed in this book, was never regarded as being a specifically female responsibility. In affluent households where men servants were kept, the butler was invariably responsible for lighting, rather than the housekeeper or maid. Thus Dr Swift, in his satirical *Directions to Servants* (1745), instructs the butler how 'to avoid burning day-light' by refusing to light any candles 'till half an hour after it be dark, altho' they are called for never so often'.[6] And in servantless households, lighting was a communal job shared by men, women, and children alike. This was because all types of artificial illumination prior to electricity were both ineffective and dangerous: they required everybody's vigilant attention if they were not to go out or cause fires, the latter being a very common occurrence. Of the 4,413 fires that broke out in London between 1833 and 1849 whose causes were ascertained, 2,876 (or 65 per cent) were the result of accidents with candles.[7]

There were many different kinds of lighting devices, especially in the country, where they were often produced at home, exploiting local resources. One of the most common types, to be found in many inland areas of England, Wales, and Ireland until the late nineteenth century,[8] was the rushlight or rush-candle, 'a small blinking taper, made by stripping a rush, except one small stripe of the bark which holds the pith together, and dipping it in tallow'.[9] Its light was extremely feeble, but it had the advantage of being cheap and easy to make.[10] Elderly labourers, women, and children would cut the rushes while still green, soften them in water, peel them, bleach and dry the pith and coat it with whatever fat or grease was readily available. The scummings of the bacon pot, any kind of animal fat, and bee's wax or mutton suet mixed with grease were all recommended.

According to Alfred Burton, author of an authoritative book about rushes published in 1891, an old lady he knew in Cheshire made her rushlights by:

. . . gathering the long pliant rushes growing in very wet places, and dressing them by the side of a pond, wetting them several times a day in the manner thatchers do for straw for thatching. When sufficiently cured, she peeled them (the pith alone being used). The grease was 'dripping', which she got from her better-provided neighbours, and she mixed with it a little mutton fat, boiling it in a large pan on the fire. Then, taking several rush piths, and tying one end to a stick with thread, so that they hung down, she dipped them into the pot, which stood on the 'hob' to keep the grease warm, afterwards hanging the stick on something to cool, whilst she went on with another lot, alternately dipping and cooling till they were thick enough to her liking.[11]

In some counties, there were special pans for melting the grease. In Sussex, for instance, it was melted in boat-shaped grease-pans that stood on three short legs in the hot ashes in front of the fire. They were made of cast-iron and were just the right shape and size for greasing about a dozen peeled rushes at a time.[12]

A rushlight required little attention once it was lit. A well-made specimen, 28½ inches long, burned for 57 minutes.[13] A smaller one, 15 inches long, lasted for about half an hour.[14] During this time it required no snuffing, as it was held in a slanting position in a notch or spring and the burnt wick fell off by itself as its coating was consumed by the flame. All that was required was to move the rushlight up when it had burned down to its holder, a job usually performed by children. ('Mend the light' or 'mend the rush' was an instruction that they knew well.)[15] When used as a night-light, the length of time a rushlight burned could be regulated very exactly by putting two pins through the pitch at the desired extinguishing point.[16]

Because of their cheapness and feeble glow, it is often assumed that rushlights were burned only by the poor. But this was not the case at all. Rushlights were frequently used to light the domestic offices, servants' quarters and lesser bedrooms of the gentry. In the eighteenth century, for example, Sir Solomon Simon and his bridge went to bed on their wedding night by rushlight;[17] and in the 1830s, Charlotte Brontë's heroine Jane Eyre got up and dressed by it.[18] Nor was the use of rushlights confined to the countryside. They were also sold in towns and cities. When John Byng (later fifth Viscount Torrington) toured England and Wales between 1781 and 1794, he was billed for rushlights at the urban inns where he stayed overnight;[19] and they were still on sale in London in the mid-nineteenth century.[20]

64 *'The Chandler's Shop Gossips, or Wonderful News', black and white mezzotint, c. 1770. 'Dame Prattle', the shop-keeper, relates the news and 'Doll Drab', gin bottle in pocket, listens, unaware that her skirts are on fire. Meanwhile 'Jack Filch' prepares to make off with her cash. Note the bunches of tallow candles hanging on the wall above Doll Drab's head.*

Tallow candles were often burned in conjunction with rushlights, sometimes sharing the same holder. They lasted longer than their humble companions, and shed a little more light, but were much more expensive. This was partly due to their ingredients. Their wicks were made of cotton or linen, which, unlike rushes, could not be got for nothing, and tallow from sheep and bullocks was needed for other purposes such as cooking, soap-making and leather-dressing. (Hogs' tallow could not be used because candles made from it guttered, smoked, and gave off an evil smell.) Tallow candles were also taxed from 1709 to 1831 and, officially at least, could only be bought from licensed chandlers.[21] Candles made out of bees' wax and spermaceti were also taxed, but at a much higher rate: this meant that they were a luxury which only wealthy households could afford, and then only for burning in their main reception rooms.[22]

Because of the tax, families only made their own candles between 1709 and 1831 if they had collected a sufficient number of candle-ends to be worth melting down and remaking; or, if they happened to have surplus tallow or keep bees and live in a remote place where they were unlikely to be caught by the tax man. Thus when Samuel Johnson went to the isolated island of Col off the west coast of Scotland in 1773, he noted that: 'In every house candles are made, both moulded and dipped. Their wicks are small shreds of linen cloth.'[23]

Although making candles out of left-over stubs was quite common, few households bothered to make candles from scratch, even when they could do so legally. Nicholas Blundell of Little Crosby, Lancashire, bought all his tallow candles in the early 1700s, despite the fact he had numerous servants and ample supplies of fat from his estate. Between June and December 1704, for example, he bought 246 lbs of candles at 3½d a pound; to reduce his bill he contributed 175 lbs of his own tallow to the chandler, whose business was in Liverpool.[24]

The few descriptions of home candle-making that survive show that this household activity was restricted to the most poor, rural parts of Britain. Josephine Callwell, for example, who was brought up in an Irish land-owning family in Galloway in the 1830s and 40s, says that the moulded candles for the parlour and drawing room were made out of mutton tallow. The wicks were 'drawn tightly through long narrow moulds fixed in rows to a board, and the melted fat poured in afterwards'. For the kitchen and nursery dips, 'lengths of loosely twisted wick were tied round a stick, a dozen or more at a time, and dipped into a great saucepan of grease upon the kitchen fire, allowed to cool and dipped again, till they had sufficient thickness'.[25] Along the border between England and Scotland, farming families made candles in similar fashion, the children joining in with gusto. The dips were hung in bundles from the rafters, along with the bacon, and 'the men would often carry a bundle of dips with them to the public house, with which to pay their score or to settle a wager'.[26]

In addition to being more expensive than rushlights, tallow candles were far more trouble to maintain. Their wicks were only partly consumed in the course of burning and had to be 'snuffed' (i.e. pinched or cut off) at frequent intervals if they were to remain bright.

The first person to demonstrate in a scientific way how often this had to be done, or rather should have been done, was Count Rumford. In 1789 he became interested in the art of lighting which, in his view, had 'been little cultivated'.[27] He accordingly invented a 'photometer' to measure the relative intensities of light emitted by luminous bodies. Using this instrument to examine fluctuations in candlelight, he established that if the light of an ordinary tallow candle, 'of rather an inferior quality, having been just snuffed and burning with its greatest brilliancy', was taken as 100: 'in eleven minutes it was but 39; after eight minutes more had elapsed, its light was reduced to 23; and in ten minutes more, or twenty-nine minutes after it had been last snuffed, its light was reduced to 16. Upon being again snuffed, it recovered its original brilliancy, 100.'[28] Thus, to keep tallow candles burning brightly it was necessary to snuff them every few minutes. It was no wonder that many households concerned with economy and convenience used rushlights instead – or employed other lighting devices.

On the small islands lying off the British mainland and in many coastal areas, families burned fish-oil lamps.[29] The local fishermen would land their catch, cut out the largest fish-livers, store them until they were rancid, and boil them to extract the oil. In the Blaskets, a group of islands off the west coast of Ireland, most of the oil was obtained from the scad and pollack:[30] in the Shetland Islands from coal-fish (saithe, known in the U.S.A. as pollock).[31] But any kind of fish was suitable. The oil was not purified and, when lit, gave off a yellow, smoky light and a penetrating smell that repelled those who were unfamiliar with it.

In some places the fish oil was burned in shells collected from the beach. In the Aran Islands off the west coast of Ireland, and in County Galway the local people burned shark oil in large scallop shells.[32] And in the Isle of Man housewives lit their kitchens by setting scallop shells on top of jugs.[33] In areas with clay deposits the oil was burned in crude earthenware lamps. The Cornish, for instance, burned pilchard oil in a 'stonen chill' which was a kind of earthenware lamp shaped like a heavy candlestick with a well at the top. The wick was supported by a lip at the side.[34]

But most lamps were made out of tin or iron. The 'cresset' used in the Blaskets during the 1870s 'was a little vessel, shaped like a boat or canoe, with one or two pointed ends, three or four feet to it, and a little handle or grip sticking out of its side – the whole thing about eight or ten inches long. The fish or seal oil was put into it, the reed or wick was dipped in the oil and passed over the pointed end of the cresset, and as it burnt away, it was pushed out'.[35] A slightly more elaborate version of this lamp was the 'cruisie'.[36] This consisted of two iron vessels shaped like sauce boats, one fitting on top of the other. The oil went into the smaller, upper vessel, along with the wick which lay almost horizontal, projecting out of the spout. Because the wick drew up the oil faster than was itself consumed (despite frequent snuffing), some oil dripped into the vessel below. So, to keep the lamp burning, someone had to pour the oil in the lower vessel back into the top one several times an evening. According to John Hocart, writing about the Guernsey crâsset which was in common use until the 1860s, this was a tricky job: the oil frequently spilled, creating a sudden darkness which tended to set babies crying and others grumbling about the stinking mess they would have to mop up.[37]

The wicks for these crude oil lamps were often made out of rushes. John Firth, who spent his life (1838–1922) in Orkney, describes how these were gathered from the moors and fens at full moon during Lammas time,* bound into sheaves, and carefully carried home. 'The youngsters were employed to strip the green peel off, leaving the white pith, "as saft as silk", which, swimming in sillock [saithe] oil, barely made darkness visible.'[38]

The use of oil lamps, as an alternative or supplement to rushlights and tallow candles, stretched quite far inland. John Urie, the son of a Paisley weaver remembered that oil cruises illuminated his father's looms in the 1830s and 40s,[39] and in Carmarthenshire cruises were still a living memory in 1910.[40] However, not all of these lamps burned fish oil. Tallow and vegetable oils were also used in some places.[41]

* i.e. around August 1.

65 *'The humble meal', painted by George Washington Brownlow sometime between 1856 and 1875. There is a crusie hanging from the rafter, to the right of the fire-place. Note the earth floor and the empty creel for carrying peat beside the chair.*

A few traditional rural lighting methods were extremely localized. For example, in areas where 'cannel' or 'candle' coal was available,[42] people deliberately burned it in their fire-places for the sake of its brilliant white light. Celia Fiennes found that cannel coal was burned in this way in Staffordshire, Lancashire and Wales in the late seventeenth century. She thought it produced a very good light.[43] Her contemporary, Roger North, commented that the cannel coal round Wigan, in Lancashire, was burned in a central grate at the very front of the chimney: 'the folk sit about it, working and merry-making.'[44] Another traveller to remark on it was Thomas Pennant. Passing by Wigan at the end of the eighteenth century, he observed that the neighbourhood's abundant supplies of cannel coal served as 'cheap light for the poor to spin by', especially during the long winter evenings when they also needed to keep warm.[45] It seems that poor people in the North continued to burn cannel coal for light well into the nineteenth century, for Thomas Webster said it remained common in 1844.[46]

In Yorkshire, the cottagers dug up immense quantities of resinous fir and oak wood out of the moors, carried it home in cart-loads, cut it into long splinters, and made it serve as candles. According to Joseph Hughes this practice carried on until the 1790s. The bituminous matter in the wood 'gave out a strong bright flame, which had the

66 *Splinters of resinous wood burning in an iron lamp above the fire in a blacksmith's cottage in the Highlands of Scotland, 1774. From Bathélemy Faujas de Saint Fond's* Travels in England, Scotland, and the Hebrides, *1799.*

twofold virtue of diffusing heat as well as light throughout their dwellings'.[47]

In the same way, the Scottish Highlanders dug large pieces of resinous fir wood out of their peat bogs, splitting them into long rods, for use as torches, and splinters 1 to 3 feet long to burn as candles. The sticks were sometimes simply burned on a slab of stone or added to the peat fire, but most households burned them in special holders: a small, round block of stone with a hole in the middle placed on the floor, or an iron lamp shaped like a shovel, hung from the chimney by a long handle.[48] The most sophisticated varieties could hold splinters of wood in mid-air and at different angles. If a very bright light was wanted, the piece of wood was held upright with the lighted end at the bottom and the flame was allowed to spread upwards rapidly. If a more gentle light was required, which would last as long as possible, the splinter was lit on top and burned its way downwards.[49] Visitors to Highland homes noted that the preparation and tending of 'fir candles' fell to the young members of the household.[50]

It seems that even when the 'better sort of people' in the north of Scotland acquired conventional candles[51] in the early nineteenth century, they continued to burn resinous wood.[52] The son of the 5th baronet and 12th laird of Gairloch, Osgood Hanbury Mackenzie, who was born in 1842, remembered that there was always 'a big heap of carefully prepared bog-fir splinters full of resin' in the corner of the main living room during his childhood: 'a small boy or girl did nothing else but keep these burning during the evening, so that the women could see to card and spin and the men to make their herring-nets by hand'.[53] The Irish peasantry also continued to burn 'fir candles' well into the nineteenth century.[54] In Ulster the bog deal splits were sometimes coated with tallow, in which case they resembled rushlights.[55]

Perhaps the most localized of all lighting methods was practised on the remote islands of St Kilda, Borrera and Soa perched way out into the Atlantic, west of the Outer Hebrides. Here the fulmar, a particularly fatty kind of sea bird, lived in hundreds of thousands. It provided the islanders with a source of light because, to quote Alexander Buchan, a missionary who landed on St Kilda in 1705, 'if 'tis approached, when ready to take wing, [it] ejects the quantity of a Mutchkin* of pure oil out of its bill'. To obtain this the islanders surprised the fowl from behind, equipped with a wooden dish fixed to the end of a rod. Sometimes they captured the bird, tied up its bill with thread, and got the oil out at home.[56] According to nineteenth-century visitors, there was also a third method favoured by the most intrepid St Kildian men. Here, the bird catcher would descend down a precipice on a heather rope armed with a sort of fishing rod having a slip noose at the end made from horse hair stiffened with the shafts of solan-goose feathers. This he would dexterously throw over the fulmar's head and haul it up from the rocks below. He would then dip the bird's beak into a leather bag suspended at his waist to catch the oil that was duly vomited.[57] Whatever the technique used, obtaining the oil was a feat requiring considerable skill, cunning, and dexterity.

When these different lighting methods faded away from rural Britain during the last decades of the nineteenth century, their place was taken not by gas and electricity (as in urban areas), but by lamps burning mineral oil. The existence of mineral oil had been known since antiquity and several eighteenth- and nineteenth-century scientists and entrepreneurs had conducted experiments on distilling it from coal and other bituminous substances. But it was not developed commercially as an illuminant until the 1840s. In the United States, Abraham Gesner distilled 'kerosene' from coal and sold it as lamp oil in 1846; and in Britain James Young did the same with 'paraffin' a year later, although he was not selling it on a large scale until 1856. After vast reserves of petroleum were discovered in North America in 1859, mineral oil became very cheap indeed[58] and inexpensive oil lamps with burners designed to eliminate any risk of smell, smoke, or explosion, flooded on to the market.[59]

In Britain, their adoption in rural households was remarkably quick. As early in 1862, the gas industry was remarking on 'the very general adoption' of paraffin lamps among the working classes, 'especially in those places where the conveniences of gas have not yet been made available'.[60] By 1891 Britain's mineral oil industry was so large and well established that *Chamber's Journal* concluded: 'There are few industries which in the space of forty years can show a progress so marvellous, or have added more to the material well-being of the nation.'[61] This eulogy failed to mention the hard work involved in cleaning and filling paraffin lamps, which could be a full-time job: at the Duke of Rutland's estate at Belvoir 'no less than six men were kept constantly employed

---

* The fourth part of the old Scots pint, or about three quarters of an imperial pint.

at nothing else but looking after the lamps' in the late nineteenth century.[62] Even so, mineral oil lamps had certainly added to Britons' domestic convenience.

In contrast to the country, lighting was virtually never produced at home in urban areas. The great majority of town and city dwellers burned only rushlights, candles, and oil lamps, all of which they bought ready-made, and the quality of their illumination was better.[63] In part this was a reflection of higher urban living standards. It was mainly townspeople who had the money to buy wax candles, which burned with a much brighter and less guttering flame than tallow candles and, marvel of marvels, did not require frequent snuffing. They could also afford more conveniences, such as glass lanterns for carrying their candles and ingenious candlesticks which made it possible to have light at a variety of different levels. The crude oil lamps to be found in coastal backwaters were almost unheard of; lamps with proper burners, albeit unsatisfactory in design, were available instead.[64] Furthermore, these were not fuelled by fish oil but by whale oil from the Greenland fishery, such as was used for streetlights, or the much more desirable spermaceti oil imported from the North American fisheries from the early eighteenth century.[65]

But urban wealth was not the only reason for superior urban lighting. Most improvements and innovations in this field were the product of an international circle of scientists working in urban centres on both sides of the Atlantic, whose researches naturally made an impact on large population centres long before reaching the countryside. The Argand lamp, for instance, which was a major breakthrough in the art of illumination, was invented in France in the early 1780s. Its creator, Ami Argand, solved the age-old problems involved in constructing a bright, smokeless, fuel-efficient lamp by designing a burner with a cylindrical wick. This simple but brilliant device allowed air to pass through both the inside and outside of the flame, thus permitting perfect combustion to take place.[66] The result was dazzling: according to Count Rumford, Argand's lamp gave out as much light as nine good wax candles. It also consumed at least 15 per cent less oil than 'a Lamp on the Common Construction, with a Riband wick' when both were producing an equal amount of light.[67]

The new lamp made rapid progress in Britain because Argand came to London in 1783 to promote it. He succeeded in giving George III a private demonstration of its virtues at Windsor Castle and by 1784 it was being manufactured in London and, with the cooperation of Matthew Boulton and James Watt, in Birmingham too. From these two centres of industrial innovation it soon spread to affluent households throughout Britain, where it rivalled even the best wax candles.[68] It was such a success that it inspired others to take a practical interest in lamp construction. Until then the subject had mainly concerned classicists tortured by an abstruse academic question: did the ancients really enjoy the use of 'perpetual' lamps and, if so, how might these have been constructed and fuelled?[69]

Count Rumford, the most notable inventor inspired by Argand, constructed his portable *Illuminator* according to Argand's principles but introduced several new improvements. He made sure that it could not possibly spill, a hazard that Argand had failed to eliminate. He also added a glass chimney, which meant that the lamp could not be blown out by a draught or gust of wind, and made it possible to adjust the amount of light the lamp emitted by turning a knob. To solve the persistent and annoying problem of the light fading as the lamp's oil level dropped, he introduced reservoirs which stored the oil at the same level as the wick. And he also proved that the use of translucent shades to diffuse the lamp's shadows and disperse its light did not markedly reduce its lighting efficiency.[70]

Foreigners were also largely responsible for the great improvements in candle manufacturing that occurred after 1710. For example, at some point between 1712 and 1740, whalers in New England discovered that the wax contained in the cavity of the spermaceti whale's head made excellent candles which burned with a bright light and even flame. They manufactured them for export to England[71] where they outshone wax candles in the drawing- and dining-rooms of grand households.

Similarly, it was a French chemist, Michel Eugène Chevreul, whose research into fats and oils (1811–23) gave candle manufacturers the means to analyze chemically the new vegetable and mineral oils that were to become available as illuminants during the following decades.[72]

Of particular importance was Chevreul's discovery that fat was not, as had been generally supposed, a simple organic substance but a mixture that could be broken down into different components. Manufacturers now knew how to separate the more inflammable material in fats, known as fatty acids, from their comparatively uninflammable glycerine base. This was a vital revelation, because candles made from fatty acids were greatly superior to those made from ordinary tallow.[73] Furthermore, when they were made with plaited cotton wicks – a development of the 1820s – they did not require any snuffing. They equalled the quality and illuminating power of wax candles at less than half the price.

British candle manufacturers were, however, slow to take commercial advantage of these findings; M. de Milly's famous self-snuffing 'bougies de l'étoile' were on sale in Paris from 1831, several years before Britain industrialists started to make the new 'stearine', or 'stearic acid' candles as they were called.[74] It wasn't until Queen Victoria's marriage to Prince Albert in 1840 that E. Price and Co. (later Price's Patent Candle Company) succeeded in creating a substantial market for them; their special 'composite' candles sold for the celebratory window illuminations were self-snuffing, bright, and comparatively cheap.[75]

By this point, of course, gas-lighting was becoming common in small towns. By 1849 there were 775 establishments manufacturing and selling gas in Britain.[76] However, most of this gas was used to light streets, shops, business premises, factories, and public buildings. Only a few eccentrics and pioneers were eager to have it in their homes. This was partly due to widespread suspicion and fear of gas. In the Yorkshire town of

Honley, for example, the new illuminating power was considered a black art by the local populace: 'it was thought to be so dangerous, that people could not sleep in their beds when they knew of its existence in their midst.'[77] But there were also more rational grounds for keeping gas out of the home; gas-lighting was undeniably hot, smelly and dirty. This didn't matter out of doors or in commercial buildings. But indoors it did: people did not want the inconvenience of having to ventilate the lights 'by the lowering of a sash, or the opening of a door for a short time', as one enthusiast suggested they do.[78] Nor did they enjoy the offensive smells that arose when the gas had not been properly purified or escaped, without being burned, from defective fitments.

For these reasons, domestic gas-lighting made little headway in urban Britain until an Austrian chemist, Dr Karl Auer (later Baron von Welsbach), invented his first 'incandescent mantle' in 1884. This consisted of a small, incombustible gauze-like tube containing rare earths which, when fixed over a burning gas jet, began to glow with heat, emitting a bright, steady light.[79] It was a considerable advance on the existing, highly unsatisfactory types of gas-burner. An incandescent mantle emitted up to 35 candle units of light compared to 10 from a 'regenerative' burner or 3.20 from a standard Argand burner;[80] and in doing so, it consumed 70 per cent less gas.[81] Although it was not trouble-free (it was prone to break and to scatter some soot), it was far less troublesome than other models. In short, once the incandescent gas mantle went on sale in 1887, domestic gas-lighting became an attractive proposition for the first time.

Although the precise proportion of urban households lit by gas between 1890 and 1950 is not known, it is clear that gas-lighting became very widespread after 1900. A large sample of working-class houses in London in 1937 showed that 40 per cent were gas-lit.[82]

Somewhat paradoxically, the spread of gas-lighting to middle- and working-class homes was as much due to the spread of prepayment meters and the gas companies' increasingly sophisticated sales policies as to the spread of the Welsbach incandescent mantle. For, because of the monopoly exercised by the English Welsbach Company, its price was kept artificially high. In 1900, for instance, an incandescent burner and mantle cost 4 shillings, as opposed to the crudest type of burner (a 'union jet nipple') which cost a penny.[83] This meant that the majority of working-class families had to put up with inferior burners and all the soot and cleaning these generated. In London it was estimated that less than 20 per cent of gas-lit homes had incandescent mantles at the turn of the century, although in Germany 80 to 90 per cent of families had them.[84]

Although electric lighting posed an immediate and serious threat to gas-lighting, it took several decades to vanquish its rival. Its progress was initially impeded by distrust and scepticism stemming from ignorance. In 1884, for example, Rookes E. B. Crompton, the pioneer electrical engineer, related that:

At the recent Crystal Palace Electrical Exhibition, a couple from the country asked the price of an incandescent lamp at one of the stalls, and being supplied with it for 5s., expended a box of matches in trying to light it, and then declared the whole thing was a swindle.[85]

67 *An advertisement for gas-lighting, c. 1885, showing how a typical middle-class couple of the time might spend their evening.*

But technological and financial problems were mainly responsible for the tortoise-like pace of its spread from city to town to village to hamlet. Thus electric lighting only superceded gas-lighting in the late 1920s and early 30s: in 1919, only half a million houses, about 6 per cent of the total, were wired for electricity, but by 1938 65 per cent were.[86] The amount of gas sold for domestic lighting fell by about half between the two world wars [87] and by 1949, when 86 per cent of British homes were lit by electricity, it hardly counted any more.[88]

It seems that women prized electric lighting more for its convenience and cleanliness than the quality of illumination it offered. For when they acquired it in their homes, they

68 *This was the sort of notice which had to be hung up in the early days of electric lighting.*

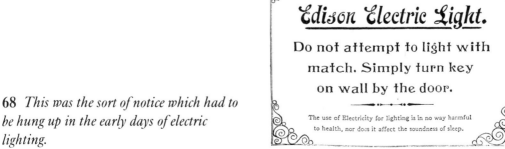

This Room Is Equipped With
Edison Electric Light.

Do not attempt to light with match. Simply turn key on wall by the door.

The use of Electricity for lighting is in no way harmful to health, nor does it affect the soundness of sleep.

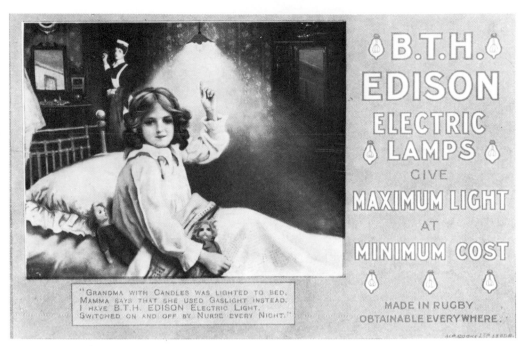

69 *An advertisement from the beginning of this century.*

consumed it at wattages which, by today's standards, were extraordinarily low. An inquiry into electric lighting in nearly 24,000 urban homes conducted in 1944 showed that many women were still doing their most demanding housework in semi-darkness: almost all the women used a single bulb of less than 75 watts to light their sculleries and kitchens and nearly a third of them installed bulbs of less than 25 watts.[89] They were so used to feeble lighting conditions that they found it hard to adjust to good ones.

The spread of electric lighting was not only important because it eliminated an entire household task. It also affected other aspects of domestic life. A whole range of characteristic lighting smells vanished from British homes, for example. Of no practical importance, this nonetheless had a significant effect on their atmosphere. Another effect, which became most evident in the post-war era, was a new flexibility that entered into women's household routines. No longer did they have to do their major housework during daylight hours: they could do it in the evenings, if they preferred. Cobwebs and layers of dust could be spotted and removed under the merciless rays of electricity in a way that they never could when concealed by rush, candle, oil and gas-light. Even more importantly, the main meal could be cooked in the evening, after sunset, rather than at mid-day.

Chapter 6 CLEANING

It is surprisingly difficult to generalize about the comparative cleanliness (or dirtiness) of our ancestors' homes, for cleanliness is not an absolute concept: it varies from place to place and time to time.

In the eighteenth century many foreigners thought that the English had very high standards of cleanliness. When the Frenchman César de Saussure visited London in 1725, he noted that 'Not a week passes by but well-kept houses are washed twice in the seven days, and that from top to bottom; and even every morning most kitchens, staircases, and entrances are scrubbed. All furniture, and especially all kitchen utensils, are kept with the greatest cleanliness. Even the large hammers and the locks on the doors are rubbed and shine brightly.' The farmhouses that Saussure visited were also clean, and he concluded that the English, though 'not slaves to cleanliness, like the Dutch' were still 'very remarkable for this virtue'.[1] Pehr Kalm, the Swede who was in England in 1748, reacted in the same way. He was impressed by the sheen on iron and brass implements, the results, he said, of frequent scouring and polishing with brick-dust. He also noted that 'English women generally have the character of keeping floors, steps, and such things very clean'. 'They are not particularly pleased' he added, 'if anyone comes in with dirty shoes, and soils their clean floors'.[2] (He had presumably made this mistake and learned his lesson!)

Yet in some ways this cleanliness was superficial. Bed-bugs, which thrive on filth, were ubiquitous: 'There are . . . few houses in London in which these least welcome guests have not quartered themselves' Kalm reported.[3] The aristocratic François de la Rochefoucauld, who stayed at several country houses in Suffolk and Norfolk during 1784, felt that the English only cleaned what people were likely to notice. At first he was overwhelmed by 'the cleanliness which pervades everything'. He couldn't get over the way houses were 'constantly washed inside and out' and was astonished at his inability to find a speck of dust anywhere. But on entering the kitchens of these apparently spotless houses, he was always disillusioned. The women who worked there were as black as coal and the dirt was 'indescribable'.[4]

Standards of cleanliness deteriorated once travellers left the south of England. The Scots, for example, were often criticized for their slovenly ways. John Loveday, a gentleman from Berkshire, who travelled in the Lowlands of Scotland in 1732, relates that the natives never emptied their close-stools* until they were 'full to ye top'. As their apartments contained close-stools in practically every room, the smell was unbearable. Loveday also says that the Scots rarely washed their rooms; 'large heaps of nastiness'

---

* A stool concealing a chamber-pot.

70 *This coloured etching, 'The Scotch Cottage of Glenburnia', by Isaac Cruikshank, 1810, reflects the traditional English belief that the Scottish were dirty and slovenly. The print illustrates the experiences of Mrs Mason when she goes to stay with the MacClartys in Elizabeth Hamilton's novel,* The Cottagers of Glenburnie, *published in Edinburgh in 1808. Mrs Mason is first horrified by the dung hills outside the front door and the absence of paving stones. Then, when she gets inside, she sees nothing but filth: black pewter plates and dishes on the dresser, butter with hairs in it, blankets with moth holes in them, etc. Mrs Mason attempts to organize a major house-cleaning, telling her hostess that 'habits of neatness, and of activity, and of attention, have a greater effect upon the temper and disposition than most people are aware of '. But to her consternation, Mrs MacClarty and her indolent daughters resist all attempts at reform: they simply can not be 'fashed'.*

were simply 'swept into one corner, Or – be it a Bed-chamber – more commodiously under ye beds'. He does, however, give them credit for clean linen.[5]

Further north still, standards of cleanliness sank lower and lower, until they disappeared altogether. The oppressed tenants of Harris in the western Hebrides, who shared their huts with cows, goats, sheep, ducks, hens, and dogs, did not even know what dirt was, according to the missionary John Lanne Buchanan who visited the island in the 1780s. They only cleaned out the animal droppings that accumulated in their huts once a year, in spring, spreading them over the fields 'as manure, for barley crops'. Buchanan did say that the islanders took pains to keep their huts as dry as possible 'by attending on their cows with large vessels to throw out the wash'; but no argument could convince them to get rid of the dung on a daily basis as well.[6]

The Irish were also accused of being oblivious to dirt. Arthur Young, writing in the 1770s, found that Dublin's lower ranks had 'no idea of English cleanliness, either in apartments, persons, or cookery'.[7] By the time James Whitelaw took a census of the city's population in 1798, overcrowding had resulted in an inconceivable amount of squalor and stench. It was not uncommon for Whitelaw to stumble across ten to 16 people, of all ages and both sexes, crowded into tiny rooms, where they slept on wads of filthy straw swarming with vermin. This was shocking enough. But what confounded him even more was the apathy and indifference of the poor: 'In the course of the survey, I frequently remonstrated with the inhabitants, and particularly when I found them unemployed and idle, on their not attempting to remove their dirt; but the universal answer was "It is not my business; if I remove it, who will pay me?" '[8]

Standards of cleanliness thus varied enormously in eighteenth-century Britain, just as they did in the other centuries covered by this book. By contrast, attitudes to cleaning were remarkably uniform. With a very few exceptions, such as the demoralized Dubliners described above, most people aspired to cleanliness. Even if it was impossible, they wanted to wear freshly washed clothes, sleep in well laundered sheets, walk on clean floors, admire bright pots and pans, and contemplate a pure white hearthstone.

One of the most important reasons for these aspirations was the ancient and deep-rooted association in most people's minds between cleanliness and spiritual purity. (When John Wesley (1703–91) proclaimed in one of his sermons that 'Cleanliness is indeed next to godliness', thus coining the favourite cliché of nineteenth-century sanitary reformers, he was drawing on Judaic and Christian traditions that went back for thousands of years.)[9] The force of the association was such that people tended to be taken aback or confused if cleanliness and virtue did not accompany each other. Thus Francis Kilvert, the Victorian clergyman and diarist, was surprised to find a married couple who had once lived in sin inhabiting a scrupulously clean cottage; he had expected it to be dirty.[10]

The importance of this association for housework was considerable. Cleaning, unlike any other household task, was widely considered to be a moral duty.[11] People were shocked if women cleaned on a Sunday; it was, after all, their job to ensure that the entire household was cleansed before the Lord's Day began.[12] This helps to explain, incidentally, why increasing amounts of cleaning were done as the week progressed and why Saturdays were so often devoted to last-minute efforts.[13]

There were also compelling aesthetic reasons for cleaning. A home looked nicer and more attractive if it was clean and for housebound wives who wished to retain their husbands' affections and stop them drinking their earnings away at the pub, this was an important consideration.[14] The tremendous urge that women felt to beautify their surroundings by cleaning them can be seen in a number of activities which, though categorized as 'cleaning', were actually done for their decorative effect. Many women,

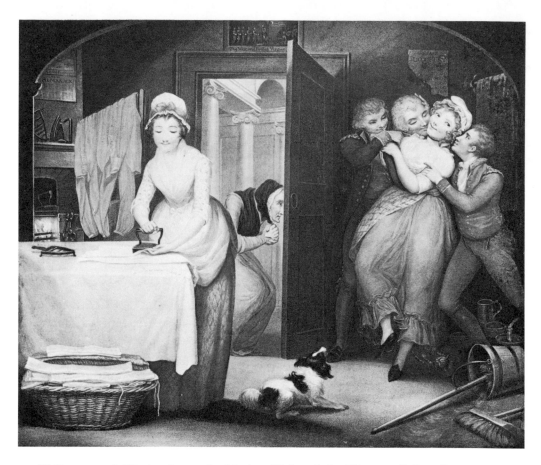

71 *'Diligence and Dissipation – the Modest Girl and the Wanton, Fellow Servants in a Gentleman's House', mezzotint engraving, 1796. The diligent girl is shown ironing snowy white linen and the dissipated wanton with her bucket knocked over (i.e. failing to clean), enjoying the attentions of no less than three men servants. The old woman looking through the key hole reminds the viewer of Death and that inevitable Day of Judgement.*

for example, used to take considerable pride in polishing their metalwork and, during the nineteenth and twentieth centuries, in having a gleaming range. Yet most of their polishing and rubbing did not make the metals cleaner. It simply delighted the eye of the beholder, who could see all sorts of interesting shapes and colours reflected from their surfaces.

This creative aspect of cleaning was particularly evident in humble homes with stone, flagged, brick or earthen floors. These usually lacked any type of covering[15] and so the women added decorations after washing them. In some places they simply added a uniform colour. Wiltshire cottage floors, for example, were given a weekly whitening with freestone* at the beginning of this century.[16] In the Yorkshire village of Morley,

* *Freestone*: any fine-grained sandstone or limestone that can be cut or sawn easily.

where brownstone* was applied in the 1830s, a narrow border of clay was added round the edge of the walls on special occasions.[17] In most households, however, women preferred to make patterns on the floors. James Harvey Bloom, an expert on Warwickshire customs between 1860 and 1930, describes how the women in his county decorated flagged floors with rubbing-stones in a myriad of different designs that were handed down within families. The most basic patterns consisted of broad white lines applied to the edges of the stones or simple twisted flourishes in the centres and round the edges. But others were much more complex; a circle in the centre of the stone and circles on the edges, looped lines drawn across the diagonals of the stone, series of lozenges, and rows of double loops.[18]

72 *Decorative floor patterns in Wales and the Marches, drawn by Eurwyn William of the Welsh Folk Museum, St Fagan's, Cardiff.*

Rubbing-stones were not the only means by which floors were decorated. The dark juice of dock leaves was used to work patterns in nineteenth-century Cheshire farmhouses;[19] while in parts of Caernarvonshire, the earthen floors were washed with water containing soot, to give them a smooth, shiny surface.[20] Wet pipeclay was applied in the tenements and closes of Glasgow in the 1920s and 1930s: 'After they wash it, the women give the stone flags a finish of wet pipeclay that dries bold and white and shows every footprint. Then, round the edges, they add a freehand border design drawn in pipeclay; sometimes a running loop like a blanket-stitch, sometimes tortuous key patterns, always mathematically accurate'.[21]

Another related cleaning activity which was certainly more aesthetic than hygienic was the practice of whitening stone hearths and door steps with hearth-stone.†[22] The latter job was usually done very early in the morning. 'If the mistress of a house would for once rise at five o'clock, she might behold a set of squalid beings engaged in whitening the steps of the doors' wrote John Thomas Smith in 1839.[23] Rich people living in towns and cities had their steps whitened daily, but in the country only about once a week.[24] Most urban housewives without domestic help did it conscientiously early each morning, using any left-over water heated from washing the breakfast dishes.[25] In Pontypool, Wales, for instance, 'Chalking the doorstep was the first duty of the morning' in the early 1900s, 'many housewives believing that evil spirits would not enter a house thus protected'.[26] The poor and destitute, however, only managed to do it on Saturdays.[27] Because their steps had to last a full week, these women often coloured

* *Brownstone*: a naturally occurring mineral, hyper-oxide of manganese.
† *Hearth-stone*: a soft kind of stone used for whitening.

their steps rather than whitening them. In the Salford slums they used brownstone and a chalky substance called 'blue mould' at the beginning of this century. The work was worthwhile because it 'helped to project the image of a spotless household into the world at large'.[28] In Huddersfield and environs, women used ruddle-stone, which was coloured a rich orangey-ochre. They sometimes combined this with 'donkey-stone', a white scouring stone pressed into a rectangular block, so called because of the donkey stamped in low relief on top. The most assiduous housewives also scoured and ruddled their windowsills and even the public pavement in front of their doors.[29] Nearby, in Honley, housewives bought 'idle-back' for whitening their hearthstones and yellow-stone for colouring their doorsteps.[30]

Finally, but not least, there were strong practical incentives to clean; it helped to promote good health and prevent disease. It was common knowledge among the educated that the progress of plagues and epidemics was impeded if certain elementary rules of hygiene were obeyed. Also, every dairymaid knew that rigorous cleanliness was essential to keep milk sweet and make good butter and cheese. Thus on a remote farm in the Highlands of Scotland, where all the dairy utensils were made of wood in the early nineteenth century, the women went to great lengths to keep them clean. First they rinsed them out with cold water and scrubbed them hard with heather brushes; then they filled them with cold water and with the help of tongs inserted red-hot *dornagan*. These were fist-sized stones they had collected from the seashore by the hundred and heated in a huge glowing furnace of peat. Three or four red-hot stones were sufficient to make the cold water boil over in each vessel and thereby sterilize it before next use.[31]

House cleaning was almost always done by women. Men were extremely loth to scrub floors and never dusted if they could avoid it. A telling, if unusual example of this traditional male antipathy to cleaning (although not to cleanliness) comes from Ellen Titterington, Thomas Hardy's parlour-maid in the 1920s. As everybody who has read Hardy's poetry knows, the man was obsessed with cobwebs. According to Ellen, this fascination with decay even entered everyday life. Hardy 'had a whim, a game almost, of hunting cobwebs at night with a little oil lamp . . . When he found a cobweb he would call "Nellie", "Elsie" (we two maids): whoever was nearest went to him, when he would point to the cobweb without saying a word, illuminating it with the little hand-lamp. The meaning we knew well. It was: I notice things and shall not expect to see the cobweb tomorrow night'.[32]

Men only cleaned if they lived alone and could not afford to pay a charwoman to do it for them, or if they happened to be butlers in grand households. The duties of the butler and his male assistants were, however, normally rather light. Men servants only cleaned plate, boots, and lighting devices. They did not work nearly as hard as the housemaids whose duty it was 'to keep every corner of the abode free from dust and soot, from damp and rust, from insects, bad smells, and disorder of every kind'.[33] Men servants in and around London provided a rare exception to this rule; their duties in the

73 *A nineteenth-century advertisement which illustrates the traditional division of labour between men and women servants.*

late eighteenth and early nineteenth centuries sometimes included dry-rubbing oak floors with lead. One writer said that the high wages paid to female servants made them too 'impertinent and slothful' to do this strenuous (and poisonous) job themselves. In the country, however, where wages were lower, women servants considered 'this sort of work theirs beyond dispute'.[34]

What cleaning did women actually do? If manuals of household management are to be believed, they cleaned everything. These publications not only list the elaborate procedures by which houses in an ideal world were to be cleaned, but provided numerous recipes for cleaning potions capable of removing every conceivable type of dirt.[35] Reality was of course rather different. Most women, whether housewives or servants, engaged in a limited range of regular cleaning activities. They cleaned the fireplace and hearth, swept, washed floors and steps, dusted, and scoured pots and pans. The majority of other cleaning jobs, such as furniture polishing, curtain washing and carpet cleaning were done much less frequently and in any case only applied to households with relatively high living standards.

Unlike many other kinds of housework, cleaning methods were astonishingly uniform throughout Britain, at least until the end of the nineteenth century. Most women cleaned their floors and fireplaces with strikingly similar mops, brooms, and brushes. These were often homemade: the mops out of woollen rags, the brushes from hogs' bristles, and the brooms from birch or heather.[36]

The only women to dispense with any of these classic cleaning implements were the

Scots. Edward Burt, an Englishman who recorded their ways in the 1750s, found that they liked to do as much housework as possible with their feet, including laundry, parsnip and turnip washing, barley grinding, and floor mopping. 'First they spread a wet cloth upon part of the floor; then, with their coats tucked up, they stand upon the cloth and shuffle it backward and forward with their feet; then they go to another part and do the same till they have gone all over the room. After this they wash the cloth, spread it again, and draw it along in all places, by turns, till the whole work is finished. This last operation draws away all the remaining foul water.' Burt adds that when he first saw this floor cleaning method he ordered a mop to be made 'and the girls to be shewn the use of it'. But his efforts were in vain: 'there was no persuading them to change their old methods.'[37]

Just as almost all women in Britain possessed the same cleaning equipment, so too they all used the same cleaning agents. Floors and stairs, for example, were kept clean with sand. It soaked up grease and droppings, as well as mud and dirt tramped in from the outside. In opulent households surfaces were normally sanded just before sweeping,[38] an even distribution being achieved by means of a sieve. Dr Swift, in his satirical *Directions to servants* (1745), instructs the housemaid responsible for cleaning the parlour hearth each morning to 'throw the last night's ashes into a sieve; and what falls through, as you carry it down, will serve instead of sand for the rooms and stairs'.[39] But in houses without pretensions to grandeur, the most heavily trodden floors were usually kept sanded all the time. Depending on local tradition and taste, the sand was either applied as a thick golden carpet or in intricate and highly decorative patterns.[40] In these households the sand was swept out and renewed on Saturday.[41] The floor, whether stone, brick, or wood, was left remarkably free of stains thanks to the sand's absorbent and abrasive action, which made the weekly wash and scrub much easier than it would otherwise have been. It is important to remember that women usually had to do their washing and scrubbing with cold water, and without the benefit of soda or soap until the early nineteenth century.

When women lived by the seaside they usually fetched fresh supplies of sand themselves. The Irish playwright J. M. Synge spent some time in west Kerry in the early 1900s and records how '. . . in our cottage the little hostess swept the floor and sprinkled it with some sand she had brought home in her apron'.[42] Inland, the sand was brought to the door in sacks by special hawkers called 'sandmen'. In Cornish villages, for example, sand was sold, well into this century, by blinded miners or old women, who transported it on donkeys.[43]

Sand was also used for scouring metals. Robert Plot, in *The Natural History of Oxfordshire* (1677), says that the finest sand dug in the parish of Kingham was used for scouring pewter 'for which purpose 'tis so very excellent, that the Retailers sell it for a penny a pound'.[44] It could also be used, in conjunction with ground oyster shell, for imparting a gleam to brass,[45] for cleaning china, or, more prosaically, to remove food adhering to the bottoms of cooking utensils. This explains, incidentally, why cook books

74 *An old woman servant scouring a cooking pot in front of the kitchen fire. The mistress of the household is about to hand a recipe to the cook. Frontispiece from* The Town and Country Cook; or, Young Woman's best Guide to the whole Art of Cookery, *c. 1780.*

75 *'Do you want any brick-dust?', 1799. This coloured etching is one of Thomas Rowlandson's 'Cries of London'.*

often warned their readers to 'Be sure that your pots and cover are well tinned, very clean, and free from sand'.[46]

Many women, however, found other cleaning agents more satisfactory. In Cornwall, for instance, where sand was freely available, housewives scoured their pots and pans (as well as their bedroom floors) with 'gaird' or 'growder', local granite reduced to a powder.[47] Steel was usually polished with emery paper or, like brass, with white brick,* brick-dust or rotten-stone.† Silver and plate were cleaned with white clay, or 'whiting' as it was called. If the silver was particularly tarnished it was washed with lye‡ first.

---

* *White brick*: this was the same as Bath brick, a preparation of calcareous earth moulded in the form of a brick, made at Bridgwater in Somerset and used for cleaning metal.
† *Rotten-stone*: a powder of decomposed limestone.
‡ *Lye*: water made alkaline with vegetable ashes (see pp. 142–4).

Rebecca Price, of Westbury, Buckinghamshire, noted in 1680: 'First wash your plate in a strong lye with flanell cloaths then rence it in clean water with whiteing in it, and set it by the fire to drye, and then rub it clean with a drye linnen Cloath.'[48] But by the early eighteenth century, soap and spirit of wine* were being substituted for lye. Lady Grisell Baillie, for example, told her butler to wash the plate in soap suds 'or spirit of wine if it has got any spots'.[49]

In the country women tended to make use of vegetable rather than mineral substances; they cleaned their cooking utensils with straw or a handful of wood ashes, occasionally boiling them in lye.[50] On farms it was quite a common practice to 'wash-up' with bran; the husks absorbed any fat or food remains and made excellent pig food.[51]

Cleaning was hardly affected by technological change until the middle of the nineteenth century. It was only at this point that towns and cities started to get to grips with their water supply problems and to improve sanitation. The advent of piped water supplies and drains had a substantial impact on cleaning, as did the introduction of water-closets.

The spread of cheap alkali in the nineteenth century also helped to make cleaning easier. An economic way of mass-producing soda from salt had been developed by Nicolas Leblanc of France at the end of the eighteenth century and the first British plant to use the process opened at St Helen's, Lancashire in 1814. Within a few decades almost all books on domestic economy recommended that floors, kitchen tables, and cooking utensils should be scrubbed with soda and it rapidly became a fixture on the average family's shopping list. The availability of cheap soda also boosted Britain's nascent soap industry which lacked a cheap supply of alkali. However, people were so used to thinking of soap as a luxury (it was taxed until 1853) that ordinary household soaps such as William Lever's 'Sunlight' and 'Monkey Brand', Joseph Watson's 'Matchless Cleanser' and Joseph Crosfield's 'Perfection' did not reach a mass market until the 1870s and 80s. Even then the extent to which these soaps actually helped to dissolve grease and ease women's cleaning burden is doubtful, give the fact that very few households had ready supplies of hot water before this century. The 1961 census, which was the first to enquire about hot water taps, showed that 22 per cent of the population still lacked this essential convenience.[52]

The impact of the patent pastes, liquids and polishes that became available during the nineteenth century for cleaning metals, stoves, and furniture is also questionable. (Anyone interested in seeing how many types the Victorians could buy and in reading about their miraculous properties, should visit the John Johnson Collection of Ephemera at the Bodleian Library, Oxford.) Products such as Goddard's silver plate powder, which came into use in about 1810, and Reckitt's 'Zebra' black lead grate polish launched in 1890, were effective and did save time and labour. But their ingredients were not new. Nor were their results particularly long-lasting.

---

* *Spirit of wine*: alcohol.

76 *An advertisement for Monkey Brand soap dated 1888.*

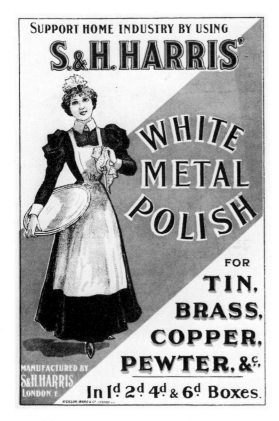

77 *A late nineteenth-century advertisement.*
78 *The carpets have been taken up and the furniture shrouded in dust covers in this advertisement of 1888. Spring cleaning enjoyed a brief vogue among the middle classes in the late nineteenth century.*

A far more radical innovation that really did revolutionize British cleaning methods was Cecil Booth's invention in 1901 of the vacuum cleaner – the first device to suck up dirt effectively. As Booth readily acknowledged, his vacuum cleaner was the culmination of almost 75 years of inventive effort. 'Like other mechanical inventions, the vacuum cleaner was preceded by many attempts to achieve similar results. The idea of removing dust and dirt from surfaces by means of a current of air produced by suction was by no means new . . . [and] . . . crude ideas of some of the elements necessary to successful operation had already been indicated.'[53] Booth, however, was the first to combine a power driven suction pump and dust collecting filter in a single workable machine.

A London engineer specializing in wheel construction, Booth was not particularly interested in cleaning problems until he happened to see a demonstration of a new American machine for cleaning railway carriages, cushions and carpets. It consisted of a compressor driven by an electric motor which blew air through a pipe; the displaced dust collected in a box above. Booth's immediate reaction was that suction would be a simpler and better method of removing it. The American who was demonstrating the machine dismissed this idea out of hand; it had been tried before and had failed, he said. Booth, somewhat annoyed, returned to his office and experimented on his carpet. According to Charles Hitchins, his business partner, 'He spread a white handkerchief on the top of the carpet, went down on his knees, and sucked on the top of the handkerchief for a few seconds, then took the handkerchief up. On the side which had lain on the carpet there was a dirty mark, which was dust'.[54] Booth likewise relates how he sucked the back of a plush seat in a restaurant in Victoria Street, on this occasion without a handkerchief, and almost choked.[55] In short, his intuition had been correct.

The vacuum cleaning machine Booth subsequently devised and marketed was acclaimed a success, not only by the hotels, theatres, and railway companies that were his initial patrons, but by royalty too. (King Edward VII and Queen Alexandra helped to promote vacuum cleaning by installing a system at Buckingham Palace.) Before long Booth and Hitchins were also running a popular 'house to house' cleaning business too. Their bright red vacuum cleaners, which were transported round London by horse-drawn vehicles, could periodically be seen outside all the most fashionable houses of the day. Uniformed operators carried hoses into the houses while the maids looked on in awe. The Bissell Carpet Sweeper, an American invention patented in 1876 which some of their more enlightened mistresses had bought, certainly did not compete in efficiency.

Around 1909 and 1910 Booth and Hitchins began to market small portable machines. They started off by making hand-operated 'Bellow' cleaners that could be worked by a couple of servants and cost £5 each. Then they produced an electrically powered vacuum cleaner which could run off an ordinary lighting circuit. By this point firms in the provinces began to acquire licences to establish local vacuum companies and the new cleaning method spread outside the metropolis for the first time. After the First World War, when domestic electricity supplies became more common and American manufacturers of vacuum cleaners started to exploit the British market, the design of small electric vacuum cleaners improved steadily. Despite their expense, 40 per cent of families with an electricity supply had one by 1948.[56]

In 1950 most women in Britain were still cleaning their houses with the same basic equipment and materials that their ancestors had used 300 years earlier. It is, however, misleading to conclude from this that the scope and importance of cleaning as a household task remained unchanged during this time. For between about 1670 and 1820 the status of cleaning was transformed; it ceased to be a peripheral aspect of housework and became one of central importance.

The first harbinger of change was the unwelcome spread of the bed-bug (*Cimex lectularius*) in Britain.[57] According to John Southall, author of a book about these blood-sucking insects published in 1730, bugs had been well known in England for over

79 *An advertisement of* c. *1938, encouraging women to buy vacuum cleaners on hire purchase. Hoover Ltd was established in 1919 – the British subsidiary of an American company.*

60 years.[58] In fact they had been present since the sixteenth century;[59] but in the late seventeenth century their numbers started to provoke public concern.[60] (The eminent London firm of bug-destroyers, Messrs Tiffin and Son, was founded in 1695.)[61] Nobody knew where the bugs had come from. Southall thought they were the result of increased foreign trade. 'This to me is apparent', he explained, 'because not one Sea-Port in England is free; whereas in Inland-Towns, Buggs are hardly known'.[62] He was probably right. Soon, however, bugs started to make their way inland. By 1824 they were so common that Anthony Haselmore, 'many years cook in a nobleman's family', said it was 'next to an impossibility' to guard against them in large towns and cities.[63]

His words were amply confirmed by the experience of Jane and Thomas Carlyle when they moved, in 1834, into 5 Great Cheyne Row, Chelsea (then, as now, a respectable London address). Jane expected, as a matter of course, to find the house infested with bugs. When she didn't find any, she wrote to a friend 'We have no bugs yet, to the best of my knowledge', adding 'I do not know of one other house among all my acquaintances that so much can be said for'.[64] Within a year she realized that she had been mistaken and, during the next 32 years, she had to battle against bugs on many occasions. In 1843, for example, she discovered bugs in the servant's bed:

I flung some twenty pailfuls of water on the kitchen floor, in the first place to drown any that might attempt to save themselves; when we killed all that were discoverable, and flung the pieces of the bed, one after another, into a tub full of water, carried them all into the garden, and let them steep there for two days; – and then I painted all the joints, had the curtains washed and laid by for the present, and hope and trust that there is not one escaped alive to tell. *Ach Gott*, what a disgusting work to have to do! – but the destroying of bugs is a thing that cannot be neglected.[65]

In addition to trying to drown the bugs, she also had them boiled to death. When she discovered bugs in her own bed (or her husband's) she invariably sent all the bedding, hangings, and curtains to the dyers' for this treatment.[66] On some occasions, however, there were simply too many bugs, and furniture had to be thrown out. In 1852, for instance, she found that a servant's bed was swarming with 200 bugs and she simply gave up. The bed was sold and replaced with one made out of iron. 'The horror of these bugs quite maddened me for many days' she commented afterwards.[67]

For most working-class women the horror was perpetual. Bugs contrived to hide themselves not only in bedding and upholstery, but behind wallpaper, picture rails and skirting boards, in cracks in wood and plaster work, under floor boards, and even inside nail holes and knobs.[68] 'Mrs Pember Reeves', who in 1913 published a study about life in the London districts of Lambeth and Kennington, found that bugs were a pressing problem in all small houses. 'No women, however clean, can cope with it' she said. Apparently some women had their bedrooms fumigated before their confinements, only to find bugs dropping on to their pillows.[69] In the Salford slums, where the inhabitants were really poor, the omnipresent bugs appeared 'in battalions' as soon as

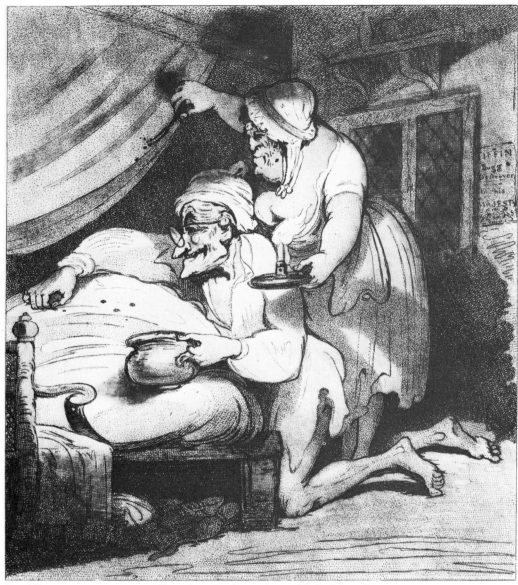

80 *'Summer amusement – Bugg hunting', a print published in 1782.*

the weather grew warm. People bravely lime-washed their bedrooms and disinfected them with 'Klenzit Kleener' and applied blow lamps to cracks in the floor boards, walls and ceilings. But to no avail. The bugs crept along joists and through party walls 'until even the valiantly cleanly housewife gave up in despair and prayed for cold weather'.[70]

Mercifully, bugs ceased to be a national pest after the Second World War, thanks to slum clearance schemes, the growth of council housing, and debugging programmes initiated by local authorities in the 1920s and 30s.[71] Although many housewives had barely managed to keep them at bay and innumerable others had failed altogether, the ubiquity of bugs did have a significant effect on attitudes to cleaning. This was because bugs could not be exterminated by traps or repelled by fumes and vile liquids.[72] Strict and regular attention to household cleanliness was shown, again and again, to be the only effective way of preventing their arrival and of getting rid of them.

The spread of coal supplies was another development that increased the amount of cleaning women had to do. Coal was much dirtier than wood or peat and, until the adoption of 'clean' fuels such as gas, electricity and coke, it was responsible for an enormous amount of household dirt and atmospheric pollution. This was remarked on by Tim Nourse in 1700. As a devotee of wood and charcoal fires, he could not abide the 'vast number of coal-dust carts trotting up and down' that scattered coal in London's streets or the 'Tartanous Smoak' that emanated from the city's chimneys:

'Twere endless to reckon up all the Mischiefs which Houses suffer hereby in their Furniture, their Plate, their Brass and Pewter, their Glass, with whatsoever is solid and refin'd, all of which are Corroded by it. A Bed of Fourscore or one Hundred Pounds Price, after a dozen Years or so, must be laid aside as sullied by the Smoak, which in the Country might have been preserv'd fresh, and in its Primitive Lustre for many Ages. All sorts of Hangings, especially Tapestry, are in a few Years totally defil'd by it, losing their Beauty, and stinking richly into the Bargain . . .[73]

Two hundred years later there were no four-posters or tapestries to worry about. But there was so much smoke and grime in the atmosphere of industrial towns that women had to wash their windows once a week and their net curtains once a fortnight. Grace Foakes, who spent her childhood in the East End of London, says that curtains got so black that it was necessary to soak them first in salt water: 'when this water was poured away it was as black as soot.'[74]

Increasing affluence also transformed the scope of cleaning by adding to the number and categories of things that required attention. Most people lived in larger and more complicated houses in 1950 than they had in 1650; and the majority of the population had far more material possessions to clean and tidy than their ancestors. This can be seen very vividly by comparing pictures of houses and their interiors over the three centuries, by studying inventories, and by reading travelogues. Thomas Pennant, for instance, on his tour of Wales in 1778, found that the mountain people of Snowdonia lived in single-room, windowless houses with a hole at one end to let out the smoke from their fires. The furniture was extremely simple: 'stones are substitutes of stools, and the beds are of hay, ranged along the sides'.[75] Arthur Young, who was travelling in Ireland at this time, found that Irish cabins were very similar one-room constructions. Their inhabitants, however, were marginally better off when it came to furniture, this consisting 'of a pot for boiling their potatoes, a bit of a table, and one or two broken stools'. Beds were not very common: as in Snowdonia, families lay on straw, along with their animals.[76]

The impact on cleaning of even small increases in living standards should not be underestimated. For example, Mary Shackleton Leadbeater, in her annals of Ballitore, a Quaker village near Dublin, writes that in the 1760s 'all the parlours had earthen floors; the hall doors opened with iron latches, and were without knockers; and most of the windows were casements'. But, she relates, as the inhabitants grew more prosperous, 'a taste for elegance arose' and the earthen floors were covered over with wooden boards and carpets. The casements gave way to sashes and 'grinning lions' heads guarded and ornamented the hall-doors'.[77] Small changes, perhaps, but they created a great deal of new cleaning; the floor boards had to be maintained in good condition, the carpets cleaned with dried tea leaves and beaten, the windows washed, and the door knockers polished.

Many additions to women's cleaning load were the result of economic growth within specific industries. For instance, the emergence of 'washing-up' with soap and water as a cleaning job dignified by its own name and its own domestic office (the scullery) followed the expansion of the Staffordshire potteries at the end of the eighteenth century. Until then almost everybody ate off pewter plates or wooden trenchers which were only rinsed in cold water or wiped clean with bread, straw or bran. Poor people shared a communal cooking pot or bowl which was practically never washed at all. There was very little china or pottery in everyday use. However, thanks to entrepreneurial potters such as Josiah Wedgwood, a large market for all sorts of inexpensive ceramic wares was established by the end of the eighteenth century. By the middle of the next century, many agricultural labourers and urban artisans could not only afford to buy ceramic plates to eat off, but ornaments to decorate their mantel-pieces and window-ledges as well. Communal eating habits continued to survive in many places, however. In 1832 Sir James Philips Kay-Shuttleworth found that the workers employed in Manchester's cotton factories always ate their meals out of a communal dish and had no cutlery other than spoons.[78] William Richard Le Fanu described Irish peasant habits in County Limerick before the great potato famine of 1847 as follows:

The potatoes were boiled in a huge iron pot, from which they were thrown into a big open-work wicker basket, shaped like the bowl of a spoon; this was placed over another large pot or over a trough, till the water was drained off; the potatoes were then turned out on the middle of the table in a heap. There was sometimes a coarse table cloth, more often none. There were no knives or forks, nor any plates, but one on which the herring if one was there, lay.[79]

In the same way, the Reverend Marmaduke Charles Frederick Morris described communal eating habits surviving in Yorkshire until the mid-nineteenth century. On one farm near Tibthorpe, for example, the wooden dining-table had a thick top which had round holes 2 inches deep, about the size of a dinner plate cut into it. 'Into these the broth and meat were poured and eaten with wooden spoons. The table had to be washed after each meal with hot water and soda.'[80] Morris also records that in the village of Nafferton in the Yorkshire Wolds, agricultural labourers ate their meat off wooden trenchers, drank tea from mugs, and milk from wooden basins as late as 1850.[81]

The mechanization of the textile trades in the late eighteenth and early nineteenth centuries also expanded the scope of cleaning. Curtains, upholstery, and carpets ceased to be luxuries solely enjoyed (and cleaned) in wealthy households. By the 1840s, for example, a comparatively modest middle-class couple such as Jane and Thomas Carlyle could expect to have fitted wall-to-wall carpeting. The Carlyles' carpets were nailed into place and only removed once a year for cleaning, incidentally.[82]

The iron trade provides yet another example of an industry's growth affecting the amount of cleaning women had to do. Its aggressive expansion in the late eighteenth and early nineteenth centuries led to a phenomenal increase in the number and size of iron grates and ranges in Britain, all of which needed regular black-leading to look presentable.

What did women feel about the cleaning they did? As might be expected, a large proportion found it a creative, satisfying and thoroughly moral activity, in which they took considerable pride. Men's descriptions of women's cleansing efforts suggest this, as does the popularity of 'decorative' cleaning activities. It should be stressed, however, that women's pride in their cleaning prowess was often mixed with servility. Arthur Munby (1828–1910), the eccentric civil servant who was fascinated with the lives of working women, records in his diary how Hannah Cullwick, the housemaid he eventually married, positively revelled in filth and the lowly status of her work. She had little self-esteem, and appeared to believe that hard manual labour would be her only salvation. Even when she was married to Munby, she continued to behave like a servant and to do all the housework.[83]

But for women living in squalid, over-crowded urban accommodation, often without access to piped water supplies, cleaning was a real and never ending nightmare. No matter how hard they worked, they never ended up with clean homes. Housewives in these miserable circumstances (and even in slightly better ones) often became hysterical cleaners. They wore their lives away in an endless round of scouring, scrubbing, and polishing, much of which was completely unnecessary.[84] Jennifer Stead, for example, reports that her Auntie Mabel (who came from Huddersfield) used to black-lead the coal shovel, scrub the coal cellar floor and, upon the return of her husband from work, turn out his pockets and trouser turn-ups to brush them down![85] Similarly, Betty Palmer relates that: 'We had a neighbour, when I was a child, who polished her dustbin with metal polish and her painted front gate with furniture polish. After her poor husband had a stroke, he was put in the garden shed all day'.[86] Sadly, some of these compulsive cleaners ended up by going truly mad. Robert Roberts, whose youth was spent in the Salford slums in the early 1900s, knew two women who suffered this fate and who were incarcerated in the local lunatic asylum. One of them he remembers vividly, 'passing with a man in a uniform through a group of us watching children to a van, still washing her hands like a poor Lady Macbeth'.[87]

81 *Women and chimney sweeps occasionally rebelled against cleaning, as this print of 1772,
'The Unfortunate Beau', shows. The maid who is twerling her mop in the air to dry it out
(just as the books instructed her to do) carefully avoids looking in front of her. The deformed
boy by her side does his bit by blackening one of the dandy's stockings with his sooty brush.*

Chapter 7 LAUNDRY

There were great obstacles to doing laundry in the past. Soap was highly taxed until 1853 and piped water supplies unusual until the latter part of the nineteenth century. But despite this, clothes-washing was an important and regular part of housework for all social classes between 1650 and 1950, even though standards were not always as high as they are today. Whatever their station in life, everybody wanted to enjoy the comfort of clean clothes as well as freshly laundered household linen. Servants frequently got a clothes-washing allowance in soap as part of their wages and complained loudly if their employers withheld this perquisite; and poor families, whose members often had literally no change of clothing, willingly retired naked to bed while their clothes were washed. George Edwards, the son of a farm worker in Norfolk, described how he had to do this in the 1850s and 60s:

My sister and I went to bed early on Saturday nights so that my mother might be able to wash and mend our clothes, and we have them clean and tidy for the Sunday . . . This work kept my mother up nearly all the Saturday night, but she would be up early on the Sunday morning to get our scanty breakfast ready in time for us to go to Sunday school.[1]

Moreover, it is clear that most households were prepared to spend a high proportion of their income on laundry. In 1844 the washing expenses of labouring families in London amounted to about half the sum they spent on rent; for middle-class families the proportion was a third.[2]

Yet another piece of evidence is the ubiquity of washer-women. The job of going to other people's homes to help with the washing was one of the most common female occupations until the twentieth century. Indeed, there were so many washer-women about that they were usually credited with providing the main route by which neighbourhood gossip and scandal travelled from house to house! According to John Thomas Smith, they seldom left their employer 'without gaining the secrets of the family', which they acquired by telling fortunes 'by the manner in which the grouts of the tea adhere to the sides of the tea-cup'.[3]

Washer-women, not washer-men; in the British Isles laundry was always a female occupation. As the chap-books popular in the seventeenth, eighteenth and early nineteenth centuries make plain, men only did laundry if there was something wrong with them. For instance, if a man helps a woman at the wash-tub, he will jump in and shit in it, thus proving that he is a fool;[4] and if he is so simple-minded as to let his wife get the better of him, he will find that he is left at home while she goes out to gossip with her cronies, with instructions 'to make a fire, and hang the kettle with water in order to wash the cloaths'.[5] Normal, virile men never even helped with laundry, although some

82 *'A Scanty Wardrobe', detail of a humorous sketch by Theodore Lane, c. 1820, showing how desperately the poor wanted to have clean clothes. The dialogue between the man lying naked in his garret bed and the boy goes as follows: Boy: Please sir, Mother says its impossible to wash your shirt any more without rubbing it in two. Man: I wish she could rub it into half a dozen my man. Boy: But it won't bear touching. Man: Then let her pin it against the wall and fling water at it for I must have it again in half an hour.*

of them enjoyed making love to laundry maids.[6] So strong was the taboo against men washing, starching, or ironing that when they were in the unhappy position of having to do so – for example, if they were widowed with young children and too poor to employ a washer-woman – they normally did it in secret, in the small hours of the morning, for they did not want their neighbours to know.

Until this century, laundry was divided into two categories. The most important consisted of personal and household articles made out of cotton and linen, and known collectively as 'linen', which were washed on a regular basis.* The second category, to be discussed later, included fabrics which either had specific spots and stains requiring special treatment or were too delicate or insufficiently colour-fast for ordinary washing and required cleaning in other ways.

* The term could be stretched to include articles made out of wool and silk.

83 *A widower washing his children's clothes by candle-light as they sleep. A journeyman paviour by trade, he was too poor to afford the services of a servant or washer-woman. From J. Wight's* Mornings at Bow Street, *illustrated by George Cruikshank, 1824.*

Washing

There were four basic methods of washing linen between 1650 and 1950, each reflecting a different stage of economic development and domestic sophistication.

The simplest of the four methods was a really primitive procedure: women took their laundry down to the nearest source of water and, without using any soap or other cleansing agent, simply pounded it clean. If they were washing near a well they often beat their linen against a wooden washing-block with a smooth or ridged bat-like implement called a beetle or a battledore. Thus when William Richard was en route from London to Wales in 1682, he passed a washing-block 'where the she-Vulcans were hammering out with Battle-door the filth of the linnen, whose unctuous distillations were the Nile that water'd the little Egypt of the adjacent garden'.[7]

Alternatively, if they were washing by a stream or a river, they would stand in the water and beetle their laundry against a stone or boulder. When Arthur Young, the famous agricultural writer, toured Ireland between 1776 and 1779, he was shocked to find that this practice ruined women's legs: 'by washing their cloathes nowhere but in rivers and streams, the cold, especially as they roast their legs in their cabbins till they

84 *A Welsh peasant woman kneels by a stream, beetling her laundry on the rocks. Her companion holds a basket of linen. From* The Costume of Great Britain *by William H. Pyne, 1808.*

are fire spotted, must swell them to a wonderful size and horrid black and blue colour always met with both in young and old.'*[8]

In Scotland women washed their laundry by trampling on it with bare feet in tubs of water, much to the astonishment of English visitors who were accustomed to the technique of beetling. Sir William Brereton, who visited the Highlands in 1635, was one of the first to record the sight. 'After their linnen is putt into a great broad lowe tubbe of water, then (their cloathes being tucked uppe above their knees), they steppe into the tubbe, and tread itt and trample itt with their fete, (never vouchsafeing a hand to nett, or wash itt withall), until itt bee sufficiently cleansed in their apprehensions'.[10] Sir William scorned this washing technique as being ineffective. But Scottish women did not agree with him; many continued to trample their washing in tubs quite unabashedly through-

---

* This horrifying account is confirmed by Hely Dutton, author of the *Statistical survey of the county of Clare*, published in 1808: 'In every part of this county the clothes (I mean those of the lower rank) are washed by beating them in a river on a large smooth stone with a flat board, called a beetle; for this purpose they will stand for hours up to their knees in water, even in cold weather; after this they run to the fire; this causes the legs to be full of black and blue spots, and to swell up to a great size . . .'[9]

85 *'Scotch washing', a print by Isaac Cruikshank, 1810. The Scottish beetle was much longer than the Welsh and Irish types, probably because of its additional use in banishing* voyeurs.

out the eighteenth and nineteenth centuries. They normally washed in groups, two women to a tub, supporting themselves with their arms thrown over each other's shoulders, while they danced up and down and sang rousing songs.[11] Foreigners tended to suspect that they washed in this way for lascivious reasons (it was, after all, rather immodest to show so much leg in public). But this was unfair. Scottish women preferred to wash with the full weight of their feet because it was more efficient. It may also have been easier to keep blood circulating in the feet than the hands, especially in winter. For Scottish women washed all the year round, even, as Edward Burt wrote in 1754, 'in the hardest frosty weather, when their legs are red as Blood with the Cold'.[12]

After the laundry had been beetled or trampled, it was wrung out and laid on the grass or a convenient hedge to dry. There the sun's rays helped to whiten the linen further, and the end results were usually quite creditable. Mr and Mrs Samuel Carter Hall, experts on Irish domestic life between 1825 and 1840, thought that beetling was one of the most effective modes of washing they knew, and even the sternest critics of the Scots' alleged sluttishness usually gave them credit for clean linen.[13]

Although this primitive washing method had disappeared from most places in England by the late eighteenth century, it was not to vanish completely from the more

86 *Irish peasant women beetling their linen in a river. From Mr and Mrs Samuel Carter Hall*, Ireland: its scenery, character etc. . . ., *1841–3.*

remote parts of Britain until after the First World War. One of the last people to describe it was the Irish playwright, J. M. Synge, who spent much time on the Aran Islands off the west coast of Ireland in the 1890s and early 1900s. 'As I walk round the edges of the sea', he wrote, 'I often come on a girl with her petticoats tucked up round her, standing in a pool left by the tide and washing her flannels among the sea-anemones and crabs. Their red bodices and white tapering legs make them as beautiful as tropical sea-birds, as they stand in a frame of seaweeds against the brink of the Atlantic'. However, he had one more prosaic comment to add. 'Their habit of using the sea-water for washing causes a good deal of rheumatism on the islands, for the salt lies in the clothes and keeps them continually moist.'[14]

A second laundry method consisted of washing linen in a solution containing some bleaching or cleansing agent. Stale urine, which contains ammonia, was very commonly used for this purpose. The urine went by different terms according to locality. In Lancashire, for example, it was called 'lant' and there was a 'lant-pot' for collecting it in every yard and a 'lant-trough' built into most garden walls, while in Yorkshire it was called 'weetin' (wetting) or 'old waish' (old wash).[15] Poor people used it for washing themselves as well, apparently with excellent results.[16]

Because urine was free, and easy to collect and store, it was employed in town and country alike. Dr David Boswell Reid, who investigated living conditions in the northern coal-mining towns of England during the early 1840s, found that streets or groups of houses frequently collected their urine in a common barrel, from which each family was supplied on wash-day. 'Where this practice continues, the state of the atmosphere on washing days is altogether unaccountable to those who are not aware of the cause.'[17] Like many respectable gentlemen who documented this rather smelly washing method, Dr Reid implied that it was dying out. But he was wrong: the custom continued in some working-class communities for at least another half century.

Dung, added to cold water, produced a similar cleansing effect, and was sometimes used as an alternative or addition to urine. (The clothes were rinsed thoroughly in fresh water afterwards, of course.) When Joseph Taylor, a London lawyer, visited Edinburgh in 1705, he found that the Scots 'put their cloaths with a little cow dung into a large tubb of water, and then plucking their pettycoats up to their bellyes, get into the Tubb, and dance about it to tread the cloaths . . .'.[18] In the same way, 'the neater sort' of Welsh peasant was reported to be using 'Swine's Dung instead of soap' in 1738 and the common people of Ireland and Scotland to be whitening their clothes with it in the early 1800s.[19] Dung, however, was never as popular as urine. This was partly because dung had other valuable uses (as manure, fuel, and building material) and partly because people suspected it of causing the 'itch'. Thus its use as a cleansing agent vanished from most parts of Britain in the early nineteenth century.

The other major cleansing solution was lye. This consisted of water impregnated with alkaline salts extracted from wood or plant ashes. It cleaned linen quite effectively for when grease or oil comes into contact with alkali it becomes more soluble in water and therefore easier to remove. The 'buck-wash', as this laundry method was called, was so common in households burning wood fires in the seventeenth and eighteenth centuries that it is hard to find a household inventory which does not mention a wooden lye or bucking tub or an account book that does not refer to the sale or purchase of ashes.

Lye was often made by passing water through clean wood ashes, two or three days before the buck-wash began. William Clift, the son of a farm labourer in Bramley, Kent, described how this was done in his family in the 1830s and 40s:

A wooden frame about 18 inches square was used, in which a layer of clean wheat straw was placed, at the bottom; and on this a coarse cloth of large size was laid, and filled full of the ashes. Then water was poured on it, as much as it would hold, and the water would drip slowly through into a large vat or tub. It was a long job, and took from the Friday to the Monday afternoon.[20]

Lye was also made out of ferns – especially in the rough and heathy districts where these were plentiful and wood in short supply. People collected them while still green, round about harvest time in July or August, half-dried them in small heaps in the open air, and burned them into fine reddish-grey ashes, usually in pots – hence the word potash.

87 *'The Fern Gatherers', coloured mezzotint, 1799.*

According to Robert Plot, author of *The Natural History of Staffordshire* (1686), the ashes were then made into balls of about 3 inches diameter (with the help of warm water) and sold at a penny the half dozen.[21] Making ash balls was a profitable cottage industry. In 1698, when Celia Fiennes passed by Cannock Wood in Staffordshire, which was overrun with fern, she found that almost everybody in the county was employed in making ash balls. The local people used them for washing and scouring all the year round and also sold large quantities in London.[22]

In Ireland, thistles, docks, and weeds of all kinds were mixed in with the fern as well. James Hall, on his tour of the country's interior in the early 1800s, found that the ashes were sifted after they had been burned, mixed with water, and 'formed into a kind of loaves, shaped like brick-bats, with a hole in the middle of each, through which a string is put with a view to hang them up to dry'. The loaves kept for up to 20 years, if properly dried.[23]

A great improvement on washing with urine, dung, or lye was to use soap, which was gentler on the linen and considerably more efficacious in cleaning it. Soap, however, was expensive. It could not be collected or made for nothing. The animal fats or vegetable oils that went into its making were also required for other purposes, such as cooking and candle-making; indeed, the demand for them was so great that additional supplies were already being imported from abroad in the late seventeenth century. To make matters worse, soap was subject to substantial excise duties periodically from 1643 to 1853.[24]

Thus until about 1850 most households economized by washing with a mixture of lye and soap. The account books for Chirk Castle in Denbighshire, Wales, for example, are typical in showing that regular payments were made for soap, wash balls and fern ashes between 1666 and 1753.[25]

Women seem to have varied the order in which they used lye and soap according to personal whim. Some like to save their soap for washing their small linen and favourite clothes and left everything else for bucking. Thus Elizabeth Purefoy (1672–1765), who lived in a Buckinghamshire manor house, divided her washing into two: 'one day soap and another day ye Buck . . .'.[26] But others preferred to soap all of their linen, boiling it in lye afterwards. Susannah Stacey (1812–93), the mistress of Stantons Farm in east Sussex, used 'soap for the soaking tub' but 'saw to it that a muslin bagful of white wood ashes was put into the copper to boil with the clothes, holding that this softened the water and whitened the linen'.[27]

Women who did their laundry with a combination of lye and soap also exercised two further options. They could, if they wished, add 'blue' to their final rinsing water when washing white fabrics to make them appear whiter.* They could also give their linen extra body and stiffness, by starching it, a practice introduced into England from Holland in the sixteenth century.†

During the second half of the eighteenth century the upper classes stopped using lye and began to wash exclusively with soap. Their social inferiors soon followed their example.[29] The development of this fourth, and last, laundry method was closely linked with the growth of Britain's soap industry. According to most historians, this expansion was an early nineteenth-century phenomenon.[30] They argue that the industry only 'took off' after the French chemist Michel-Eugene Chevreul showed that soap was not simply a mixture of fat and alkali but the result of a chemical reaction between them; and after another Frenchman, Nicolas Leblanc, developed a cheap way of mass-producing alkali (soda‡) from salt, thus freeing soap-boilers from their dependence on ashes and barilla (sea-weed). Once the first plant using Leblanc's process was established at St Helen's, Lancashire (1814), and once soap manufacturers started to experiment with new vegetable oils imported from abroad, only the soap tax remained

* *Blue*: a powder containing a blue pigment. The latter was obtained either from smalts (powdered glass coloured deep blue by cobalt) or from ultramarine (extracted from the mineral lapis lazuli or made artificially). Blue was sold on its own or combined with starch.

† According to John Stow's *Annals*, starching was first taught in England by an enterprising Flemish woman, Dinghen van den Plasse, who came to London as a refugee in 1564. Some of the 'best and most curious wives of that time' who wished to emulate 'the neatness and delicacy of the Dutch for whiteness and fine wearing of linen' paid her the staggering sum of £5 to learn the art. Starch soon became so fashionable among wealthy women that Philip Stubbes dubbed it 'the devil's liquore' in his *Anatomie of Abuses* of 1583.[28]

‡ *Soda*: sodium hydroxide. This was used by economical women who wanted to restrict their soap consumption and gradually took the place of lye during the course of the nineteenth century.

to impede the progress of a great new industry . . . Or so the conventional argument runs.

But in fact the soap industry had started to expand and to increase its sales much earlier than this. By the late seventeenth century, London's soap boilers were already serving 'a great part of the kingdom' despite competition from the Dublin makers of Castle soap and country chandlers in the north and west of England who were making substantial quantities of 'Cake Soap, Ball Soap, and white soap of Wood and Fern Ashes and Kitchen-stuff'. John Houghton, a contemporary trade expert, found that respectable households were using 'about as many pounds of Soap as there be heads in the family' when they washed all their clothes at home. He pointed out however, that respectable households were greatly outnumbered by poor ones and argued that if 'a strategem could be found to alter the use of bucking and hogs-dung' soap consumption would be much greater.[31]

One stratagem would clearly have been to abolish the excise duty on soap. But this was not to be; the government was always more concerned to increase its revenues than to help the poor be clean. Soap consumption only continued to rise because of the wiliness of underground soap-makers (who made a mockery of official production figures) and because women could not make lye from coal ashes. As Henri de Valbourg Misson observed when he visited England in the late seventeenth century, 'at London, and all other parts of the country where they do not burn wood, they do not make lye. All their Linnen, coarse and fine, is wash'd with soap'.[32]

By 1747, when *A General description of all trades, digested in alphabetical order* appeared, soap-boiling was mostly carried on in 'very large Concerns' and esteemed as one of the 'uppermost Trades, by which many a fair Estate has been acquired'. The soap boilers were, apparently, 'dealing much into the Country as well as in Town . . .'.[33] Account books tend to confirm this picture. Eight different types of soap were bought on an Aberdeenshire estate in Scotland in 1735, for example.[34] Contemporary budgets also assumed that washing would be done with soap. In 1741 it was estimated that a bachelor earning £238 a year from a small business would spend £12 annually on his soap, starch and blue.[35] And, a few decades later, all but the destitute were buying soap on a regular basis, if only in small quantities to supplement their use of lye, urine and dung. David Davies, a clergyman from Berkshire, who made a detailed study of agricultural labourers' expenditure throughout England in the late 1780s, found that the majority bought soap once a week and his findings were confirmed by Sir Frederick Morton Eden's monumental study *The State of the Poor* (1797).[36] Soap was only home-made on some large farms and estates which had surplus animal fat available.[37] The process of boiling the lyes and fat was so long and tedious that most women much preferred to leave it to professional soap-makers.

Washing with soap, unlike other laundry methods, required hot water. In upper-class homes water was usually heated in a large copper, set in brickwork with a fire underneath. The copper, which was normally installed in the wash-house but was

88 *'How are you off for soap', 1816. Betty the laundry maid is surprised at the wash-tub by Lord Vansittart, the Chancellor of the Exchequer, who had just raised the soap tax. The print suggests that Betty is nearing the end of her wash: the line outside the window is fully loaded; the last load of 'whites' is in the copper; and the bar of soap in the dish is wearing thin.*

sometimes to be found in the kitchen or scullery, contained about 20 gallons and fulfilled two functions. It was used to heat the washing water which was then ladled into wooden tubs or earthenware pans. And it was also the vessel in which the laundry was boiled after it had soaked in the tubs, been soaped, beaten with a dolly* or peggy† and scrubbed, either by hand, or on a ridged washing board. By 1790, when *The Ladies' Library: or, Encyclopaedia of Female Knowledge, in every branch of domestic economy* was published, it was conventional wisdom that every family ought to have a copper, if only for reasons of economy 'as it will save almost two-thirds of the coals otherwise consumed'. Providing the stove drew well, it had the advantage of burning cinders and almost every kind of refuse and, 'when the water is once made to boil, a small fire will make it continue'.[38]

Quite apart from its economy, the copper was extremely practical; families could use it to heat water for other purposes, for brewing, and to boil large puddings. Its

* *Dolly*: this was a two- to six-legged pole, which was used for beating and rotating especially dirty washing. It was used on its own or incorporated into a strongly hooped wooden tub somewhat reminiscent of a churn.
† The *peggy* or *possing stick* was a somewhat similar device, but its plunger was perforated with holes and it acted by suction.

89 *A woman washes linen while another tends to the fire that is heating water in a large iron boiler. The scene is Sandpit Gate Lodge, Windsor Castle, c. 1754. Pen and water colour drawing by Paul Sandby.*

introduction into the houses of the labouring classes was thus vigorously advocated by philanthropists and reformers throughout the nineteenth century. However, despite their enthusiasm, coppers were adopted only slowly in these homes. Families without coppers simply heated water in their largest available receptacle. The agricultural labourers living in the village of Harpenden in Hertfordshire during the 1860s and 70s were typical in using the large iron boilers in which they cooked their food. The women transferred hot water from these boilers to large wooden troughs 3 to $3\frac{1}{2}$ feet long with sides sloping inwards and a shelf for soap in the corner. The washed linen was then moved to the cauldron for boiling.[39] The system was very similar to using a proper copper except that it was less economical and practical. The receptacle was apt to boil over,

90 *'Mrs Grosvenor laundry-woman to the Queen'. Washing out of doors was not confined to the poorer classes, as this late eighteenth-century black and white mezzotint shows.*

filling the kitchen with ash and steam; lumps of soot often tumbled down the chimney, blackening the white linen boiling below; and those unfortunate cottagers who only possessed one boiler were unable to cook any food while washing was in progress.

Because of these disadvantages the poorer classes often did their laundry out of doors, especially when they lived in the country. The medical officer of health for Essex between 1889 and 1919 found that 'very few cottages have a detached wash-house with a copper and in fine weather the usual plan is to boil the water in the largest available vessel over an open fire held together by a few loose bricks, and to do the washing in the open air'.[40] In Cornwall, women often took their washing to the nearest well, along with a 'brandis' (trivet) and boiler, 'the surrounding furze brakes providing them with the necessary fuel'.[41]

Washing out of doors could be an immensely enjoyable social occasion, as this description, given by a shoemaker's daughter who was brought up in Cefn Mawr, Wales, during the 1860s, shows. 'Some of the happiest days of my childhood were when my mother packed us off with food for the day with other children, and to take the clothes to wash. Then, by the River Dee, we would take a bucketful of coal and get a few boulder stones and make a fire to boil the clothes in the bucket and rinse them in the water, for there was plenty of water and we hadn't to carry it.'[42]

In exactly the same way, James Inglis describes the annual blanket washing that took place in his Scottish sheep-farming parish during the nineteenth century as 'one of the most joyous occasions of the whole year'. Before going off to work, the men built a fire of logs, peat and brushwood by the river-side for boiling the water in an enormous cauldron. The women then boiled their blankets and woollen clothing with soap and soda and trampled them clean in wooden tubs. At lunch time, when the washing had been wrung out and spread out to dry over the bushes and bracken, the men returned for an exuberant picnic.[43]

Laundry days

Laundry was the only household task to have a definite day of the week assigned to it; the majority of women washed on a Monday or, failing that, a Tuesday. Those who washed later in the week were considered rather slovenly as this Scottish laundry rhyme makes plain:

They that wash on Monanday
Hae a' the week tae dry;
They that wash on Tyseday
Are no far by;
They that wash on Wednesday
Are nae sair tae mean; (i.e. are well enough off)
They that wash on Thursday
May get their claes clean;
They that wash on Friday
Hae gey muckle need;
They that wash on Setterday
Are dirty daws indeed.[44]

The usual explanation for the tendency to wash on Mondays or Tuesdays is that women needed most of the week to get their clothes laundered in time for Sunday, when everybody was meant to be dressed in their best for church. But in fact most women had their laundry finished by Wednesday, or Thursday at the very latest. It seems more likely that women chose to wash on the same day for reasons of solidarity and companionship (after all, in many places they washed together); and that they favoured Monday, as opposed to any other day of the week, because the more prosperous among them had just been fortified by a large Sunday dinner and a day of relative inactivity. In addition, the common timing of market days on Thursdays and Saturdays provided many women with an incentive to dispose of their laundry at the beginning of the week.

The frequency with which the Monday and Tuesday wash-day recurred was largely a matter of income and social class. The poor, who often lacked more than one change of clothes, had to wash once a week; but the rich, who possessed large reserves of linen, could keep going for weeks. In the *Merry Wives of Gotham*, an eighteenth-century chap-book, a rebellious and lazy housewife makes this point quite clearly when she says: 'I spare my husband's lye and soap, for whereas I should wash once a week, I wash but once a quarter.'[45] The gentry certainly never waited quite so long, although they did wash infrequently during most of our period. In 1695, John Houghton found 'upon inquiry' that 'in good citizens' houses, they wash once a month'.[46] While the diary of Mary Hardy, the wife of a well-to-do Norfolk farmer, reveals that she washed every two, three, or (most commonly) four weeks during the 1770s, 80s and 90s.[47]

The subtleties involved in the frequency of wash-day are nicely brought out in Flora Thompson's *Lark Rise to Candleford*. In the poor hamlet where her heroine, Laura, grew up in the 1890s, washing was done once a week, on a Monday. But when Laura moved to a more prosperous village, she soon discovered that the postmistress with whom she was lodging 'kept to the old middle-class country custom of a huge washing of linen every six weeks . . .'. Laura, who did not have a stock of clothes capable of lasting so long, sent her washing home to her mother each week.[48]

The upper-class habit of infrequent washing started to disappear in the eighteenth century. An early aristocratic household to break with tradition was that of Lady Grisell Baillie in Edinburgh. The memoranda and directions which she laid down for her servants in 1743 ordered a weekly wash: 'one week the body linnin is washt, the second week table and bed linnin.'[49] This change probably occurred because an increasing proportion of wealthy households were living in towns and cities where, unlike the countryside, there was not enough space to dry large quantities of linen. It is reasonable to suppose that these households, having adopted the weekly wash in town, then transferred the practice to their country houses. Whatever factors were at work, the weekly wash had certainly become the norm in most households by the end of the nineteenth century. The only odd-women-out were miners' wives and mothers who washed pit-blackened clothes daily, usually in the evening.[50]

The loathing of laundry explained

One striking feature of laundry that set it apart from the rest of housework was the tremendous amount of antipathy it aroused. This is very evident, both in the songs that were written about washing[51] and in the descriptions of 'wash-day' left to us in diaries and memoirs.[52] It is clear that women dreaded this event because of the very hard work and long hours they had to put in; and their families loathed it too, knowing that the household routine would be turned upside down and that those directly involved in the process were likely to be out of sorts until it was all over.

91 *'Matrimonial comforts – Washing day', a print by Thomas Rowlandson, 1810. The man of the house greets his friend (in hat and overcoat) as follows:*
'Ah! my old Friend. I wish you had called at some more convenient time but this is a washing day. I have nothing to give you but cold fish, cold tripe & cold potatoes . . . you may smell soap suds a mile! Ah Jack, Jack you don't know those comforts! You are a Bachelor!'

When considering this antipathy to laundry (although not to its results), it is important to understand what a tough job it was. To get their washing done in a day, women often had to start work in the small hours of the morning. The mid-nineteenth-century farm servant girls in the Yorkshire Wolds who rose at 1 am and washed until tea time were not untypical.[53] Nor were the professional laundresses who arrived at their clients' houses before dawn.[54] Women doing laundry also had to carry considerable weights, even when convenient water supplies were close at hand. Kate Mary Edwards, a mill-hand's wife who brought her family up in Lotting Fen, Huntingdonshire, during the 1870s and 80s, found that:

You had to be as strong as a man to lift the great wooden wash tubs, allus left full o' suds, to keep 'em binged [i.e. soaked], even without the weight o' the wet clothes; and then you had to lift the great iron pot, full of water, on and off the pot hook over a hot turf fire, and drag the wet washing in a clothes basket to the line down the garden, and put it in and out again, perhaps four or five times if it were a wet day.[55]

To make this back-breaking labour even worse, there was the constant irritation of wet and damp, not to mention unpleasant smells. (Interestingly, there are few cases of women complaining about the pungent odour of dung and urine or the astringent fumes of bubbling lye, but many instances of their being nauseated by the smell of soap-suds!)

The work involved in doing laundry did not simply consist of washing and drying but involved a series of finishing processes as well. These all required extra work and time, a theme that was emphasized in the most famous and popular of all washing songs, 'Driving away with the smoothing iron', which begins:

'Twas on a Monday morning
When I beheld my darling;
She looked so sweet and charming
In every high degree
Yes! She was neat and willing O,
A-picking up her linen clothes;
And driving away at the smoothing iron,
She stole my heart away,
And driving away at the smoothing iron,
She stole my heart away.

On Tuesday the darling is 'a-soaping' her linen clothes, on Wednesday she is 'a-starching', on Thursday 'a-hanging out', on Friday 'a-rolling down', on Saturday 'a-ironing', and finally, on Sunday 'a-wearing'.[56]

These stages never took a whole week as the song suggests, but they certainly took longer than a day. James Woodforde, of Recton Longville in Norfolk, noted in his celebrated diary on Monday 10 June, 1799 that 'Washing week [is] with us this week. We wash every five weeks. Our present washer-women are Anne Downing and Anne Richmond. Washing and ironing generally take us four days. The washer-women breakfast and dine the Monday and Tuesday, and have each one shilling on their going away in the evening of Tuesday'.[57] In William Clift's family the washing for 10 people was done once a month in the 1830s and 40s. 'The actual washing was commenced at 3 o'clock on Monday morning' and, with three women at work, 'was finished about mid-day on Tuesday'. The ironing took one and a half days 'and by Thursday all articles would be finished and put away, clean . . .'.[58] Discounting the time spent on preparing the lye, the entire operation took four days. Similarly, a survey of several hundred labouring families in London conducted in the 1840s showed that the time occupied was rarely less than two days, and more often extended into a third day. In this case laundry was done once a week, beginning on a Monday, and each housewife washed by herself.[59]

The time and labour spent on each finishing process varied according to circumstances. Bluing was very little extra trouble for women with piped water supplies; but for those who had to fetch the water for this third, final rinse it was hard work. Similarly the time devoted to starching depended on the number of articles to be starched, which varied according to income and prevailing fashion;[60] on the trouble women were prepared to take in making up the starch to exactly the right consistency;* and on whether the starch was bought or homemade. Although most women bought it – the industry was already well established by the late seventeenth century[62] – some economized by making their own out of wheat, potatoes, horse-chestnuts, or rice. Allan Jobson, for example, remembers how his grandmother, a Suffolk farmer's wife, made hers from old potatoes in the early 1900s. 'They were grated under water and the resultant mash left for twenty-four hours. The dirty water was then strained off and the deposit set on a tray and dried.'[63] Nineteenth-century Irishwomen beat most records for thrift by using the left-over gratings to make a kind of potato bread called 'stampy'.[64]

When it came to drying, all women were at the mercy of the weather. It was frustrating to have to remove linen from hedges or clothes-lines because it was about to rain and even more so to discover that it was already drenched. But to dry indoors was even worse, for very few houses had enough space and the inhabitants had to put up with damp clothes draped over the fire guard or dripping onto them from clothes-lines suspended overhead.

It was particularly demoralizing to dry linen in towns and cities, especially those with manufacturing industry. For their atmosphere was so polluted that the linen was soon covered with little specks of soot. In addition, there was the difficulty of finding space to hang it out of doors. Lady Hugh Bell, in her study of early twentieth-century Middlesborough, describes what the town's working-class women had to put up with. 'When it is not raining, they hang the linen, if they have no backyard, across the little narrow street, or rather alley, which runs between the two rows of back doors, where it forms a series of damp flapping barriers. The carters who sometimes drive along these back streets have assumed a sort of prescriptive right to get the hanging obstacle out of the way in any fashion they choose, either flicking it over the clothes-line, or even twitching it off and throwing it into the road'. If the linen was thrown to the ground, the women picked it up and washed it again. Tiresome as this was, it was far preferable to drying the linen indoors in their cramped houses.[65]

* Starch was usually made out of wheat. It had to be boiled before use, a tricky process because it had to be done in a hurry and the starch often burned or thickened too quickly. But when the Irish potato famine forced up grain prices in the 1840s, manufacturers were forced to use alternative sources of starch. Their predicament resulted in what must have been the only benefit of the potato famine for British housewives – soluble rice starch. As George Reckitt, a partner in the starch manufacturing firm Reckitt and Sons Ltd, wrote in 1849:
'In the south of England the rice starch is obtaining a large sale . . . it is a starch which possesses the greatest strength and I know of no instance of anyone who has introduced it where they have gone back, almost all tell me they could not do without it, the beauty of it is it can be used either with or without boiling.'[61]

92 *A woman hanging out her laundry, a print by George Morland first sold in 1793. From Francis William Blagdon,* Authentic memoirs of the late George Morland, with remarks on his abilities and progress as an artist, *1806.*

93 *Clothes drying by the fire in a northern interior, sketched by Caroline Elizabeth Hamilton in the summer of 1839. The woman is sewing and the girl is resting from her book.*

Smoothing techniques

By far the most common smoothing technique was ironing. It was done even by comparatively humble people. Farm and cottage inventories from central Essex dating from 1635 to 1749 contain frequent references to the flat smoothing iron which was heated over the fire, and the hollow, box or lock, iron which was kept hot by an internal piece of pre-heated iron or a lump of charcoal or coal.[66] Similarly, many of the late seventeenth-century inventories that survive from Devonshire yeomen, husbandmen, tradesmen and craftsmen include 'smoothing' and 'stiling' irons.[67]

Women who did not have metal irons smoothed their linen in other ways, some of which were quite ingenious. One method was to trample on it. When Elizabeth Isabella Spence visited Dumfries in Scotland at the beginning of the nineteenth century, she noticed groups of women washing their linen along the banks of the River Nith. Some had their 'dried linen spread smoothly on a blanket' and were 'tramping it with their bare feet'. She said they used this process 'instead of an iron or mangle'.[68] In Shetland and Orkney they used smoothing stones, oval in shape with a wooden holder, as late as 1876.[69] These were heated in the fire or in boiling water. In other places, the work was done with wooden rollers. In 1803, Dorothy Wordsworth was shocked to see a 'most indecent practice' going on in a Scottish graveyard. Several women had brought their linen to the flat tombstones and, 'having spread it upon them, began to batter as hard as they could with a wooden roller, a substitute for a mangle'.[70] Another technique using the wooden roller was to wind the damp linen round the cylinder and to roll this on a flat surface. Once the linen was completely tight and wrinkle-free, it was unrolled and laid flat to dry.

The proper mangle, a machine for pressing flat, heavy linen such as sheets and table cloths by passing it between rollers, was sometimes used as an alternative to ironing. It took two quite different forms. The earlier kind consisted of a large rectangular box, 7 feet long and 3 feet wide, filled with several hundredweight of stones. It rested on two loose rollers and was moved backwards and forwards on them. The linen was either wrapped round the rollers or spread flat on a polished base beneath. This was an expensive item and at least two people were normally required to work it. Its use was largely restricted to the houses of the nobility and gentry in the seventeenth and eighteenth centuries. When Anne, Duchess of Hamilton, ordered one from Edinburgh in 1696, she paid £53 (Scottish) for it (a substantial sum) and insisted that the wright should accompany it to her estate in case it needed repairs on arrival and so that he could 'teach the women how to make it go'.[71]

However, the box mangle became much more common in the nineteenth century after George Jee devised a method in 1797 of moving the box back and forth by turning a handle one way. This simple innovation meant that it was no longer necessary to have two to three adults operating the mangle; a woman aided by a child sufficed.[72] Professional laundresses often bought this improved model and mangled their neighbourhood's linen for a small fee.[73] Mangling was also taken up by women who needed to supplement their income. Louise Jermy, for instance, describes how her father, a fishmonger, bought her mother a Baker's patent box mangle in the 1880s.[74] It succeeded in stretching the family's meagre resources, but Louise was a cripple by the age of 13, a misfortune she attributed to the hard work involved in operating the machine.[75]

The second type of mangle, developed in the nineteenth century, was upright and much more compact.[76] It consisted of an iron stand supporting two or more rollers through which the linen was passed; levers and weights provided the necessary pressure for both wringing and smoothing it out. Because this kind of mangle served a dual purpose, could be worked easily by one person, and took up such little floor space, it proved far more popular than its predecessor. The iron industry, ever eager for new products to mass produce, seized upon the new design and a vast mangle/wringer industry grew up round Keighley in Yorkshire and Accrington in Lancashire. The prices of wringers, mangles, and combined wringing and mangling machines fell steadily; and between 1870 and 1930, the period of the industry's heyday, millions were sold each year.[77]

Ironmongers also eased the 'smoothing' process in other ways during the late eighteenth and nineteenth centuries. In their desire to capture as large a portion of the

94 *'A Servant Ironing' with a box iron, painted by Henry Robert Morland.* c. *1767. She is not yet fully dressed: she has not pinned her gown to her stays or put the shawl on the back of the chair round her shoulders. This sort of* genre *painting was very popular at the time.*

95 *George Jee's improved mangle, submitted to the Society for the Encouragement of Arts, Manufactures and Commerce in 1797. From the Society's* Transactions *of 1798.*

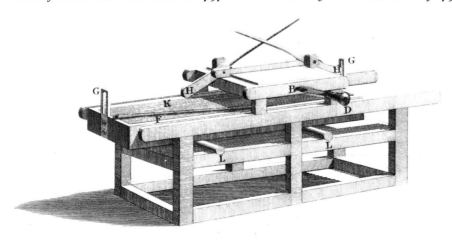

96 *A combined wringing and mangling machine advertised in the 1897 catalogue of W. Summerscales and Sons.*

'ironing market' as possible, they competed to produce as many models of iron as they could reasonably hope to sell. As a result, housewives could choose from a super-abundance of irons in all shapes and sizes, many with highly specialized functions. Puffing, egg and mushroom irons vied with 'Italian', 'French', 'Spanish', and 'German' irons, not to mention those for flounces, sleeves, hats, fluting and piping. This fantastic boom in the production of iron smoothing devices is well illustrated in the catalogues of contemporary ironmongers. Archibald Kenrick and Sons of West Bromwich, for example, sold a handful of irons at the start of the nineteenth century, 27 different kinds by 1836 and 39 by 1876.[78] The boom was also evident in the appearance of special heating devices for irons, mostly for use in kitchens lacking a range with a suitable hot plate.

However, the 'smoothing' process did not become really easy until the appearance of electric irons in the early 1900s. These had the great advantages of being quick and easy to heat and free of fumes and smells (such as those emanating from the gas irons which enjoyed a brief vogue in the 1880s and 90s). In addition, their bottoms were rust-proof, so that it was not necessary to clean them after each use, as was the case with ordinary irons. Although the majority of irons sold before the Second World War were non-thermostatic and cost much more than traditional kinds, they were snapped up enthusiastically; by 1948, 86 per cent of households with electricity had one.[79]

Other laundry methods
So much for the different ways in which women washed and 'finished off' their linen. How did women remove stubborn spots and stains that did not come out by ordinary washing? And how did they clean dyed materials that were not colour-fast (a common

problem until this century)? The numerous books of 'secrets' and manuals of house-hold instruction dealing with these subjects[80] show that there were plenty of methods available before the advent of commercial dry cleaning with petrochemical solvents in the late nineteenth century.[81]

Grease and oil were removed by using turpentine, either on its own or mixed with an absorbent powder such as ground sheep's trotters, fuller's earth,* chalk, or pipe-clay. Drops of wax were drawn out by a hot coal wrapped in a linen rag or piece of brown paper. Ink was removed by lemon or onion juice, chamber lye (i.e. urine), or white soap dissolved in vinegar. Wine and vinegar stains were usually immersed in warm cow's milk, and iron-mould† was bleached away with citrus or sorrel juice. Fruit stains were rubbed with butter and washed in hot milk.

In addition there were all sorts of multi-purpose stain-removing soaps and liquids, which provident housewives were supposed to make at home and apply when needed. But whether many actually did so is a debatable point, because the recipes for these soaps and liquids were complicated, involving numerous different ingredients. Take one of Hannah Glasse's mid-eighteenth-century recipes for spot-removing soap; it calls for 1 lb of burned alum,‡ 6 oz of ireos,‡ 2½ lbs of white soap, half an ox's gall,‡ two egg whites, and a dash of sal nitrum or saltpetre.‡ In another receipt for 'a Water which will take all manner of Spots out of Cloth of any colour' she said it was necessary to pound together two old ox galls, 2 scruples‡ each of roach allum and alumen fecis, 4 oz tartar of white wine,‡ and a scruple of camphire.‡ These were then simmered with 2 quarts of clear soft water until the mixture was free of scum and froth. Three ounces of aqua vitae‡ of three distillings were added at the last moment; and the liquid was kept in a well-stoppered glass vessel.[82]

Some kinds of dyed cloth had their own particular treatments. Dark silk, for example, was cleaned with vinegar applied on a dark cloth or, if it was red or white, with spirit of wine (alcohol) and egg white. Wool and linen were often washed in sorrel juice and fabrics made out of silk and 'gold and silver stuffs' were rubbed with stale bread or bran.

Despite the plethora of published instructions about these specialized cleaning methods and their many variations, it is difficult to tell how widely they were known and practised. For, in contrast to the numerous descriptions of linen-washing that survive,

---

* *Fuller's earth*: a hydrous silicate of alumina.

† *Iron-mould*: a spot or discolouration, usually caused by iron-rust.

‡ *Burned Alum*: alum calcinated over the fire (i.e. deprived of its water of crystallization) so as to become a white powder. Alum is chemically a double sulphate of aluminium potassium. *Ireos*: the white flowered iris. *Ox gall*: the substance also known as bile. It collects in the animal's gall-bladder and contains soda, which dissolves grease. *Sal nitrum* or *saltpetre*: potassium nitrate, a crystalline substance. *Scruple*: a very small quantity, 1/24th oz Apothecaries weight. *Roach allum*: rock alum. *Alumen fecis*: some form of alum? *Tartar of white wine*: bitartrate of potash (acid potassium tartrate), present in grape juice, deposited in a crude form in the process of fermentation, and adhering to the sides of wine-casks in the form of a hard crust. *Camphire*: camphor, a whitish translucent crystalline volatile substance belonging to the vegetable oils distilled from *Camphora officinarum* (*Laurus camphora*), and purified by sublimation. *Aqua vitae*: alcohol distilled from beer or wine.

one never finds an account of a woman spilling wax on her dress and rushing for a hot coal or a description of a laundry-maid's skill in removing an obstinate spot from a valuable piece of silk.

It is also difficult to judge how efficacious the methods were. The fact that they hardly changed from the sixteenth century, when the first English book on the subject was published, to the early twentieth century, and that many of the simpler old remedies are still used today, is to their credit.[83] Chemical analysis of the agents used also suggests that many of them were effective. But, without testing all the methods out on different textiles it is not possible to be certain.

Nor is it known how many women practised them successfully at home and how many gave up in despair: it was always possible to send a particularly difficult garment to be scoured professionally. William Tucker, one of the very few scourers to divulge the secrets of his trade, showed how thorough the process of scouring was at the beginning of the nineteenth century, in these instructions for cleaning a man's coat:

First dry about two ounces of Fuller's earth by the fire, then pour a sufficient quantity of boiling water on it to dissolve it to the consistence of molasses or honey; take a sufficient quantity of this on top of your three fingers, and plaster thinly over such spots of grease as may be on the coat, particularly remarking the cuffs, collar, the pocket holes, and under the arms etc . . . This done, if you have time, dry it by the fire or in the sun; prepare a pennyworth of bullock's gall, mix with it a half a pint of stale urine; add to this, if required, a little boiling water, to make the quantity of alkaline liquor sufficient for your purpose . . . Dip your hard brush in this liquor, and brushing the spotted places in your coat, you will find it produce a white froth, like soap lather. After this, you must dip the coat in a bucket of cold water, spring water is best, to wash off the filth and bad smell.[84]

Finally, if this course failed, there was a last resort: the garment could be redyed a darker colour! It was no coincidence that professional scourers were usually dyers as well.[85]

The unchanging history of laundry between 1650 and 1950

Laundry was not greatly affected by technological change during these three centuries. The drudgery of washing was lightened to a certain extent during the nineteenth century by the spread of cheap soap, wringers, and piped water supplies. And 'smoothing' was certainly facilitated, first by the upright wringer-mangle and later by the electric iron. But the really basic problem of providing ready supplies of piped hot water had not been solved. The Heating of Dwellings Inquiry, which surveyed over 5,000 working-class households in 1942, found that three quarters still had to heat their washing water specially; 31 per cent of them used a copper, 28 per cent a gas boiler, and 16 per cent a pan or kettle over the kitchen fire or stove.[86]

Furthermore, the washing process remained almost completely unmechanized. The majority of women did their washing by hand, aided only by a dolly or peggy and a ridged scrubbing board. When the Political and Economic Planning group looked at

97 *An advertisement of c. 1909 showing the joys of washing with Borax. Note that the washing is already on the line at six minutes past ten in the morning.*

the market for household appliances in 1945 it found that these two aids, along with wringers, were the staples of laundry equipment.[87] The electric washing machine was to be a rare curiosity until the 1950s and 60s; in 1948, only 3.6 per cent of families in the United Kingdom had one,[88] compared to 29 per cent in 1958,[89] 64 per cent in 1969, and 77 per cent in 1980.[90]

Why did it take so long to develop this liberating appliance? There were many attempts to devise an efficient washing machine during the seventeenth, eighteenth, and nineteenth centuries. Sir John Hoskins, a fellow of the Royal Society, had invented a washing machine of sorts by 1677. Robert Hooke's diary for that year refers to Hoskins' 'way of Rinsing fine linnen in a whip and bag, fastened at one end and strained by a wheel and cylinder at the other. N.B. whereby the finest linnen is washt wrung and not hurt'.[91] And by 1758, the inventor William Bailey was speaking of 'the Machine Washing-Tubs, which were some time since much in Use', which implies that Hoskins had not been working alone. It seems that these early machines had not been successful. Bailey dismissed them as being extremely 'unhandy and laborious', adding that he 'almost despaired of making any Use of them'. His own invention was supposed to a great improvement. Operated by one person, it could perform the work of three or four washer-women with much saving of fuel and soap and it could be made by a common carpenter or cooper for 50 shillings.[92]

98 *An early washing machine invented and drawn by William Bailey. From his* Treatise on the better employment and more comfortable support of the poor in work-houses, *1758.*

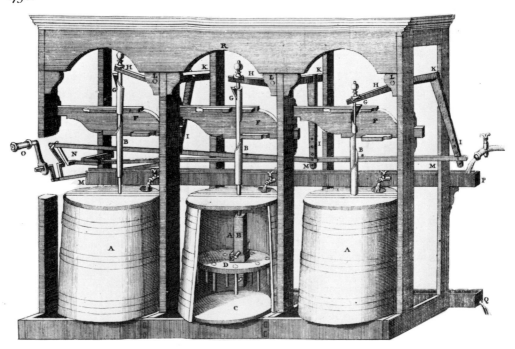

But although domestic washing machines were both patented and marketed from the late eighteenth century onwards, there was little enthusiasm for them, even among servants,[93] and very few households bought them. The handful of manufacturers producing them in the nineteenth century sold them to the owners of mansions, large country houses, hotels, schools, and commercial laundries. W. Summerscales and Sons Ltd., who in their catalogue of 1897 claimed they were the largest makers of laundry machinery in the world, concentrated almost exclusively on producing washing machines for institutional laundries.

The domestic washing machine could not become a success until two problems had been solved. Firstly, it had to be connected to hot and cold water supplies and equipped with a waste pipe; otherwise machine washing was little different from using a dolly or peggy in an ordinary wash tub. Secondly, it was necessary to provide a source of motive power. Steam power, which was used successfully from the early nineteenth century, was only viable in large-scale institutions, commercial laundries and public wash-houses.[94] Electric power, distributed to people's homes, was the answer. But this did not become widely available until the late 1920s and early 30s. So, although electric motors capable of heating water and rotating or oscillating a machine's contents were available in the early 1900s,[95] the market for them was minute. And the same was true of spin-driers and drying machines, the other mechanical aids which were to transform laundry after the Second World War.[96]

Another striking aspect of laundry is the way in which it remained very much part of housework throughout the three centuries. Although most women could send their laundry 'out' to be done by a professional laundress or, from the early nineteenth century, to a commercial laundry,[97] very few chose to do so. Nor did they frequent the 'public' laundries that were set up in cities in the second half of the nineteenth century unless they absolutely had to.* A survey of working-class households in 1942 showed that 73 per cent did all their laundry at home[99] and the proportion of better off households making use of commercial facilities was similarly low.[100] This reluctance on the part of women to let their laundry out of the house is rather puzzling, given the fact that so many of them positively hated the whole process of washing and ironing. It certainly cannot be explained away in terms of cost, because commercial and public laundries were keenly priced. Nor can the unpopularity of sending laundry 'out' be attributed to women's fears that their clothes would be 'borrowed' and worn by the washers and their families,[101] or to their dislike of the idea of their linen being washed in the same water as other people's. No, the explanation is a moral one. If 'cleanliness was indeed next to godliness', women wanted to create that moral worth with their own hands, or if this was not feasible, at least in their own homes.

* Public wash-houses were never very common, unlike the public baths with which they were associated. In 1913, for example, they only existed in London, 16 provincial towns in England and nine towns in Scotland. They were most densely concentrated in Lancashire, Yorkshire and London. Provision was virtually non-existent in many parts of the British Isles, including Ireland, South Wales and Durham.[98]

Chapter 8 SERVANTS

The greatest plague of life . . .[1]

In 1834, Jane and Thomas Carlyle moved into 5 Great Cheyne Row, Chelsea. They were a respectable, childless couple in their thirties. Although not rich, they had sufficient means to employ a domestic servant, and one of Jane's first tasks on arrival was to hire one. She knew, from experience, that it would not be easy to find the 'jewel' they were looking for, but she little dreamed that she would have a succession of 34 servants during the next 32 years, as well as innumerable charwomen and temporary, make-shift helps.[2]

Servants were, in fact, to be the bane of Jane's life, as her letters make plain. She started off, in June 1834, with Bessy Barnet from Warwickshire, 'by far the orderliest, cleverest worker we have ever had in the house'. But Bessy left after a few months, for family reasons. Her replacement, Jane Ireland from Lancaster, was amiable enough, but hopelessly incompetent and had to be sent home. By June 1835, Jane had already taken on her third servant, this time an Irish Protestant, who left a couple of months later 'to attend a sick mother'. Jane made do with local charwomen for three or four weeks before hiring another Irish girl, this time a Roman Catholic. Unfortunately, she proved to be 'a mutinous Irish savage' and was dismissed a month later. October 1835 saw the arrival of Sarah Heather, nick-named 'Sereetha the Peesweep', who was willing but feeble.

For the following 21 months, the Carlyles were under the care of Anne Cook of Annandale. In July 1837, however, she was sent home in disgrace. Ellen, 'a sweet girl' who 'did her very best to please' filled in until Helen Mitchell from Kirkaldy arrived in December. She was an excellent servant and stayed with the Carlyles for almost nine years. But after her departure in November 1846, to housekeep for her brother, a manufacturer of coach fringe in Dublin, the Carlyles' domestic life was again plunged into turmoil. Helen's first successor, Isabella, only stayed a fortnight; she refused to help with the laundry and accused Jane of treating her like a slave. A 'half dead cook' with a fiery temper filled in for another two weeks until the arrival of Anne II. This cheery Cockney stayed until the autumn of 1848, when she married a butcher's assistant and moved to Jersey. Meanwhile Helen Mitchell from Kirkaldy had quarrelled with her brother in Dublin and returned to the Carlyles. She had taken to drink though, and Jane was eventually forced to dismiss her in February 1849.

Elizabeth Sprague served for the next 19 months. Jane at first described her as 'far the most loveable servant I ever had'; but by the time Elizabeth departed, she had 'murdered sleep'. Eliza, a little girl who had never been in service before and 'who could not cook a morsel of food or make a bed' without having Jane at her heels, came for a fortnight. From August to September 1850, Emma from Essex was in charge; but as she was incapable of absorbing more than one order at a time and could not make mutton broth or roast meat properly, Jane was forced to get rid of her. By February 1851, three other young women had been tried out; one who 'roasted fowls with the crop and bowels in them', another who arrived ill and had to be sent to hospital, and a third who went deaf. May saw the arrival of Ann III, 'a thoroughly good, respectable woman' who stayed 14 months until July 1852. A great beauty, whose physiognomy appealed to Thomas, was then engaged, but left after a week. At the end of August, an Irish Fanny was hired. A good cleaner and cook, she stayed for about a year, before running away to get married.

In August 1853 Ann III returned to Cheyne Row and remained there for nearly five years. The Carlyles enjoyed a second, much deserved, era of domestic stability. However, after Ann's departure in March 1858, Jane's monotonous routine of trying out different servants resumed. There was a Miss Cameron from Inverness, the daughter of a lieutenant. She promised well, but was convicted of lying and theft and ran out of the house late one night, never to be heard of again. Old Jane was a flop too; at the age of 71, she insisted on 'a pair of young legs' to assist her and she stole ale on the sly.

So the saga went on. Servant after servant passed through the Carlyle household, nearly all of them departing after short stays. Sometimes they left on their own accord – for family reasons, through illness, or because they were going to marry. But more often than not, they were dismissed by Jane for incompetence and/or dishonesty.

By 1860, Thomas had become such a well known and prosperous writer that Jane was able to employ two servants. But this development, instead of making life easier, simply added to her problems. For she had to make sure that the two servants she employed got on well together and complemented each other's skills. She also had to train them to Thomas's exacting ways and, as he grew older, he became increasingly spoiled, cantankerous and intolerant. It was this, more than anything else, Jane admitted, which made 'a change of servants, even when for the better, a terror to me in prospect, and an agony in realization'.

Anyone unfamiliar with Jane's sterling qualities might conclude from this account of her servant problems that she was a difficult, if not impossible, mistress to work for. But this was not so. She was kind and spent a considerable amount of time training her servants and sharing the housework with them. Her experiences, far from being unique, were typical. For servants were very much a mixed blessing; and in many cases, they were far more bother than they were worth.

The trouble was that most servants were very young. Girls entered service when they reached their teens (if not earlier), and left it, for the most part, as soon as they could. The 1851 census revealed that 40 per cent of the female domestic servants in England and Wales were under the age of 19 and that 66 per cent were less than 24 years old.[3]

In addition, of course, most domestics came from inferior socio-economic back-grounds to their employers'. They therefore had to make all sorts of cultural adjust-

99 *'Anger. This unruly passion shews itself in a forcible degree in a termagent mistress scolding her maid servant.' It is significant that Thomas Rowlandson chose the relationship between mistress/servant to represent anger in this coloured etching of 1800, one of a series entitled 'LeBrun travested: or caricatures of the passions'.*

ments on entering service which, due to their inexperience and minimal education, were far from easy. In Charlotte Adams' book *Little servant maids* (1851), there is a vivid description of how difficult these adjustments could be. The heroine, Jessy Joslin, comes from a poor family living in overcrowded, filthy conditions. When she begins work at Mrs Sewell's, she is at first overwhelmed by the luxury and strangeness of her new surroundings. She finds it hard to understand or adhere to Mrs Sewell's high standards of cleanliness and she does not know how to do the jobs expected of her. Although her mother had taught her how to nurse the baby, fetch water, scour floors, light fires, and mend and make clothes, Jessy had never dusted, swept, whitened front door steps or washed up tea things before. Nor had she done any ironing. As a result, she starts off by doing her work very badly: Mrs. Sewell's snowy white linen is symbolically covered with black scorch marks.[4]

Because the great majority of servants were young and uneducated, employers were

100 *A royal servant: Bridget Holmes at the age of 96, painted by John Riley in 1686. She was in royal service from the reign of Charles I until her death in 1691 at the age of a hundred in the reign of William and Mary.*

Pub.^d July 25 1801. by R. Ackermann N.º 101 Strand.

THE MAID OF ALL-WORK'S PRAYER!!

O All ye HOUSEHOLD GODS who preside over cleanliness and good management, aid me in my arduous undertaking. *Scrub* away from me, I beseech ye, all false pride, and vain consequence, and *brush* me up to laudable exertion. Let the *smoothing iron* of good nature, give a *polish* to my countenance, and *lather* within me the *soap-suds* of innocence, so shall I appear white as a new washed shirt in the eyes of my master. *Mop* from him, O cleanly Deities, the *foul water* of wickedness, when he comes home late from the tavern, and cleanse him with the *brick-dust* of reformation, so shall I remain as chaste as the *children* in the *Nursery;* but if he is permitted to bear about him the *roaring fire* of iniquity, the *pure flame* of my virtue, may be obliged to *give warning,* and quit its *place* for ever!

Erect in my bosom, I beseech ye, a *register-office* for all good actions, so shall I *boil-over* with gratitude for the numerous favors you have *cooked* up for my acceptance: And should a handsome *fellow servant* gain the heart of your humble worshipper, may he be *diligent, sober,* and *honest;* shake us then together in the *frying-pan* of matrimony, that we may become *fritters* of purity, free from broils and dissensions, and fit to *wait* at the tables of the good and virtuous, and be as it were *warming-pans* to each other.

Let these be my *wages,* and I shall submit cheerfully to my labours, nor shall I breathe a sigh for greater liberty, but *make my bed* in peace and sleep contented.

SPRAGG, PRINTER, 27, BOW-STREET, COVENT-GARDEN.

101 & 102 *The aspirations of servants, as recorded in a couple of broadsides published in 1801. The coloured illustrations were designed by G. M. Woodward and etched by Thomas Rowlandson.*

THE COOK'S PRAYER!!

Oʜ! all ye Gods and Goddeſſes, whoſe celeſtial appetites are not too refined to reliſh the good things of this world, liſten to a votary at your altar.

Twelve years have I been Cook to Alderman Gobble, and never was a better maſter, the *kidney* of good-humour, a *raſher* of generoſity, and a *taſte*, delicate as a *boiled chicken*, in ſhort, he is a *Salmagundy* of all that is eſtimable.

Continue me, I beſeech you, a twelve-months longer in his ſervice, and then, with the little per-quiſites I have *haſhed* together, I may be able to enter on the *eating-houſe* in *Pye* corner, which I have longed for theſe three years. Should that be the caſe, ſtir up, I pray you, the *flames* of love in the boſom of John the Coachman, make him *hiſſing-hot* with affection, and *boiling over* with tenderneſs for the melting charms of my delectable perſon:—long have I *waſted* myſelf away to a mere *ſhadow*, in ſad and hopeleſs deſpair, and at preſent he minds me no more than a *turkey* does a *rabbit* roaſting on the ſame ſpit, or a *gooſe* the *gridiron* on which it is broiled. Yet there is a time for all things; he may yet have compaſſion for my youth; nor let my beauty wither like a ſprig of *ſweet marjorum* in a chimney corner. What an acquiſition he would be to my ſhop! he would create an *appetite* to look at him through the window; not like the puny *raddiſh* ſtalks of the pre-ⁿt age, but a hale able-bodied man, capable of ſtanding fire, and round as a copper-pot lid. Grant me but this, ye Gods, and raiſe the price of kitchen-ſtuff, and Dolly Diſhwell ſhall ever praiſe ye.

SPRAGG, PRINTER, 27, BOW-STREET, COVENT-GARDEN.

forced to spend an enormous amount of time and energy on training, directing and supervising them. When Katie Nicol of Hartleap Farm, Sunderland, agreed to train eight-year-old Janet Greenfield in 1814, she was committing herself to giving endless directions for a whole year. 'See lassie, be clever, and get the dishes washed, and gang oot into the yaird and cut some greens and take the graip and howk up some leeks and take them to the burn and wash them, and bring them in and shear them for the kail, and then take the tatty creel and wale a wheen tatties and wash them at the burn . . .' was typical of the torrent of instructions that continually gushed from her lips.[5]

The effort that employers put into training their servants was often wasted, however. For another characteristic of domestic servants was that they did not usually remain with their employers for long. A survey of 2,443 servants in England and Wales (excluding London), completed in 1898 showed that 35 per cent had worked in the same household for less than a year, and a further 19 per cent for less than two years. Only 5 per cent of the servants had worked for the same mistress for between four and five years and only 8 per cent for over 10 years. The average length of service was 1.4 years.[6] The reason for this mobility lay in servants' desire to better themselves. Apart from marrying, the most effective way of doing this was to keep moving on to more attractive jobs. A maid of all work would hope to join a household with several other servants so that she would not have to work so hard, just as a scullery or chamber maid would dream of becoming a cook or housekeeper, the two most highly paid jobs in the female servant hierarchy.[7]

This rapid turnover in domestic employment was by no means unique to the Victorian period. The household books of Lady Grisell Baillie, wife of the Receiver-General of Scotland, mention the names of at least 60 different servants employed between 1694 and 1704. Of these, 31 remained in service for less than a year and 17 for less than two years.[8] Nicholas Blundell's diurnal likewise reveals that he and his wife faced a continual coming and going of servants. 'Jane Smith who had not been three months my Servant left her service, she was first Cook and now Dary-Maid and is suckseeded by Bridget Sumner', reads a typical entry in July 1704.[9] It was quite possible for Betty Atherton to go away 'in a Passion', return and leave again, for Mary Molineux to disappear in the middle of the night, and for Mary Brown to depart, all within the space of two months, July and August 1707.[10]

The other problems that Jane Carlyle experienced were similarly universal. Every mistress knew the frustration of losing a servant as soon as she had become good at her job. For this reason, some employers only gave their maids the minimum of training. One servant who wrote her autobiography describes how in her second job, which she entered in 1803 at the age of 16, 'My mistress made me nurse the child, and do everything that was laborious; but all that required any art or knowledge, she not only would not let me do it, but would send me out of the way, with the little boy, while she did it herself. This was done that I should not leave her, or think myself qualified for a better place'.[11]

Most mistresses were also confronted, now and then, with an uppity servant who did not know her place. The maid in question would wear clothes that were too fine for her lowly station, refuse to do certain tasks, sulk, answer back, and sometimes even demand higher wages. 'Susan and I have been discussing the problem of the domestic servant, which is becoming very serious in every part of the country', wrote Henry William Polderoy in 1886. 'In earlier years we could reckon upon a supply of modest, willing, trustworthy girls, who, for the priviledge of working in a gentleman's household, were ready to accept a reasonable sum in the way of wages. Now, thanks to the pernicious diffusion of Radical ideas, everything is different. Servants ask double wages if they are called upon to leave London . . . and . . . are commonly sluttish and rude'.[12] Like many others of his generation, Polderoy thought there was something new about the servant problem. There was not. Daniel Defoe (alias Andrew Moreton) had attacked servant insubordination at great length in the early eighteenth century; and countless man and women had complained about it in their letters, diaries and account books.[13]

Servants' dishonesty was another perennial problem. It was all too common for servants to make deals with tradesmen, and to pilfer food, drink and household linen.[14] Indeed, servants delighted in bamboozling their employers; or at least this is what popular writers suggested.[15] For example, an eighteenth-century chap-book entitled *The parson and the fowls: or, the maid too cunning for her master*, describes how a clergyman orders his pretty young maid to spit-roast two fowls for his Sunday dinner. While he is at church, the maid's sweetheart comes to visit and eats the birds himself. When the parson returns home, the maid pretends that an intruder has made off with his dinner. Pointing to 'an empty smeer'd dish upon the table', she tells the parson that 'I no sooner brought the fowls to the table, but he snatch'd them both out of the dish, and cram'd 'em into his breeches, and away he scower'd out of the back door as if the devil were in him'. The parson attempts to chase the intruder and returns home 'puffing and blowing, having nothing left but batchlor's fare, viz. bread and cheese and kisses for his Sunday dinner'. The maid, of course, is tickled pink.[16]

The usual recourse employers took, upon discovering their servants' dishonesty, was to dismiss them. But occasionally they took more drastic action. In 1736, for example, Elizabeth Purefoy and her son, Henry, of Shalstone Manor, Buckinghamshire, discovered that four of their servants had stolen five hogsheads of stale beer from the cellar. They placed an advertisement in the newspaper offering a guinea's reward to anybody who would bring one of the ringleaders, Mary Davis, to justice and had a warrant sent out for her arrest.[17] Another solution was to reduce the number of servants kept. John Mill, minister of three Shetland parishes between 1743 and 1803, found that his servants were so 'thievish and mischievous', and 'liker wild beasts than Christians' that they constituted the greatest plague of his life. Because his wife had a delicate constitution, she could not control the monsters and they ended up by keeping only one servant in the house.[18]

The dishonesty of servants often came to the fore in the absence of their mistresses,

103 *'Quae Genus, in the service of Sr Jeffery Gourmand'. As can be seen, Quae Genus is not behaving himself: his pocket is bulging with a piece of fruit he has stolen and he is giving the maid a drink of Sir Jeffery's best port. Another maid servant brazenly helps herself from behind the door. From William Combe,* The History of Johnny Quae Genus, the little foundling of the late Doctor Syntax, *illustrated by Thomas Rowlandson, 1822.*

as Thomas Wright, a clothier and weaver from Birkenshaw in Yorkshire, discovered when his wife died in 1777. He had two servants. 'One was an incurable drunkard, and proved very expensive to me; the other, the greatest liar and the greatest thief that ever fell under my observation. She turned the house upside down, and plundered it through every time I turned my back, and carried out (whenever I was absent) to her father's and relations, meal, flour, butter, eggs, ribbons, small linen, beer and bottles of rum . . .' By 1781, Thomas Wright had lost such a lot of money that he was forced to remarry to avoid ruin.[19]

Clearly there were many disadvantages in having servants. Only a small minority of wealthy employers who could afford to pay a steward or housekeeper to manage their servants did not suffer from them. Lady Breadalbane of Taymouth Castle, Scotland, for example, had a steward in charge of her servants. In the household regulations she drew up in 1829, she outlined his role as follows: 'John Ferguson, who acts as secretary and house steward, conveys all orders respecting the management of the household, likewise all the orders for the outdoor servants and others which Lord or Lady Breadalbane desire him to communicate. It is expected he will take a general charge (as far as possible) of seeing the orders he receives are attended to . . . In short that the servants do their duty.'[20] Most employers, however, were never in the fortunate, luxurious position of Lady Breadalbane. Even when a mistress had good servants, she still had to devote time to directing them. The cook had to be told what food to prepare for each meal, the parlourmaid informed about prospective guests, the house-maid exhorted not to cut corners when cleaning, and so on.

This raises the interesting question of why people bothered with servants at all. The main and most obvious reason was, of course, that they needed help with their housework. A farmer's wife could not possibly manage her cows and poultry and attend to all her domestic concerns without several pairs of extra hands. Nor could a society lady entertain large numbers of guests without a great deal of support from below stairs.

However, the employment of servants also had a lot to do with social status. The richer and more important you were, the larger the number of servants you were expected to employ. Furthermore, the wealthier you were, the more likely it was that you could afford to have men servants working indoors: these were an impressive status symbol for they did far less housework than their female colleagues and received twice the pay.[21] Thus Mrs Beeton, in her famous *Book of Household Management* (1861) said that a wealthy nobleman would have 12 men servants and 13 women; a family with an annual income of about £1,000, a man-servant and four women servants; and a family in the £750-a-year bracket, a foot boy and three women. All other households, with annual incomes of less than £750, could not afford to employ a man at all and had to make do with one, two, or three women servants, as their circumstances permitted.[22] This was also true of the mid-eighteenth century. When 'Madam Johnson' estimated 'the necessary charge of a family in the middling station of life' in 1754, she assumed that the family would consist of 'a man, his wife, four children, and one maid-servant'.[23]

The relationship between a household's status and the number of servants it employed was so important that even very poor people would go through the motions of having a servant. For example, at the end of the nineteenth and beginning of the twentieth centuries, the London poor often employed a 'step-girl' on Saturday mornings to scrub their front door steps and surrounding pavement area. The girl, dressed in a sack to protect her clothes from the dirt, would be duly noted by the neighbours.[24]

Servants' practical impact on housework
How did servants affect the actual conduct of housework? Were they responsible for introducing and popularizing new ways of doing it? Should fashions in domestic life, such as whitening front door steps or starching bed linen, be attributed to their influence? After all, servants worked long hours and had plenty of time to innovate, and they might have wished to break the monotony of their daily routines. Furthermore, they changed jobs so frequently that they could spread new ideas and techniques, like bees laden with pollen, from one place to another. Unfortunately, the evidence required to answer these questions is remarkably scanty. Very few servants wrote about

their lives and those who did preferred not to dwell on their work: their employers' testimony is more plentiful, but hardly more illuminating.

The only area of domestic life where servants were clearly creative and influential was cookery. Nearly all manuscript recipe collections contain items attributed to servants and many eighteenth- and nineteenth-century cook books were actually written and published by them.[25] The authors were frequently cooks in royal or aristocratic households and thus in an especially powerful position to change culinary taste. Mrs Mary Eales, whose *Receipts* appeared in 1718 had been 'Confectioner to her late Majesty Queen Anne' and Robert Smith whose *Court Cookery* was published in 1723 had cooked for King William, the Dukes of Buckingham and Ormond, other members of the nobility and gentry, as well as the French ambassador D'Aumont. But this was not always the case. The woman who improved the third edition of Charles Carter's *The London and Country Cook* (1749) had been 'many years housekeeper to an eminent merchant in the City of London' and Mrs Deborah Irwin, author of *The housewife's guide* (*c.* 1830) was 'twenty-three years cook to a tradesman with a large family'.

When it comes to technology, servants were definitely not innovative. There is not a single invention, however minor, that can be attributed to a servant. Furthermore, there is no evidence that servants ever campaigned for the introduction of piped water supplies, gas or electricity or urged their employers to buy time- and labour-saving appliances to lighten their work load. Indeed there is much to suggest that servants actually resisted such innovations.

In many cases this was a result of ignorance. An old servant, writing about her career in 1917, recounts how 'when the carpet-sweeper first came out, our kind lady got one, as the house had many of the Brussels carpets and she thought it would be such a boon'. But the head housemaid and other maid-servants took against it. The carpet sweeper lay unused until one day the head housemaid angrily gave it a sudden shake. She thought that she had broken it. 'But no, she had turned out the brush, and now she could see how it had to be kept clean – a grand discovery'. Soon afterwards all the servants knew how to work the carpet-sweeper and made good use of it.[26] Such stories were quite common. According to an all-women committee which recommended, in 1923, that employers buy labour-saving devices to make domestic service more attractive to educated girls, there was 'a curious and quite unreasoning hostility among maids themselves to the use of such appliances, due presumably to that conservatism of which the British race is not infrequently accused'.[27]

While servants were certainly not at the forefront of domestic technology, their existence did not impede or retard its progress. Almost all the important developments that made housework easier occurred in the nineteenth century when servants were extremely numerous. Advertisements frequently pictured a uniformed maid with a radiant smile on her face standing by the latest model of gas stove, drawing hot water from a geyser, ironing with an electric iron, dusting with a vacuum cleaner or polishing furniture with a new brand of cream or polish. Indeed, these advertisements often bore

104 *An advertisement of c. 1910. 'No trouble with Servants where there is a constant hot water service supplied by "Ewart's Califont". Hot water always ready instantly night or day.'*

the slogan 'saves time and labour' and hinted that acquisition of the product would tempt good servants to stay. In 1889, for instance, an Oxford ironmonger wrote a pamphlet on *Economy and other advantages of gas*, in which he said 'It may be confidently stated that the use of gas for cooking, fires, bath-heating, washing and drying reduces the servants' work by one-half . . .'[28].

Of course not all the developments that transformed housework in the nineteenth and twentieth centuries proved an immediate commercial success. But this was not due to the availability of cheap servant labour. Electricity was slow to spread, for example, because it was very expensive; and washing machines did not sell well because they were ineffective unless electrically powered. If there had been a direct causal link between the size of the servant population and the rate of technological progress in the home, the 1890–1930 period, when servants were disappearing rapidly, should have been characterized by a sudden rush of household inventions. But it was not. Nor was there a significant increase in consumer expenditure on domestic appliances. (This was only to come much later, in the affluent 1960s and 70s.)

Perhaps the best way of assessing servants' impact on housework is to examine what happened to people's domestic lives when they lost their servants. This began to happen in the late nineteenth century: between 1861 and 1891 the percentage of indoor domestic servants in the population of England and Wales dropped from 6.1 to 4.9 (although their absolute numbers increased due to population growth). During the first three decades of the twentieth century, the decline accelerated. By 1911, servants constituted only 3.6 per cent of the population and by 1921, 2.7 per cent. While large establishments had little trouble in retaining their domestic staff, most smaller households that employed one or two maids could no longer do so.[29] The Depression in the 1930s provided a small and brief respite, but servants were soon to disappear from British life almost completely.[30]

How did the new 'servantless households' cope? They were obviously forced to drop some of their standards. The days in which it was possible to have a laundry maid spend an entire day ironing a single petticoat for one wearing (Annie Wilkinson's experience while working at Castle Howard during Edwardian times) were over.[31] The owners of large country houses found that it was no longer possible to keep all their silver out on their dining-room sideboards and tables and packed it away in baize bags and boxes. In some cases, of course, this was not done without a pang and 'a feeling that the old order had indeed passed, taking with it those distinguished marks of dignity, culture, refinement, beauty, . . . beloved by the old country-house class'.[32]

Most people, however, did not suffer unduly. They simply reorganized and rationalized their domestic lives. To their relief, this proved surprisingly easy. Cooking was simplified by cutting the number of courses served at each meal. Certain time-consuming cleaning jobs, such as black-leading fireplaces and whitening front door steps, were dropped. Fewer clothes were starched. Brass door fitments, taps and stair rods which required regular polishing were replaced with lacquered, painted or enamel versions. Kitchens were reorganized to include areas for washing-up, food storage and eating. Food trolleys became popular and, if the dining room was adjacent to the kitchen, a service hatch was cut into the wall. The use of both front and back doors fell out of fashion, thereby ending needless running around and confusion of two bells ringing at the same time.[33] Above all, the conventional allocation of labour within the house, whereby the wife and her servants did everything, receiving no help from the men or children, was slightly modified. As Mrs James George Frazer said in *First Aid to the Servantless* (1913), a husband had to show consideration in a servantless house. 'He need not splash in his bathtub like a hippopotamus at the Zoo' and he could put away his own clothes. Furthermore, children could be trained to help their mothers do odd jobs, like fire-lighting and shelling peas.[34]

Of course some people found it hard to adjust to their now servantless existence and complained bitterly. But many came to the conclusion that life with servants, while permitting certain luxuries, had in fact been rather inefficient and wasteful. A whole range of jobs that servants did appeared, upon examination, to be unnecessary or pointless.

It would seem from this that servants had more impact on household organization and the scope of domestic activities than on their actual techniques. Overall, however, their impact on housework was surprisingly limited.

Servants as model housewives (and husbands)

Evangelical Christians liked to think that domestic service provided young women with an admirable training for married life. In fact, if they are to be believed, the good servant made a model housewife. Not only had she learned the virtues of obedience and submission, but she had acquired useful skills which would be a blessing to her husband and children as long as she lived.[35]

The argument about obedience and submission must be taken with a pinch of salt. But what about its companion? Were servants who married and established their own homes influenced by what they had learned while in service? According to Mary Leadbeater's description of life at Ballitore, a village near Dublin, they were. They absorbed their employers' values and attitudes and practised the skills they had picked up while in service. When her father's servant, David Doyle, married her brother's cook, Winifred Byrne, in 1791, he continued to read and made sash-windows to ventilate and lighten their humble cottage. As for Winifred, 'she managed his earnings with prudence, prepared his simple meals with neatness, indulged in no luxury but the cleanliness and regularity of her house, and received him with ever cheerful looks and a cheerful fire'. Under her good influence, David stayed away from the bottle and they managed to acquire a cow, a sure sign that they were prospering economically as well as morally. The couple were, in Mary Leadbeater's view, 'a pattern to their poor neighbours' as well as an excellent example of the benefits of domestic service.[36]

A less evangelical and more honest answer is provided by Flora Thompson in her account of life in the 1880s and 90s at Juniper Hill, a hamlet on the Oxfordshire-Northamptonshire border. Here all the girls went into service when they reached the age of 12 or 13. They received a good training in the domestic arts, but when they returned home to marry, they found that there were severe limits to the usefulness of what they had learned:

The young woman laying her own simple dinner with knives and forks only could have told just how many knives, forks, spoons and glasses were proper to each place at a dinner party and the order in which they should be placed. Another, blowing on her fingers to cool them as she unswathed the inevitable roly-poly, must have thought of the seven-course dinners she had cooked and dished up in other days. But, except for a few small innovations, such as a regular Sunday joint, roasted before the fire if no oven was available, and an Irish stew once in the week, they mostly reverted to the old hamlet dishes and style of cooking them. The square of bacon was cut, the roly-poly made, and the black cooking-pot was slung over the fire at four o'clock; for wages still stood at ten shillings a week and they knew that their mothers' way was the only way to nourish their husbands and children on so small a sum.

But, as Flora Thompson goes on to explain, while poverty circumscribed their application of new cooking methods, they were able to indulge themselves when it came to interior decoration:

There were fancy touches, hitherto unknown in the hamlet. Cosy corners were built of old boxes and covered with cretonne; gridirons were covered with pink wool and tinsel and hung up to serve as letter racks; Japanese fans appeared above picture frames and window curtains were tied back with ribbon bows. Blue or pink ribbon bows figured largely in these new decorative schemes. There were bows on the curtains, on the corners of cushion covers, on the cloth that covered the chest of drawers, and sometimes even on photograph frames. Some of the older men used to say that one bride, an outstanding example of the new refinement, had actually put the blue ribbon bows on the handle of her bedroom utensil. Another joke concerned the vase of flowers the same girl placed on her table at mealtimes. Her father-in-law, it was said, being entertained to tea at the new home, exclaimed, 'Hemmed if I've ever heard of eatin' flowers before!' and the mother-in-law passed the vase to her son, saying, 'Here, Georgie. Have a mouthful of sweet peas.' But the brides only laughed and tossed their heads at such ignorance. The old hamlet ways were all very well, some of them; but they had seen the world and knew how things were done.[37]

Women trained as laundry-maids usually had the least difficulty in applying their skills. They did their family's washing to perfection, and often dealt with other people's as well, for a small fee. This additional source of income could make all the difference in times of crisis. Joseph Arch, for example, describes how his mother, formerly in service at Warwick Castle, saved the family from starvation by doing laundry work when his father was unemployed in 1835.[38]

Chamber-maids, or house-maids, on the other hand, had virtually no accomplishments to display because they learned so little while in service. As Ned advised his friend Harry, in a late eighteenth-century 'penny-history' about courtship and marriage: 'Never marry a chamber-maid, for they bring nothing with them but a few old cloaths of their mistresses, and for house-keeping, few of them know anything of it; for they can hardly make a pudding or a pye, neither can they spin, nor knit, nor wash, except it be a few laces to make themselves fine withal.'[39]

The first systematic attempt to assess the value of domestic service as a training for married life was made by Miss F. A. F. Livingstone in the early 1930s. She questioned 200 London working-class girls and their mothers on the subject. But although she received many illuminating replies, they were inconclusive. The mothers were divided in their opinions; the daughters so opposed to domestic service that their answers were biased. In the end, Miss Livingstone concluded that domestic service suffered from severe defects as a training for marriage, basically because 'the girl does not have the spending of the money or the selection of the meal; it is not her own things that she spoils or for which she is responsible, and unless her duties lie in the kitchen her experience only extends over a small part of the field of housewifery'.[40]

The ideological effects of domestic service
So far this chapter has been exclusively concerned with assessing servants' practical

impact on housework in the British Isles. It is now time to consider the important ideological effects of domestic service – the ways in which the existence of servants influenced people's attitudes to housework and to women.

Servants' humble status near the bottom of Britain's social and economic hierarchy inevitably rubbed off on the work that they did; and this association was constantly reinforced by their sheer numbers. It is hard to conceive how ubiquitous domestic servants once were, now that they are so much a thing of the past. But a proposal 'for the due regulating of servants' made in the reign of Queen Anne (1698–1714) said 'It has always been computed, by common Estimation, That the Servants of both sexes in England and Wales, do amount to the Third part of the People'.[41] Given that the term 'servant' included outdoor servants, labourers, apprentices and clerks in the early eighteenth century, this 'common estimation' suggests that indoor domestic servants may have represented from 10 to 15 per cent of the population.[42] If this is so, the proportion of servants in the population and labour force was even higher in the early eighteenth century than it was in the nineteenth. For when indoor domestic servants in England and Wales were enumerated in the census of 1831 (the first to make detailed returns of people's occupations), it turned out that they represented 4.7 per cent of the population and 12.6 per cent of the work force. In 1891, when the number of domestic servants reached its all-time peak of 1,549,502, they made up 4.9 per cent of the population and 15.8 per cent of the labour force. Domestic service was the largest single occupation in the United Kingdom.[43]

The ratio of men to women servants also had great ideological significance. At no time was the ratio evenly balanced: women servants were always predominant. But in the seventeenth and eighteenth centuries, men-servants were quite common. They were especially numerous in noble households, where the mediaeval, courtly tradition of male service lingered on.[44] The *Servants' Instructions* drawn up by James Brydges, Duke of Chandos, in 1720, for instance, show that all the key positions in his household (steward, clerke of the checque, clerke of the kitchin, butler, usher of the hall) were held by men, as indeed were the majority of lesser posts. On New Year's Day, 1721, the Duke's household numbered 135 people, of whom only 12 were female domestic servants.[45]

Men were also employed by the gentry. The Disbursements Book (1691–1709) of Sir Thomas Haggerston, a country gentlemen from Lancashire, shows that he employed six men servants, three of them liveried, and five to six maids.[46] The London household of Fanny Boscawen, an admiral's wife, in 1748 included two men (a French butler and a footman) as well as seven women (a lady's maid, cook, kitchen-maid, nurse, nursery maid and two housemaids).[47] In Scotland, the domestic staff of John Hamilton of Bargeny, a landowner and industrialist, included 17 women (eight lady's maids, four chamber maids, two laundry maids, two dairy maids, and a kitchen maid) and five men (two cooks, two footmen and a butler) between 1750 and 1756.[48]

However, this widespread pattern of employing men servants as well as women came to an end during the 1780s, partly as a result of the growing number of alternative job

105 *'High life below stairs', black and white mezzotint, 1770. To employ a black man servant was a great status symbol in the eighteenth century.*

opportunities provided for men by the Industrial Revolution,[49] but mainly because of a stiff tax imposed on male domestic servants in 1777.[50] Originally set at a guinea per servant to help finance the War of American Independence and encourage men to join the navy, the tax was not repealed until 1937. During the intervening years it remained at a high level and was rigorously enforced.

As a result, almost everybody was discouraged from employing boys and men in a domestic capacity. In 1784, just seven years after the tax had gone into effect, François de la Rochefoucauld, a French aristocrat who was visiting England, found that 'while there are certain English noblemen who have thirty or forty men servants, the cooking and housework that is not seen are generally done by women, and men servants are employed only for such duties as are performed in the presence of guests'.[51]

The tax on male servants also meant that apprentices and farm labourers could not do any housework on a part-time or occasional basis without their employers taking the risk of incurring a financial penalty. This was very significant because until then, servants had often fulfilled a mixture of domestic and non-domestic functions. The account books of James Laurie, a clergyman in a remote Ayrshire parish consisting of 700 scattered crofts, show that his three women-servants and herd lassie were 'as active in the byre and the field as in the kitchen'.[52] In the same way, Elizabeth Purefoy's letters indicate that she usually wanted her servants to work indoors, as well as out. In March 1738, for example, she wrote to her agent William Holloway that she was looking for 'a footman to work in the garden, lay the Cloath, wait at Table, and go to cart with Thomas when hee is ordered, or do any other Businesses hee is ordered to do . . .'.[53]

A rare insight into the way the tax effectively stopped men from doing housework is provided by the casebook of appeals issued by the commissioners of the excise in 1781. This explained, in no uncertain terms, that a man like the Reverend Mr Humphreys of Woodbridge, Suffolk, who employed a 12-year-old footboy to run errands for him, clean shoes, sharpen knives, sweep the garden and light fires, as well as 'other occasional business in the house', had to pay the tax. In the same way, George Geree Elwick, a farmer from Kent, was liable because his servant William Lucas doubled up as footboy and gardener. Although William spent most of his time out of doors, on the farm and in the garden, he also rode out with his master and performed domestic tasks such as churning butter and cleaning boots and shoes. The case of James Champagne, a wine merchant of Melcombe Regis in Dorset, was very similar. He employed Thomas Peters as a porter in his business and for washing bottles and casks. But this did not debar him from the tax because Thomas also waited at table and cleaned knives and forks.[54]

Domestic service soon became an almost exclusively feminine occupation as employers realized how strictly the tax was interpreted and enforced. By 1851, 89.9 per cent of the indoor domestic servants in England and Wales were female and in 1911, 91.7 per cent were. The idea that housework was women's work was born out by reality, in a way that it had never been before. Only in Ireland, where the tax was never imposed, was this not the case. The ratio of male and female servants retained its traditional balance and men servants continued to do domestic work.[55] As Dorothea Conyers, an Irish gentlewoman, commented in 1920: 'Every Irish servant will do everyone else's work cheerfully, the men come in to help the maids to polish floors and shoes, and the maids are quite willing to feed the horses if all the men are out . . .'[56]

At no time was the ideological impact of domestic service on attitudes to housework and to women's place in society more starkly revealed than when the flow of young girls entering service diminished in the late nineteenth and early twentieth centuries. A veritable flood of pamphlets, tracts and books appeared on the market, trying to identify the cause. There were many explanations of course – education being a major contender. But virtually all the mistresses and servants participating in the debate agreed that the roots of the problem lay in the low status of domestic service. It was simply far less attractive than most other occupations open to women. Although the pay compared well,* hours were much longer.† Living and working conditions were often appalling

* Because women servants got free board and lodging and worked very long hours, it is difficult to compare their wages with those of women working in other occupations. Theresa McBride, however, has found that 'domestic service offered a distinct monetary advantage over other kinds of female employment in the nineteenth century'.[57]

† When the Women's Industrial Council investigated domestic service in 1914, they found that most servants were on duty from 6.30 am until 10 pm or later, with almost no free time.[58]

and there was no organization to which employers and servants could turn to resolve disputes. As Mrs Eliot James, author of *Our Servants. Their duties to us and ours to them* (1883), put it: 'the young people of the cottager and labouring class . . . look down on domestic service and seek other openings instead – they become dressmakers, milliners, clerks, assistants in shops, pupil-teachers, school mistresses, or perhaps aspire to posts in the telegraph and post office: anything rather than be servants as their fathers and mothers were before them.'[59]

As might be expected, the diagnoses were accompanied by suggested cures. Catherine Buckton, writing in 1898, thought it was necessary 'to make elementary technical instruction in practical cookery, laundry work and housewifery an obligatory subject, like the three R's, in every public elementary day school in England and Wales for all girls between the ages of 9 and 12'.[60] 'Amara Veritas', an 'experienced mistress', agreed with her, but went a step further: all transactions between mistresses and servants had to be put upon a sound business basis. She advocated unionization, franchise for women and legislation as the best methods for bringing this about.[61] By contrast, 'Justice' of North Shields thought that all would be solved if mistresses stopped treating maids as if they were a necessary evil and gave them 12 hours' free time a week.[62] An 'old-established' domestic employment agency likewise felt it sufficient to advise mistresses to stop putting three or four maids in one bedroom, to provide them with comfortable furniture, a sitting room, plenty of good food and free time, and to avoid favouritism.[63]

But because domestic service was such a common part of everyday life, and had been for such a long time, almost nobody asked whether it should continue to exist or proposed to abolish it. Mrs Havelock Ellis, author of an obscure pamphlet called *Democracy in the kitchen* (1894), was a rare exception. She believed that the servant question was 'at the very core of our national democratic problem'. In her view, servants were not to be kept in their place but liberated. The first step in this process was to make domestic service a trade, with limited hours and legal contracts. The second required the setting up of municipal domestic service facilities which 'would in ten or twenty years be as remunerative as the General Post Office . . .'. 'If every woman could have a minimum instead of a maximum of domestic spider-threads tugging at her brain year in and year out, through the municipalization of laundries, bake-houses, kitchens, and restaurants, worked under well-trained and methodical civil servants, just imagine for one moment what a new life would be on this earth,' she asked.[64]

Even more significantly, nobody questioned the assumption that housework was women's work and responsibility. Every mistress took it for granted that if she lost her servants she would be left doing all the housework by herself (albeit with some cooperation from her family and the services of a weekly charwoman).[65] And all other women made similar assumptions. Whatever their social, economic or educational background, they simply did not expect to share the housework with their husbands and children. The tradition of female domestic service died hard.

Chapter 9 TIME SPENT ON HOUSEWORK

It is not possible to compare the amount of time women spent on housework at different periods between 1650 and 1950. For the necessary evidence simply does not exist. While individual men and women often described housework at length, they almost never provided details about its timing: they had little sense of the value of time and therefore no reason or motive for recording its disposition. And there were no surveys of the ways in which British housewives filled their days until two (not very scientific) studies in the 1930s.[1]

This lack of evidence is frustrating. But even if there were plenty of quantitative evidence about the time women spent on housework before the 1930s, it would still be extraordinarily difficult (if not impossible) to make meaningful comparisons about the length of their working day because of all the different factors that need to be considered.

In the first place, housework has never been an occupation with a fixed definition. How does one take into account its changing scope and content when making comparisons? And how does one define activities which fall into the grey area between housework, leisure and paid work?

Secondly, there is the variable of living standards. It is important to be able to place households accurately in the economic hierarchy. But living standards are notoriously difficult to define and evaluate; and their effects on the time spent on housework are so complex that they defy generalization.

A third significant factor to consider is a household's location. Women living in the country usually had more to do than their sisters in the city; they lacked the amenities of urban life and had to be far more self-sufficient. It would be unfair, however, to say that country housewives always put in longer hours. Many aspects of rural housework were seasonal; pig-killing, for example, only took place once or twice a year. And urban housewives living in badly polluted environments were forced to spend far more time cleaning and washing than country women.

Fourthly, the size of a household – the number of rooms and people in them – also affects time spent on housework. But while much is known about the history of British housing between 1650 and 1950, demographers are still working out what changes in family size occurred during the period. It is logical to assume that mothers with several young children worked longer and more intensive hours than housewives without children, but there is no way of telling how much harder they worked or how much extra time per day they allowed for children of different ages.[2] The additional housework generated by having elderly relations or guests in the house is similarly hard to assess.

Finally, time spent on housework was subject to yet another variable: the amount of help women received from servants and family members.

The impact of these variables could differ so much from one household to another that it would be misleading to think of British women as having a normal or standard working schedule at any given time. This can be seen very clearly during the last three-quarters of the nineteenth century when variations, determined by social class and geography, in the content of housework and the time it required were particularly marked. Britain was by then an industrial giant and upper-class urban women could profit from unprecedented developments in domestic technology. Yet in many remote places, women continued to live and work as their ancestresses had done several centuries earlier.

In 1828, for example, an Irish peasant who lived in a one-room hut at Cloonygara spent most of her time producing food for her family. She set potatoes and sowed wheat and kept pigs, sheep, goats and a cow, as well as wood pigeons, ducks and drakes. Sometimes she went fishing for eel and pike to vary her family's basic diet of potatoes and buttermilk; and to make a little money to pay the landlord and to provide her family with clothes, she grew flax. (She spun both this and her wool into yarn.) The time she spent on housework was insignificant compared to these primary occupations. For instance, she had virtually no cleaning to do, the family possessions consisting of two spinning wheels, a box, a table, a cooking pot, a chair and a bed with coverings.[3]

The routine of this Irish peasant woman was very different from that of Susannah Stacey (1812–93), an English farmwife who lived in east Sussex. She too led a rural existence and was heavily involved in producing and processing food. But she was not operating at a subsistence level. The farm was large and prosperous and there were many labourers and visitors to feed. Susannah's pickled pork, smoked hams, cheeses, beer, and fruit wines were known throughout the county. Her cooking was never restrained by poverty. She baked regularly and for breakfast usually produced some boiled beef. For lunch, there would be a pork or beef pudding boiled in a cloth, along with some fruit pies or 'plum heavies' (pastries filled with currants and spices). On top of all this, Susannah kept a garden from which she distilled herbal remedies for every kind of human ill, washed a large quantity of laundry once a month, and made her own candles and soap. The only thing she did not do was make her family's clothes.[4]

Leaving the country for the city, women moved into a different world. Food production and processing ceased to be necessary. Fuel was delivered to the door, candles could be bought from a chandler's shop, laundry sent out to a washer-woman. Thus the women who worked 14-hour days in the Midland factories during the 1830s, could survive without doing much housework at all. They and their families existed off wheaten bread and potatoes, washed down with tea or coffee, and lived, for the most part, in filthy houses.[5] A full-time housewife like Ellen Youl, the wife of a Northampton boot factory worker at the end of the century, only had to concern herself with cooking, cleaning, keeping up a good fire, and budgeting. (This last activity was especially time-consuming, partly because Ellen's husband did not earn much, but mainly because he could never be relied upon to surrender his earnings.)[6]

Making ends meet was in fact a major feature of urban housework. Even a relatively well-off London housewife like Jane Carlyle worried about money and made earnest calculations about what she and her husband could afford. Most of her time, however, was spent in managing her servants and making up for their shortfalls. Thus if the servant could not cook, Jane prepared the meals. Likewise, if the servant was an incompetent cleaner, Jane did the more delicate or difficult tasks herself, such as dusting books, unnailing carpets for beating, and exterminating bugs. But the scope of her household activities and the time she spent on them depended not only on the quality of her servants but also on her husband's movements: Thomas Carlyle so hated any sort of domestic commotion that Jane usually embarked on ambitious spring-cleaning and sewing projects whenever he went away.[7]

She certainly did far more housework than a wealthy, society woman like Lady Frederick Cavendish, whose married life (1864–82) consisted of one long round of social engagements in London and visits to friends and relations in country houses. Yet even if Lady Cavendish did not dirty her hands, she was still, in some senses, a housewife. She had to manage her servants (her diary shows that this was no easy matter) and she was responsible for composing menus and dealing with her household accounts.[8]

One variable affecting the time spent on housework is particularly hard to fathom: this is the extent to which husbands helped their wives with housework. The evidence, unfortunately, is far from plentiful. However, it is obvious that men never helped women very extensively, except in extraordinary circumstances, such as those described by Richard Jones, a Welshman born near Ruthin in 1789:

When I was a little boy I well remember how my mother kept my father and all the family from starvation one year. Owing to a late harvest and bad weather, when it was time to carry the corn practically all of it had rotted in the fields that year. What remained was bad and useless except to feed the pigs with. Grain was very dear and we had no money to buy any. There were hundreds of families in Wales in the same case, winter coming on and famine staring us in the face. My father went mad thinking of the black winter that faced us. One night my mother broke the heavy silence and said to my father: 'I'll make a bargain with thee; I'll see to food for us both and the children all winter if thou, in addition to looking after the horse, the cattle and pigs, wilt do the churning, wash up, make the beds and clean the house. I'll make the butter myself.' 'How wilt thou manage?' asked my father, the tears running down his cheeks. 'I will knit', said she. 'We have wool. If thou wilt card it, I'll spin.' The bargain was struck; my father did the housework in addition to the work on the farm and my mother knitted. She rose early and worked late and out of the twenty-four hours she only slept for five or six. She had set herself the task of knitting three stockings a day ... And so it was that she kept us alive until the next harvest.[9]

According to Sir Charles Shaw, a similarly dire and unusual situation existed in Manchester between 1839 and 1842. Many men were unemployed and while their wives

106 *'The Welsh Curate', a hand-coloured mezzotint, c. 1760. The caption reads thus:*

Tho' lazy, the proud Prelate's fed,   *His Wife at Washing – T'is is his Lot,*
This Curate eats no idle Bread: *To pare the Turnips, watch the Pot:*
Each Faculty and Limb beside,   *He reads, and hears his Son read out;*
Eyes, Ears, Hands, Feet, are all employ'd. *And rocks the Cradle with his Foot.*

worked in factories from half past five in the morning until seven or eight o'clock at night, they remained at home, acting as cooks and nurses.[10] William Dodd, who was also investigating factory conditions in the Midlands and North at this time, reported likewise that the husbands of women employed in the cotton mills at Bolton-Le-Moors were 'in many instances being kept idle at home'. 'It is quite pitiable to see these poor men taking care of the house and children, and busily engaged in washing, baking, nursing, and preparing the humble repast for the wife, who is wearing her life away toiling in the factory' he said.[11]

Married couples did not normally expect to have their roles reversed in this way, any more than they expected to share housework on an equal basis. In the seventeenth and eighteenth centuries, however, it seems that women often received a great deal of help from their husbands. The diurnal of Nicholas Blundell of Little Crosby, Lancashire, shows that he was constantly making life easier for his wife Frances, who bore him many children in quick succession. For a start, he shared in the management and discipline of the servants and kept the household accounts. He did not do any of the cooking, but he helped to feed the pigs and preserve food. In November, 1708, for instance, he was laying apples in straw and putting 'some Black Puddings in Pickley to keep'. In August 1710 he was papering 'a great many Glasses of Sweetmeats' and in July the following year he was trying to discover the best way of keeping artichokes. ('I buried some Harty Choks in a Mug in the Ground and some I hung in the House to try to keep them but it did not answer expectation', he wrote in disappointment.) He also helped in the pantry: on one occasion, his head 'being ill', he cut bread there. More unusually, he did all the brewing of beer and ale and made other kinds of alcoholic beverage such as brandy and ratafia. When guests were expected, he was quick to lend a hand. 'I set out the Desert and helped to dress flower pots for the Chimneys', he noted in June 1705. He never did any routine cleaning, but did dust the pictures in the chapel and he cleaned out his personal closet every year before Christmas. Above all, Blundell was a great handiman: he was always fixing things. In February 1709 he mended a smoothing iron, as well as a meal chest in the storehouse; the following month, he took 'the Coffy Mill in peeses to see whot was the falt with it'.[12]

Blundell may have been an unusually assiduous husband, but his behaviour was by no means exceptional by seventeenth- and eighteenth-century standards. In the nineteenth century, by contrast, men who helped women around the house were considered either effeminate or eccentric. Indeed by the 1880s and 90s, it was a point of pride in most families that men did not lift a finger while they were at home. In Northampton, for example, working-class men did not even do minor chores such as fetching coal, chopping firewood or carrying dustbins out to the pavement.[13] In Salford, likewise, men proved their virility by avoiding anything that was considered women's work. If, on occasion, they had to lend a hand (because their wives were exhausted at the end of a long day, or pregnant) they locked the doors first so that the neighbours would not see. Those husbands who were caught in the act of scrubbing a floor, washing, or cooking were apt to be called derisive names such as 'mop rag' and 'diddy man'.[14] In rural Yorkshire, women waited on their husbands hand and foot and actually called them 'master'. The men treated them as mere child-bearing instruments and expected them to pull their weight and earn their keep just like servants. A week after childbirth, women were to be found doing heavy work, such as laundry and milking, and, however tired they might be, they were at their husbands' beck and call all day long.[15]

The reason for this change in men's domestic behaviour is not easy to explain. It may be that men worked longer hours in the nineteenth century than formerly: after all, an increasing proportion of them earned their living in towns or cities, where work was far more regimented than in the country. Many men had to spend an increasing amount of time travelling to and from work. On returning home in the evening, often in a state of complete exhaustion, their one desire was to rest. The men were the main bread-winners, whether their wives worked or not, and it seemed only fair that they should be exempt from housework. This rigid division of labour coincided with the growing feminization of domestic service and thus fitted into a definite 'trend' or 'fashion', which soon spread from the cities to the country.

It did not, however, find its way to Ireland, where industrialization was much less pronounced than on the mainland, and the ratio of men and women servants more balanced. Here husbands continued to help their wives in the traditional ways, as can be seen in the behaviour of a tailor who lived in a four-room cottage in the town of Garrynapeaka, County Cork, during the 1930s. While his wife Ansty got up at dawn to kindle the fire, carried the turf and the water, made the tea and butter, did the laundry, cleaned the house, and fed the cow, hens and ducks, he tended the fire, baked soda bread, cooked lunch, filled the oil lamps, salted butter, washed eggs, and cleaned the knives and forks.[16]

What about children? How much did they help with housework? The evidence here is also rather scanty. But it seems that children in households with servants were not normally expected to do any domestic chores and that children in families without servants were. But, because children only became useful at the age of seven or eight and usually left home in their teens, the period in which they could lighten their mothers' workload was relatively short. Take the case of Mary Somerville (1780–1872). Recalling her youth in a Scottish seaport, she remembered that: 'When I was seven or eight years old I began to be useful, for I pulled the fruit for preserving; shelled the peas and beans, fed the poultry, and looked after the dairy, for we kept a cow.' But by the time she was ten, she had left home for boarding school.[17]

The actual amount of housework children did appears to have been governed almost entirely by maternal need. The main task that James Dale Copper, the son of a Sussex carter, helped with in his boyhood during the 1890s was the weekly mangling. An enterprising businessman in the village kept a large, heavy box mangle in a wooden lean-to hut which anybody could use for a penny. James and his brother would compete with other boys to break the speed record for rolling the box over the linen from one end

107 *Children helping with housework – under the watchful eye of their mother. From* Our Village *by Mary Russell Mitford, 1879 edition.*

of the table to the other. The box would invariably fall off its rollers and the boys, unable to lift it back, would have to ask the owner for help, much to his annoyance.[18] But John Lawson, who grew up at Boldon Colliery in Durham during the 1890s, did not have nearly as much fun. His services were in constant demand because his father, a miner, worked long hours and his mother had ten children to look after. 'Until I was twelve years of age and commenced work in the mine' he recorded in his memoirs, 'I had to spend most of my time after school hours and during holidays as nurse and housemaid.' He was always washing dishes, 'dashing' pit-clothes, brushing, cleaning and greasing pit-boots, and cleaning pit lamps as well as looking after his siblings. 'I could legitimately say that I brought up several of my younger brothers and sisters' he wrote.[19] Such boasts were quite typical. Children usually spent more time tending brothers and sisters than on housework itself. This enabled their mothers to focus on whatever job was at hand with full concentration and was the most efficient allocation of labour.

Although it is impossible to compare the amount of time women spent on housework at different periods in any precise or meaningful way, it is clear that they always worked longer hours than men. Their working day began when they got up, at least an hour before men started work, and did not end at an appointed hour in the late afternoon or early evening, as was the case with men, but at bed-time. This disparity between the length of men and women's working hours was true of town and country alike but it was most frequently remarked upon by writers describing rural life. John Firth, for example, said that in mid-nineteenth-century Orkney, women 'busily prepared the wool for being woven into blankets and clothing for the family' during the long winter evenings, but the men would 'smoke and doze or spin yarns by the fireside to the humming of the spinning wheel and the rasping of cards'.[20] In her *Fenland Chronicle*, Sybil Marshall points out that if life was hard for the men in the early 1900s, it was harder still for the women. The wives of agricultural labourers were up with the lark in the morning to sweep and clean their houses and tend their numerous children. During the busy seasons they worked all day long in the fields, only returning home for tea. Their husbands might then help them by feeding the pig or fetching a yoke of water, but would then relax for the evening. The women were left to prepare the evening meal, put the children to bed and make and mend clothes.[21] In the same way, the journalist William Linton Andrews commented on what little leisure a farmer's wife in an isolated Yorkshire farmhouse had between the two world wars. She was continually cooking, baking, washing-up, and cleaning. Her husband, by contrast, was not nearly so hard working: ' . . . when the rain bursts upon him as he is making his round of the flocks he can take a rest on the hay in the nearest cowhouse, with a clear conscience . . .' and 'if the river swells into flood you will find [him] fishing his favourite pool, intent on trout fried with his morning ham.'[22]

Furthermore, just as women tended to do housework all day long, so they did it all week. Women, unlike men, usually worked Monday to Sunday inclusive. In theory, of course, the Sabbath was meant to be a day of rest for everybody. Women were supposed to ensure that they had all their housework done by Saturday evening so that they could go to Church on Sunday and be free to read devotional literature.

A minority did indeed manage to meet the ideal. Julia Curtis, in her account of life in a remote village in the west coast of Scotland in the 1880s, says that very little housework was done on the Sabbath. The day was devoted to spiritual rather than practical matters. 'The night before, boots and shoes were brushed, and most of the food cooked. Yellow backed novels and other light literature were locked up and Sunday magazines and books of a religious nature solemnly produced.' No dishes were washed and, she adds, 'on Monday morning the maids were confronted with stacks of cups and plates, which often caused much grumbling'.[23] On the island of St Kilda the women considered it sinful to draw water or milk cows on Sunday and desisted from doing so.[24] And in Abernant, Wales, miners' wives did all their cleaning on Friday and their cooking on Saturday so that they would not have to break the Sabbath. Any woman who transgressed felt that God noticed, as Maude Morgan Thomas learned when staying with her aunt Blodwyn in the early 1900s:

Your uncle had gone to church alone. I wasn't feeling well, so I stayed home. And then I remembered that I had neglected to bake a pie for dinner. So I got to work quickly, and in no time at all the pie was in and out of the oven – a nice rhubarb it was, too. I felt very guilty about baking it on Sunday, but I knew that your uncle would miss his pie. Well. I set it out on the garden bench to cool off, but when I went to get it for dinner, the chickens had eaten every speck! I have always thought that was my punishment for baking on Sunday.[25]

Most women, however, found it impractical to make a Sunday a complete day of rest. Their families still needed attention and, in any case, it was traditional to produce the best meal of the week at Sunday lunchtime. Thus, when Mr 'Worthy', a virtuous late eighteenth-century farmer, visits Mr 'Bragwell' on a Sunday morning, he is horrified to find 'an uncommon bustle in the house'. All hands were busy. 'It was nothing but baking and boiling, and frying, and roasting, and running, and scolding, and eating.' Most members of the household had no time for religious observances. 'The boy was kept from church to clean the plate, the man to gather the fruit, the mistress to make the cheesecakes, the maids to dress the dinner, and the young ladies to dress themselves.'[26]

That women normally worked longer hours than men is more than confirmed by the first surveys of the ways in which women spent their time. The earliest, in 1934, was based on 1,250 urban working-class wives. It showed that the majority got up at 6.30 am and went to bed between 10 and 11 pm, after spending 12–14 hours on their feet attending to housework and children. It did not, unfortunately, attempt to differentiate between the two activities or determine how much time was spent on different domestic tasks.[27] The second, conducted by the Electrical Association of Women in 1935, was based on an unstated but relatively small number of working-class housewives who had the good fortune to live in fully electrified homes. Although it was part of a propaganda exercise designed to promote electricity, it turned out that women who lived in ideal conditions still spent a considerable amount of time on housework: 49.19 hours a week or 7 hours a day. This broke down into 15.50 hours a week on cleaning, 14.20 on cooking, 7.53 on washing-up, 6.43 on mending and sewing, and 5.53 on laundry.[28]

A more rigorous survey, this time of 76 working-class housewives living in three different London County Council housing estates carried out in 1948, did much to confirm the finds of the 1934 study. For it showed that the average housewife's weekday consisted of about 12 hours' work, 4 hours' leisure and 8 hours' sleep. The time spent on housework varied slightly, according to family circumstances. The woman without any children spent an average of 9.3 hours a day on general housework, laundry, food preparation and consumption, mending, shopping, and animal care. As she also spent 2.2 hours in outside employment, her total working day was 11.5 hours long. The mother with one child had a slightly longer working day of 11.8 hours: but the 1.2 hours she spent on childcare and the 2.4 she put in on her job meant that she spent slightly less time (8.2 hours) on housework. With two children rather than one, the housewife worked 12.3 hours a day: she spent 9.2 hours doing housework, 1.8 looking after children and 1.3 earning money. However, once a woman had three or more children she only worked an 11.6-hour day. Of all the women in the survey, she spent the least amount of time on housework (7.9 hours) and on work outside the home (1.0) and the most on childcare (2.7).[29]

Finally, it is evident that housework obeys Parkinson's Law: 'work expands so as to fill the time available for its completion.'[30] In other words, women working outside the home always did their housework more quickly than those who were full-time housewives. They had to. In the same way, the spread of utilities and time- and labour-saving appliances did not have any discernible long-term effect on the average housewife's working hours. Time saved on one task was simply put to new use and the scope of housework redefined. A woman who gained an extra 45 minutes a day through the introduction of piped water into her house would use them to do more cleaning and washing. Similarly, a woman whose coal range was replaced with a gas stove would cook more elaborate meals than she had previously, because it was so much easier. In this way, housework remained a full-time occupation for most women in 1950, just as it had been in 1650. The old dictum 'a woman's work is never done' is subject to many interpretations and all of them are true.

Chapter 10 WOMEN'S ATTITUDES TO HOUSEWORK

To superintend the various branches of domestic management, or as St Paul briefly and emphatically expresses the same office, 'to guide the house', is the indispensable duty of a married woman. No mental endowments furnish an exemption from it; no plea of improving pursuits and literary pleasures can excuse the neglect of it. The task must be executed either by the master or the mistress of the house: and reason and scripture concur in assigning it unequivocally to the latter.*

Women's attitudes to housework did not undergo any fundamental change between 1650 and 1950. The vast majority of women accepted housework as their main occupation throughout the three centuries. That is not to say that women all had the same feelings about housework. Far from it. Some loved their work and derived great satisfaction from it. Others heartily disliked certain features of their routine, such as wash-day, supervising bad servants, or struggling to make ends meet. A few loathed everything about housework and did as little of it as they could. In 1722, for example, John Essex was driven to publish *The Young Ladies' Conduct* because he found that housekeeping had 'of late years' been 'too much neglected by Ladies of Fashion'. As a result of their 'idle education' and lamentable ignorance, these ladies thought that the government of a house and the management of servants was 'too mean and insignificant for Persons of their Quality' and only 'fit for Women of Inferior Rank and Condition, as Farmers' Wives etc'.[1] It is clear, however, that despite all the variations in women's attitudes to housework, they never questioned the basic assumption that it was women's work.

In fact, from the perspective of the 1980s, it is remarkable how content women were to spend their lives doing housework. There were no rebellions and very few rebels. The woman who turned down good marriage proposals to pursue an independent career was a rarity. And it was not often that women exhibited signs of anti-social behaviour that can be interpreted with confidence as a form of protest against housework. The 'scolds' who poured abuse on all and sundry, and who were always at the centre of any fight or brawl, were to be found in most communities until the mid-nineteenth century, when the term fell into disuse. But their venom seems to have been directed against the world in general rather than anything more specific. In any case, whenever they got out of hand, they were quickly silenced by means of humiliating public punishments.[2] In the seventeenth century, for example, a scold might find her

---

* Thomas Gisborne, *An Enquiry into the duties of the female sex*, printed for T. Cadell and W. Davies, London, 1797, p. 271. This book was very popular. By 1823 it had gone through 13 editions.

108 *A Newcastle woman wearing a brank, 1655. From Ralph Gardiner,* Englands Grievance Discovered, *1796.*

109 *A brank illustrated in Robert Plot,* The natural history of Staffordshire, *1686. Plot thought it was 'much to be preferr'd to the* Cucking-Stoole, *which not only endangers the* health *of the* party, *but also gives the* tongue *liberty 'twixt every dipp'. He explains that 'the* Letter a *shews the joynted* collar *that comes round the* neck; *b, c, the* loops *and* staples, *to let it out and in, according to the bigness and slenderness of the* neck; *d, the joynted semicircle that comes over the* head, *made forked at one end to let through the* nose; *and e, the* **plate** *of* Iron *that is put into the* mouth, *and keeps down the* tongue'.

head encased for up to 48 hours in a 'brank', a metal contraption with a spoke that immobilized the tongue, making it impossible to speak without drawing blood. She would then be led round the town on a rope or chained to one spot until she showed unmistakable signs of repentance.[3] More commonly, however, scolds were simply ducked in the local pond or river, to the jeers of the local community.[4]

In the same way, it would be wrong to take too seriously the fact that women were often depicted in the act of putting on trousers in satirical prints; they are always so deliciously plump and feminine and so obviously interested in fashion that one is left

110 *'Ducking a Scold', coloured etching by Thomas Rowlandson, 1812.*

with the impression that far from wishing to change their sex, they simply wanted to know what they looked like in a different attire.

Several tales of women who swopped roles with their husbands, forcing them to do the housework against their will while they sat back and enjoyed themselves, survive in chap-books. In *Simple Simon's Misfortunes*, for example, Margery succeeds in getting her husband 'to do anything she desir'd, as making of fire, scouring the grates, cleaning the spits, washing the dishes, making the beds, with a hundred [other] little things belonging to drudgery', through a terrifying mixture of harsh rebukes and physical violence. Whenever Simple Simon failed to obey her or did anything wrong, he was promptly bashed, dog-whipped, cudgeled or beaten; and on one famous occasion when he went off to have a drink with a friend, Margery tied him hand and foot in a basket and hauled him up the chimney, where she left him all night, to be smoked with her hams. The next morning 'he was almost roasted like a red herring'.[5] Such stories, however, are fictional and there is no evidence to suggest that they were based on the antics of real women.

Nor is there any evidence that feminists were concerned about the rights and wrongs of women doing housework. Their writings and activities were focused on other issues

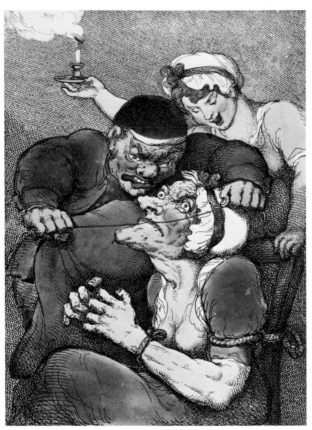

III *'The Cobler's Cure for a Scolding Wife', coloured engraving by Thomas Rowlandson, 1813.*

affecting their sex, such as education, suffrage, law reform, and birth control. They wanted to promote women's emancipation, but changing the existing allocation of labour within the home was not a priority. This was, in many ways, highly pragmatic: specific reforms are easier to contemplate and bring about than revolutions. But it also reflected the personal interests and needs of the women who became feminists. It is significant that they almost all came from relatively prosperous backgrounds and were able to afford servants. In other words, they were free to pursue their work more or less full-time, unencumbered by the domestic cares experienced by the majority of women. For them housework was not an important issue. Anything that affected them personally (such as winning the vote or taking degrees at Oxford and Cambridge) seemed far more significant.

Why was the domestic status quo so universally respected? Tradition explains a great deal. The ancient concept of society as an ordered hierarchy in which the different sexes and social classes had specific roles to play was universally accepted. It was, after all, borne out by reality and supported by an enormous weight of biblical and historical evidence. From time immemorial the main function and expectation of women was to marry and give birth to children. Any young lady who doubted this for so much as a moment had only to visit her local church and read the inscription on the grave stones and funereal monuments: the significant facts recorded in most women's lives were the date of their birth, the date of their marriage, the names of their husbands and children and the date of their death. The order of nature, the scheme by which God had created the world, could not be turned upside down. In theory, of course, the young lady might have argued (along with modern-day feminists) that there were no biological or moral reasons why women should also be obliged to do housework. In practice, however, she did not. Marriage, childcare, and maintaining a home were so inextricably linked together that it was almost impossible to disassociate them from each other.

But women also adhered to the status quo because they did not have much choice in the matter. From girlhood, their education and upbringing prepared them for a life of domesticity, rather than jobs and careers that would take them out of the home.[6] When they reached the age of employment they found that they were debarred from almost every skilled, professional, or lucrative occupation open to men.[7] They also knew that women could earn only half to two-thirds as much as men in the rare cases when comparable work was open to them.[8] In short, most women did not find that employment was very rewarding. They could not gain power and influence through their jobs, nor could they make much money. Under the circumstances, marriage, children and housework were attractive options. It was no wonder that the ambition of every young girl was to find a good husband and marry him as soon as she could.

A small minority of women did, of course, succeed against all odds in accumulating capital and setting up their own businesses. But as soon as these women chose to marry, they immediately lost all their financial independence and were forced back into the fold of housewifery. For until the Married Women's Property Act came into effect in 1883, a wife had no civil status apart from her husband's. According to common law, her property passed into his hands as soon as they exchanged their vows: he could do exactly as he pleased with all her earnings, investments, stock-in-trade, and household goods and spend any income derived from her 'real' property, although he could not actually dispose of it without her consent. Well-off, prudent women could circumvent the law by putting some or all of their property into a trust before they married. (This trust was then held and administered for their benefit according to their own instructions.) But it is estimated that only 10 per cent of all married women were able to take advantage of this loophole in the law. The majority had no right to determine what happened to their property once they were married, or to make use of it. If they continued to work, as many did, they could not enter into contracts or incur any debts and their earnings belonged to their husbands.[9]

Crippling economic injustices such as these meant that women made little headway in employment outside the home and that they spent the bulk of their working lives doing housework. They also ensured that women had no influence over the development of domestic technology. For most of the three centuries discussed in this book, women were the passive beneficiaries (or victims, as the case might be) of changes initiated and brought about by men. They played no part whatsoever in the development of the first four industries that transformed the nature of housework (coal, iron, water, gas) and little in the fifth (electricity). Nor did they invent or improve any time- and labour-saving appliances. In fact they rarely took out patents at all: and when they did, their inventions were trivial. (Devices for boiling and poaching eggs and brushes for sweeping chimneys were typical of those registered in the nineteenth century.) In addition to this, women were consistently slow to grasp the implications of new developments and to promote those that made housework easier. Indeed it was not until Caroline Haslett set up the Electrical Association for Women in 1924 that Britain had any sort of female pressure group lobbying for inprovements in domestic technology.

This extraordinary impotence cannot be blamed on the general inadequacies of female education, or the fact that women received little grounding in science and technology before the twentieth century. For a surprisingly large number of the men who contributed to Britain's industrialization were self-taught. The memoirs and biographies of many scientists, for example, show that they educated themselves by observing what was going on in the world, reading, conducting experiments and, where possible, attending public lectures.[10] Apart from convention, there was absolutely nothing to prevent women from doing the same.

Instead, the explanation lies primarily in women's lack of economic power. All the technological developments that changed housework during the Industrial Revolution and its aftermath could not have occurred without substantial capital investments. But while men had access to capital (which they either inherited or produced by their own efforts), women did not. The principle of primogeniture was strictly held and, unless a woman had no brothers, she did not stand to inherit any real estate* or much of her family's money.[12] Moreover, the average woman did not have good employment prospects; and however she earned her living, she was certain to earn much less than a man. From this it followed that a woman's savings were seldom sufficient to enable her to make investments or to set up a substantial business. No matter how hard she worked and however intelligent she was, there was no way in which she could earn enough to invest in a water supply company or become an iron founder. Then, when a woman married, she lost all financial independence and all opportunity to invest, unless her husband died and she happened to inherit his capital. This did, of course, occur occasionally. Women who ran their own businesses had usually inherited them from their husbands.

Women's inability to influence and direct the development of domestic technology

---

* Land ownership sheds a great deal of light about the distribution of wealth in Britain between 1650 and 1950 and, in particular, the relative economic status of men and women. The data provided by local historians who have studied the enclosure movement show that only a tiny minority of women owned any land at all and those who did tended to own very little of it. Take the Lincolnshire parish of North Thoresby. When it was enclosed by Parliament between 1836 and 1846, the 43 local landowners were named and ranked in order of importance. The largest landowner (a man) owned 865 acres 1 rood and 11 perches

112 *'Advantages of Modern Education', 1825. Chaos reigns in the kitchen because the cook is reading novels! The books behind the cobweb include Wate's* Hymns, *the* Whole Duty of Man, *the* Holy Bible, *and Hannah Glasse's bestseller,* The Art of Cookery made Plain and Easy. *This print is full of interesting details, such as the large roasting screen or 'hastener' placed before the fire and the rug on the stone flags.*

was also the consequence of their political impotence. The significance of the latter did not go unremarked. Mary Astell was arguing for women's political emancipation as early as 1694 in *A Serious Proposal to the Ladies For the Advancement of their true and greatest Interest* and Mary Wollstonecraft helped to popularize the cause in *A Vindication of the Rights of Women* (1792).[13] But it was not until the 1832 Reform Act was passed that the struggle for women's political rights began to gather momentum.[14] The Manchester Society for the Promotion of Women's Suffrage was established in 1865 and two years later John Stuart Mill addressed the first appeal for women's political emancipation to Parliament itself. However, women did not obtain full local government franchise until 1907; and it was only in 1918 that they finally won the right to vote and stand as candidates in parliamentary elections. But even then, women were denied the same electoral rights as men. The parliamentary franchise was restricted to women over the age of 30 who held university degrees or occupied property worth £5 or more a year.

and the smallest landowner (also a man) a mere 20 perches. The sole woman among them, Elizabeth Croft, owned 4 acres 3 roods and 17 perches and ranked number 25 in the hierarchy.[11]

113 *'Hiring a Servant', coloured engraving by Thomas Rowlandson, 1812. A young girl's desire to further her career becomes a salacious joke.*

Given these qualifications it was hardly surprising that the first woman to sit in the House of Commons (Nancy Astor) was no ordinary mortal but a sparkling society hostess married to one of the richest and most influential men in England. Another decade was to elapse before the restrictions were removed: the Suffrage Act of 1928 enfranchized all women over the age of 21.

It is interesting to speculate what would have happened to the history of housework if women had won the vote and been elected to Parliament and local government positions in the mid-nineteenth century. Would they, for example, have speeded up the reform of the laws governing family relations and women's property rights? Might they have supported the efforts of towns and cities to improve their water and gas supplies with greater enthusiasm and foresight then men? And perhaps developed a more realistic legislative strategy for the development of electricity supplies? Is it fanciful to suggest that radical members might have fought for equal educational and employment opportunities for women? It is impossible to tell. It is incontrovertible, however, that women are more effective in promoting their interests when they have economic and political power than when they do not.

CONCLUSION

There can be no doubt that the Industrial Revolution had a profound effect on housework in the British Isles.

In the first place, the growth of certain industries transformed the nature of domestic life. Heating and cooking, for example, were twice revolutionized, first, as a result of the coal-mining boom and secondly, of the manufacture of coal-gas. The phenomenal expansion of the iron industry filled people's houses with the metal. Below ground there were pipes carrying water and gas; above, every conceivable type of domestic appliance, be it a grate, range, iron, mangle, or humble cooking pot. The discovery of a cheap way to manufacture large quantities of soda (and hence soap) in the beginning of the nineteenth century made laundry a far more pleasant and efficient undertaking then it had been previously. The electrical industry illuminated Britain's homes effectively for the first time in history; and, by providing a source of energy suitable for powering time- and labour-saving machines, narrowed the gulf between factory and home.

The scope and locus of housework also changed fundamentally as a result of urbanization. Britain's swelling population crowded into towns and cities at an unprecedented rate and the amenities necessary to support it duly followed. The urban housewife found that she had a much smaller range of domestic duties than her country cousin. She also had less choice as to where she did her housework: there simply was not the space to work out of doors, and, as a consequence, she became increasingly housebound.

In addition, the improved communications that went hand in hand with the growth of urban life had a homogenizing effect on housework. The marked regional differences so characteristic of domestic life in the seventeenth and early eighteenth centuries gradually disappeared. By the end of the nineteenth century, for instance, there were few Scotswomen left who still used their feet to clean floors and vegetables and to trample their laundry. Women increasingly shared the same standards of cleanliness. Local words for common, everyday household objects were being forgotten, as were distinctive local dishes, and dialects were losing their strength.

But the main effect of the Industrial Revolution was to raise the national standard of living to an unprecedented degree and, in the process, to remove most of the back-breaking, soul-destroying drudgery from housework. While the wealthy might have lived equally well in 1650, the bulk of the population was far better off in 1950.

It would be wrong to suppose that this great 'leap forward' was made overnight. Far from it. There was usually a long time lag before new developments found their way to the home. The potential of gas for cooking and heating, for example, was recognized by a handful of people in the mid-seventeenth century, but this only became commercially viable in the 1880s. Similarly, great advances were made in the technology of water supply in the first part of the eighteenth century, but they were not fully exploited until more than a hundred years later when hordes of city-dwellers were dying from water-borne diseases such as cholera. Immense technical and financial problems impeded the development of electric lighting and electric power. In short, scientific discoveries were never sufficient to ensure progress in domestic technology; strong economic reasons for exploiting them were just as necessary.

The impact of the Industrial Revolution on housework was not the same nationwide. There were remarkable variations in the rate at which domestic innovations became accessible to different socio-economic classes or known throughout the British Isles. As might be expected, the rich were the first to benefit from progress in domestic technology and the poor invariably the last.

But geographical location was almost as important as class. Until about 1780, virtually every important innovation originated in London; it would become popular there and in the south of England before gradually spreading to the rest of Britain via a rural network of large country houses belonging to the landed gentry and aristocracy and an urban network of prosperous towns and cities. Thus, during this period, any London household was likely to be better off in terms of domestic technology than its counterpart in the north of England, Scotland, Wales or Ireland. After 1780, however, London began to lose some of its technological and economic pre-eminence and there were many more innovations in other cities. Improved communications relayed them rapidly to smaller centres, from which they advanced more slowly into the surrounding countryside, still using country houses as stepping stones.

The way in which innovations could leapfrog from one place to another meant that at any given time people living in mediaeval conditions coexisted with others who enjoyed every amenity of a subsequent period. In the early 1900s, for example, a substantial proportion of the rural population lacked piped water supplies, gas, and electricity. The central open hearth, with a hole in the roof above, still survived in parts of Ireland and Scotland; and on remote islands, such as Foula and Eriskay, women were still grinding their corn by hand in stone age querns.[1]

It is often thought that the Industrial Revolution undermined women's status. According to one common argument, this happened partly because certain types of production were wrested from women's hands. But this does not really stand up to examination. Food production, as mentioned earlier, was never an exclusively female preserve. It is true that women were generally responsible for baking, but their families shared in the work of raising pigs, and men were often to be found brewing beer, ale, and a host of other alcoholic drinks. Thus, if loss of self-sufficiency damaged women's status, it should also have damaged that of men and children. But there is no evidence that it did; almost nobody complained about the spread of commercial breweries and bakeries or the growth of the retail food market. So long as they had the money, they were glad to buy their food and drink, rather than go to all the trouble of producing it themselves.

Other types of home production, such as rushlight and soap-making, were indeed a female monopoly. But it is hard to believe that women's position in British society was enhanced by the fact that some of them waded into marshes until they were thigh-deep in mud and water to procure rushes which they peeled and dragged repeatedly through vile-smelling hot kitchen fat, sweating profusely as they did so. And it is equally hard to believe that soap-making could have added to their prestige either. Julia Curtis, who was brought up on a sheep farm on the west coast of Scotland in the 1880s, remembers that candle making was a distinctly 'unpleasant operation, owing to the nauseous odour of boiling fat' and that the results were 'crude in the extreme', bearing 'little resemblance to the civilized article'.[2] And it was with disdain and disgust that John Fairfax-Blakeborough describes the 'abominable stinking, yellow, mutton-fat dips' made by Yorkshire wives in the 1880s and 90s.[3]

It is perhaps more plausible to argue that the industrialization of textile production had an adverse effect on women's status. For here, at last, is an example of a thoroughly respected, skilled cottage industry dominated by women (though not run by them) that factories brought to rapid extinction in the late eighteenth and early nineteenth centuries. But even this case has its difficulties. Firstly, not all women were engaged in producing textiles before the Industrial Revolution. Even in 1650, the main clusters of women to be found knitting, spinning or weaving in their homes were in Scotland, the north of England, Wales and Ireland. Secondly, industrialization did not oust women from textile production at all: substantial numbers of women worked in textile-producing factories in the nineteenth and twentieth centuries.

If women's status was not necessarily undermined by their ceasing to engage in certain types of production, what about the other side of the argument? This maintains that Britain was transformed into a cash economy as a result of the Industrial Revolution. Women, no longer producing essential domestic commodities and earning at least one-third less than men, were put at a grave disadvantage. Everything that they and their families consumed had to be bought for money, and primarily with their husbands' earnings. They therefore became almost completely dependent on men, suffering a major loss of status not only in their marital relationships but in society as a whole.

At first sight this thesis sounds convincing enough, especially as women were very much the second sex when Marx and Engels developed their capitalist interpretation of industrialization. There are, however, some serious objections to it. In the first place, the theory confuses cash with capital and greatly underestimates the former's prevalence in pre-industrial Britain. It is true that the flow of money became increasingly noticeable from the late eighteenth century onwards: the population was growing rapidly; more and more people were living in towns and cities where they could not produce their own food and drink and had to buy it; and factories were producing an amazing array of new goods to buy. But that is not to say that cash was unimportant in the sixteenth and seventeenth centuries. Far from it. It is clear from account books and diaries that virtually everything, be it labour or goods, was bought for money. Bartering arrangements and payments in kind existed, of course, but only on a small scale and they were usually made in conjunction with an exchange of cash. That women lived in a world where money did count can be seen in their eagerness to sell their surplus foodstuffs and handicrafts. And they were fully aware of the monetary value of their labour: the going rates for different types of female domestic servant were common knowledge.

More importantly, the theory glosses over the fact that men rather than women owned the means of production in both pre-industrial and industrialized Britain. The housewife who 'brewed her own beer' and who 'spun her own yarn' was not the independent entrepreneuse that many would have us believe. She was processing raw ingredients derived from land owned or rented by her husband and grown through his labour and that of the servants he paid to help him. Alternatively, the raw materials had been bought with his cash. The same applied to butter, cheese, candle and soap-making: a woman did not generally own the animals from which her ingredients came. She also depended on her husband to buy the expensive equipment necessary for production (brewing utensils and spinning wheels, for example, were not cheap). Seen in this light, the Industrial Revolution did not affect the essential features of women's economic position. The only change was that the men who owned the means of production and derived their profit from women's labour were no longer relations but strangers. Meanwhile the other factors determining women's economic standing – access to skilled and lucrative jobs and the differential between male and female pay rates – hardly changed.

Nor did the Industrial Revolution revolutionize family life or disturb the traditional division of labour between the sexes. Pre-industrial Britain was no golden age in which men and women clustered round their homesteads, each sex participating in the other's activities: it was an extremely hierarchical society in which men and women had different roles to play.[4] Women bore children and took care of the home. Men went out to work to earn their living. If they lived in the country, they would generally be out of doors all day long, tilling the land. If they lived in a town or city, they would also work away from home. Some men, of course, had businesses situated in their homes or adjacent to them. However, there was usually a sharp architectural line between the business premises and the home. And the fact of proximity did not mean that a wife participated in the business or ran it on an equal footing with her husband: her place was very much at home, even if home was only next door.

This division of labour between the sexes did not change in any fundamental way as a result of industrialization and urbanization. Women were still expected to produce children and do housework and those who did not were the subject of severe disapproval. Sir Charles Shaw, for example, was horrified at the way female factory operatives in Manchester in the 1830s and 40s were 'totally unequal to fulfil any domestic duty'; they left their babies and young children in the care of neighbours, who drugged them with quack medicines, neglected to clean and rarely did any cooking, much preferring to eat out at a beer-house.[5] In the same way, men were still expected to work away from home and support their wives and children.

Does Britain, as the first country in the world to undergo rapid industrialization and urbanization, offer a model of their impact on domestic life? Can it be said, for example, that their main effect is to remove a great deal of hard physical labour and misery from women's work? And that this is due to the spread of utilities such as water, gas and electricity and the development of a sophisticated manufacturing and distribution system for food and other goods, rather than the invention of time-and labour-saving appliances?

Similarly, is it true that industrial revolutions do not have much further impact on housework? In other words, the time spent on individual household tasks may change and their scope may be redefined, but housework remains women's primary occupation. The traditional division of labour between the sexes is not fundamentally altered.

It should be added at this point that the British model does not appear to have changed significantly since 1950; the post-war era has not revealed any novel, hitherto unrecognized, facets of the industrialization process which throw the history of housework between 1650 and 1950 into a new perspective. There have, however, been several interesting developments which are worth mentioning by way of postscript. For one, the pace of change in housework has speeded up. The break-throughs in domestic technology made in the three previous centuries have rapidly become accessible to the majority of the population. By the end of the sixties, most households in Britain had water, gas, and electricity laid on and were buying time- and labour-saving appliances on a substantial scale.[6] When new products, such as detergents, or materials like plastics were developed, they immediately became available for home use: the old tendency for innovations to reach the domestic market only after other outlets had been saturated was at last broken.

In addition, the post-war era has seen a plethora of new gadgets and appliances. None of them has actually eliminated household tasks, but several have sharply reduced the time required to carry them out. Food processors, for example, have made it possible to prepare all sorts of foods at great speed and microwave ovens to defrost and cook meals in minutes.

Some interesting changes in people's attitudes to housework have also occurred, following the women's liberation movement which sprang up in the late 1960s. When a small group of radical feminists decided that women should receive wages for doing housework, they did not get a sympathetic response. But their campaign helped to spread the notion that housework does constitute a form of 'productive' labour and should, in principle, be accounted for in the gross national product. A few social scientists also became aware that housework deserves as much attention as any other occupation; by the mid-1970s, Ann Oakley had launched the sociology of housework as an acceptable field of enquiry.[7]

Leaders of the women's liberation movement have also attacked the belief that babies and small children under school age need to be looked after *exclusively* by their *mothers*, *at home*, if they are not to suffer irreparable psychological and educational harm. They have pointed out that children need the care of their fathers too, and that in other societies they are cared for by several adults at a time and positively benefit from the variety of different stimuli. As a consequence of this belief, the feminists argued, women were excluded from full participation in the work force during their childbearing years and forced to become housewives. Men had no reason to assume equal responsibility for bringing up their offspring; the state was absolved of any obligation to provide childcare facilities; and employers were under no pressure to introduce paternity leave or flexible working hours for parents who wished to leave their jobs early to collect their children from school or take unpaid leave to look after them when they were ill or on holiday.

Somewhat predictably, women's demands for free crèches, nurseries, and 'flexi-time' attracted little political support. 'Far too difficult' and 'the country simply can't afford it' was the absurd but united response from bureaucrat and employer alike. And when unemployment worsened in the late '70s and early '80s, this lack of support for working mothers hardened into opposition. The debate, however, served a useful purpose in illuminating those features of Britain's ideological, economic and institutional framework that conspire to keep women at home. Furthermore, the dogma that women are morally obliged to bear the main responsibility for childcare (and, by implication, housework) had been rudely challenged.

Finally, 'women's lib' as it is often called, has created considerable social pressure on men to do housework. Increasing numbers of men, especially in the middle classes, have started to cook, shop and wash-up, many with evident enjoyment. But the ancient taboos against men doing cleaning and hand laundry remain almost as strong as ever. And very few men have come to share housework on an equal basis with women or opted to become 'house husbands'.

Appendix:
'A Woman's Work is Never Done'

A BALLAD (*seventeenth-century version*)

Here is a Song for Maids to sing,
Both in the Winter and the Spring;
It is such a pretty conceited thing,
Which will much pleasure to them bring;
Maids may set still, go, or run,
But a Woman's Work is never done.

As I was wandring on the way,
I heard a married Woman say,
That she had lived a sollid life,
Ever since the time she was made a wife.
For why (quoth she) my Labor is hard,
And all my pleasures are debarr'd;
Both Morning, Evening, Night and Noon,
I'm sure a Woman's Work is never done.

And now (quoth she) I will relate
The manner of my Woful Fate;
And how myself I do bestow,
As all my neighbours well do know;
And therein all that will it hear,
Unto my song I pray a while give ear;
I'le make it plainly to appear right soon,
How that a Woman's Work is never done.

For when that I rise early in the morn,
Before that I my head with dressings
  adorn,
I sweep and cleane the house as need
  doth require,
Or, if that it be cold, I make a fire:
Then my Husband's breakfast I must
  dress,
To fill his belly with some wholesome
  mess;
Perhaps, thereof, I eat a little or none,
But I'm sure a Woman's Work is never done.

Next thing that I in order do,
My children must be lookt unto;
Then I take them from their naked Beds,
To put on their clothes, and comb their
  heads;
And then what hap so ever do betide,
Their breakfast straight I must provide,
Bread cries my Daughter, and Drink my
  Son,
And thus a Woman's Work is never done.

And when that I have filled their bellies
  full,
Some of them I pack away to School,
All save one sucking Childe, that at my
  breast,
Doth knaw and bite, and sorely me
  molest:
But when I have laid him down to sleep,
I am Constrain'd the house to keep,
For then the Pottage Pot I must hang on,
And thus a Woman's Work is never done.

And when my pottage pot is ready to boil,
I must be careful all the while;
And for to scum the pot is my desire,
Or else the fat will run i' th' fire;
But when th' eleven a clock bell it doth
  chime,
Then I know 'tis near upon dinner time;
To lay the Table-cloth I then do run,
And thus a Woman's Work is never done.

References and notes to text

INTRODUCTION

1 – These figures are no more than estimates; the first census was not held until 1801. For a useful discussion of demographic developments during the Industrial Revolution see Tranter, Neil L., *Population since the Industrial Revolution. The case of England and Wales*, Harper & Row, U.S.A., 1973.

2 – Law, C. M., 'Some Notes on the Urban Population of England and Wales in the Eighteenth Century' in *The Local Historian. The Quarterly Journal of the Standing Conference for Local History*, vol. 10, no. 1, 1972, pp. 13–26.

3 – For maps and a useful summary of these developments see: Darby, Henry Clifford, *A New Historical Geography of England after 1600*, Cambridge University Press, Cambridge, 1976.

4 – Tranter, *Population since the Industrial Revolution*, pp. 51–2.

5 – Harrison, George and Mitchell, Frank C., *The Book of Facts about People*, Allen & Unwin, London, 1950, p. 40.

CHAPTER I WATER

1 – Jennings, Louis J., *Field paths and green lanes: being country walks, chiefly in Surrey and Sussex*, Murray, London, 1877, p. 252.

2 – Green, John Little, *English Country Cottages: Their Condition, Cost, and Requirements*, The Rural World Publishing Company, London, 1900, p. 171.

3 – Kalm, Pehr, *Kalm's account of his visit to England on his way to America in 1748*, Macmillan, London and New York, 1892, pp. 148–9.

4 – Thompson, Flora, *Lark Rise to Candleford*, Oxford University Press, London, 1945, p. 8.

5 – Kalm, *Kalm's account of his visit to England*, p. 228. For further information about animal-powered water raising machinery, see: Elliot, J. Steele, 'Bygone Water Supplies' in *The Bedfordshire Historical Record Society: Survey of Ancient Buildings*, vol. 2, published by the society in conjunction with the Public Museum, Luton, 1933; Brunner, Hugo and Major, J. Kenneth, 'Water raising by Animal Power' in *Industrial Archaeology. The Journal of the History of Industry and Technology*, vol. 9, no.

2, May 1972, pp. 117–51; Brunner, Hugo, 'Relics of the Wheelwright's craft. Donkey Wheels as a Source of Power' in *Country Life*, Dec. 28, 1972, pp. 1770–1; Brunner, Hugo, 'Circular Horse Power. The Rotary Animal Engine' in *Country Life*, March 2, 1978, pp. 557–9.

6 – Robinson, Maude, *A South Down farm in the sixties*, Dent, London, 1938, pp. 16–20.

7 – Rowntree, Benjamin Seebohm and Kendall, May, *How the labourer lives: a study of the rural labour problem*, Nelson, London, 1913, p. 330.

8 – Royal Commission on Housing in Scotland, *Report of the Royal Commission on the Housing of the Industrial Population of Scotland Rural and Urban*, H.M.S.O., Edinburgh, 1917, p. 168.

9 – Great Britain, Scottish Housing Advisory Committee, *Report on Rural Housing in Scotland*, H.M.S.O., Edinburgh, 1937, p. 84.

10 – Fiennes, Celia, *The Journeys of Celia Fiennes, Edited and with an Introduction by Christopher Morris*, Cresset Press, London, 1949, p. 86.

11 – Colston, James, *The Edinburgh and District Water Supply. A historical sketch*, Colston and company, printers, Edinburgh, 1890, p. 49.

12 – Loudan, Jack, *In search of water; being a history of the Belfast water supply*, W. Mullan, Belfast, 1940, p. 34.

13 – Cossins, James, *Reminiscences of Exeter fifty years since*, Printed for the author by W. Pollard, Exeter, 1877, pp. 56–7.

14 – Great Britain, Health of Towns Commission, *Report on the State of Newcastle-upon-Tyne and other towns. By David Boswell Reid, Esq., M.D. One of the Commissioners appointed by Her Majesty for Inquiring into the State of Large Towns and Populous Districts in England and Wales*, H.M.S.O., London, 1845, pp. 99–100.

15 – Great Britain, Health of Towns Commission, *Second Report of the Commissioners for Inquiring into the State of Large Towns and Populous Districts*, H.M.S.O., London, 1845, vol. 2, p. 124.

16 – *Ibid.*, vol. 1, p. 220.

17 – *Ibid.*, vol. 1, pp. 90–1.

18 – Hutton, Catherine, *Reminiscences of a gentlewoman of the last century: letters of Catherine Hutton . . . , Ed. by her cousin, Mrs Catherine Hutton Beale . . .*, Cornish Brothers,

Birmingham, 1891, p. 52.

19 – Clarke, Edward Daniel, *A tour through the south of England, Wales, and part of Ireland, made during the summer of 1791 . . .* , Printed at the Minerva Press, for R. Edwards, London, 1793, pp. 348–9.

20 – Mitchell, William Cranmer, *History of Sunderland*; with a foreword by Samuel Hoole, Hills Press, Sunderland, 1919, p. 103.

21 – Colston, *The Edinburgh and District Water Supply*, p. 43.

22 – Firth, John, *Reminiscences of an Orkney Parish together with old Orkney words, riddles and proverbs*, Orkney natural history society, Stromness, 1974, p. 11.

23 – Pacey, Arnold (ed.), *Water for the thousand millions. Written by the Water Panel of the Intermediate Technology Development Group founded by Dr. E. F. Schumacher*, Pergamon Press, Oxford, New York, 1977, p. 34.

24 – Great Britain, Health of Towns Commission, *Second Report . . . for Inquiring into the State of Large Towns and Populous Districts*, vol. 2, p. 37.

25 – Great Britain, General Board of Health, *Report by the General Board of Health on the supply of water to the Metropolis (presented to both Houses of Parliament)*, H.M.S.O., London, 1850, pp. 150–3.

26 – Royal Society of Arts, London, *National Water Supply. Notes on Previous Inquiries, prepared in connexion with the Congress, held Tuesday and Wednesday, 21st and 22nd May, 1878*, Bell, London, 1878, part 5 'On the supply of rural districts and small towns'.

27 – Thresh, John Clough, *Housing of the Agricultural Labourer With special reference to the County of Essex*, Rural Housing and Sanitation Association, Chelmsford, 1919, p. 42.

28 – Great Britain, General Board of Health, *Report . . . on the supply of water to the Metropolis*, p. 136.

29 – Great Britain, Health of Towns Commission, *First Report of the Commissioners for Inquiring into the State of Large Towns and Populous Districts*, vol. 2, p. 125.

30 – Great Britain, Health of Towns Commission, *Second Report . . . for Inquiring into the State of Large Towns and Populous Districts*, vol. 2, p. 14.

31 – *Ibid.*, vol. 1, p. 89.

32 – World Health Organization, 'Community Water Supply and Sewage Disposal in Developing Countries' in *World Health Statistics*, vol. 26, no. 11, 1973. (The figures, given in litres, are here converted into gallons to facilitate comparisons.)

33 – United States, Water Resources Council, *The Nation's Water Resources 1975–2000*, Washington D.C., 1978, vol. 2, part 3, p. 20. (The figure, given in U.S. gallons, has been converted to the British measure.)

34 – Bathgate, Janet, *Aunt Janet's legacy to her nieces; recollections of a humble life in Yarrow in the beginning of the century*, G. Lewis, Selkirk, 1894, pp. 54, 62.

35 – Marshall, Sybil, *Fenland Chronicle: recollections of William Henry and Kate Mary Edwards collected and edited by their daughter*, Cambridge University Press, London, 1967, pp. 172–4.

36 – Johnson, Clifton, *Among English hedgerows*, Macmillan, London and New York, 1899, p. 232.

37 – Browne, J. H. Balfour, *Water Supply*, Macmillan, London, 1880, pp. 48–51.

38 – Great Britain, General Register Office, *Census 1951. England and Wales: Housing Report*, H.M.S.O., London, 1956, chapter 8.

39 – Morton, John, *The natural history of Northamptonshire; with some account of the antiquities. To which is annex'd a translation of Dooms-day book so far as it relates to that county*, R. Knaplock and R. Wilkin, London, 1712, p. 495.

40 – James, John, *The Theory and Practice of Gardening: Wherein is fully handled All that relates to Fine Gardens, commonly called Pleasure-Gardens, As Parterres, Groves, Bowling-Greens*, etc . . ., Geo. James, London, 1712, p. 191.

41 – Mons. Sorbière, *A Voyage to England, Containing many Things relating to the State of Learning, Religion, And other Curiosities of that Kingdom*, J. Woodward, London, 1709, pp. 15, 29.

42 – Hatton, Edward, *A new view of London; or, An ample account of that city, in . . . eight sections. Being a more particular description thereof than has hitherto been known to be published of any city in the world . . .* , Printed for J. Nicholson [etc.], London, 1708, pp. 791–3.

43 – Sorbière, *A Voyage to England*, pp. 32–3.

44 – Galloway, Robert L., *Annals of Coal Mining and the Coal Trade. The Invention of the Steam Engine and the Origin of the Railway*, The Colliery Guardian Co., London, 1898, p. 158.

45 – J. C., *The compleat collier; or, The whole art of sinking, getting and working, coal-mines, etc., as is now used in the northern parts, especially about Sunderland and Newcastle*, G. Conyers, London, 1708, p. 24.

46 – Sorbière, *A Voyage to England*, p. 29.

47 – Dickinson, Henry Winram, *A short history*

of the steam engine, Cambridge University Press, Cambridge, 1939, pp. 14–15.

48 – For details about Morland see: Dickinson, Henry Winram, *Sir Samuel Morland Diplomat and Inventor 1625–1695*, Heffer, Cambridge, 1970.

49 – Dickinson, *A short history of the steam engine*, pp. 18–28.

50 – Savery, Thomas, *The Miner's Friend; or, An Engine to raise Water by Fire, described. And of the manner of fixing it in mines; with an account of the several other uses it is applicable unto; and an answer to the objetions made against it*, Printed for S. Crouch, London, 1702, pp. 30–1, 41–5.

51 – Bradley, Richard, *New Improvements of Planting and Gardening, both philosophical and practical . . .*, W. Mears, London, 1720, pp. 175–9.

52 – Desaguliers, John Theophilus, *A Course of Experimental Philosophy*, W. Innys etc., London, 1745, vol. 2, pp. 466–7.

53 – For an account of the steam engine's development see: Triewald, Mårten, *Short Description of the Atmospheric Engine Published at Stockholm, 1734, Translated from the Swedish with foreword, introduction and notes*, Newcomen Society, London, 1928; Farey, John, *A treatise of the steam engine, historical, practical and descriptive*, Longman, [etc.], London, 1827; Dickinson, *A short history of the steam engine*, 1939; Stowers, Arthur, 'The development of the atmospheric steam engine after Newcomen's death in 1729' and Mott, R. A., 'The Newcomen Engine in the 18th century', in *Transactions of the Newcomen Society for the study of the history of engineering and technology*, vol. 35, 1962–3, London, 1964; Rolt, Lionel Thomas Caswell and Allen, J. S., *The steam engine of Thomas Newcomen*, Science History Publications, New York, 1977.

54 – Williamson, F., 'George Sorocold, of Derby. A pioneer of water supply' in the *Journal of the Derbyshire Archaeological and Natural History Society*, Kendal, 1936, vol. 10.

55 – Desaguliers, *A Course of Experimental Philosophy*, vol. 2, pp. 414, 528.

56 – Vream, William, *A description of the air-pump, according to the late Mr Hawksbee's best and last improvements*, Printed by J. H. for the author, London, 1717, advertisement at end.

57 – Switzer, Stephen, *An introduction to a general system of hydrostaticks and hydraulicks, philosophical and practical*, T. Astley and L. Gilliver, London, 1729, vol. 2, pp. 351–2.

58 – Desaguliers, *A Course of Experimental Philosophy*, vol. 2, p. 414.

59 – The main sources for Desaguliers' life are his numerous books and articles, the Brydges manuscripts at the Huntington Library, Pasadena, California, and the D.N.B.

60 – Desaguliers was not the first person to write seriously about waterworks. In addition to the books already cited see: Caus, Isaac de, *New and Rare Inventions of Water-Works Shewing the Easiest waies to Raise Water Higher then the Spring* [translated from the French by John Leak], Joseph Moxon, London, 1659; D'Acres, R., *The art of water-drawing, published by Henry Brome, at the Gun in Ivie Lane, London 1659 and 1660, with introduction and diagram by Rhys Jenkins*, Newcomen Society, Cambridge, 1930; Mandey, Venterus and Moxon, J., *Mechanick powers: or, The mistery of nature and art unvail'd, shewing what great things may be perform'd by mechanick engines, in removing and raising bodies of vast weights with little strength, or force*, Printed for the author, London, 1696; Ozanam, Jacques, *Cursus mathematicus: or, A compleat course of the mathematicks* [translated from the French by John Theophilus Desaguliers], J. Nicholson, London, 1712; Switzer, Stephen, *Ichnographia rustica; or, the nobleman, gentleman, and gardener's recreation*, D. Browne, London, 1718; Mariotte, Edmé, *The motion of water, and other fluids. Being A treatise of hydrostaticks . . . Together with little treatise of the same author, giving practical rules for fountains, or jets d'eau* [translated from the French by John Theophilus Desaguliers], J. Senex etc., London, 1718; Barlow, Edward, *An exact survey of the tide . . . To which is added, A clear and succinct description of an engine, which fetcheth water out of the deep, and raiseth it to the height design'd, progressively, by the same motion*, T. Woodward, London, 1722; *The builder's dictionary: or, Gentleman and architect's companion . . .*, A. Bettesworth and C. Hitch etc., London, 1734.

61 – The Chelsea Waterworks Company, for example, was forced to build a series of steam engines along its stretch of the Thames during the second half of the eighteenth century because the current was not sufficiently strong to turn water wheels and because horse engines were too expensive. Faulkner, Thomas, *An historical and topographical description of Chelsea, and its environs . . .*, T. Faulkner etc., Chelsea, 1829, vol. 1, pp. 48–50.

62 – For further details about the growing demand for water closets and baths during the first two decades of the nineteenth century see: Matthews, William, *Hydraulia; an historical and descriptive account of the waterworks of London, and the contrivances for supplying other great cities,*

in different ages and countries, Simkin, Marshall and Co., London, 1835, p. 64 and Great Britain, Health of Towns Commission, *Second Report for Inquiring into the State of Large Towns and Populous Districts*, vol. 2, pp. 101–2.

63 – Matthews, *Hydraulia*, pp. 66–71.

64 – Cleland, James, *Annals of Glasgow, comprising an account of the public buildings, charities, and the rise and progress of the city*, James Hedderwick, Glasgow, 1816, pp. 397–8.

65 – Hemingway, Joseph, *History of the city of Chester, from its foundation to the present time*, Chester, 1831, p. 340.

66 – Faulkner, *An historical and topographical description of Chelsea*, pp. 50–2.

67 – See introduction p. 2.

68 – Great Britain, Health of Towns Commission, *First Report of the Commissioners for Inquiring into the State of Large Towns and Populous Districts*, vol. 1, pp. 122–3.

69 – Chadwick, Edwin, *Report on the Sanitary Condition of the Labouring Population of Great Britain* contained in the *Report to Her Majesty's Principal Secretary of State for the Home Department, from the Poor Law Commissioners, on an Inquiry into the Sanitary Condition of the Labouring Population of Great Britain; with appendices, Presented to both Houses of Parliament, by Command of Her Majesty*, July, 1842, H.M.S.O., London, 1842, p. 63.

70 – See Great Britain, Health of Towns Commission, *First* and *Second Reports*.

71 – Snow, John, *On the mode of communication of cholera*, 2d ed., much enl., J. Churchill, London, 1855.

72 – Great Britain, General board of Health, *Report . . . on the supply of water to the Metropolis*, p. 15.

73 – Stewart, Alexander Patrick and Jenkins, Edward, *The Medical and Legal Aspects of Sanitary Reform, with an introduction by M. W. Flinn*. Leicester University Press, New York, 1969, p. 76.

74 – For a general account of municipal trading in the nineteenth century see: Dolman, Frederick, *Municipalities at work; the municipal policy of six great towns and its influence on their social welfare*, Methuen, London, 1895.

75 – As the Rivers Pollution Commission of 1868 proved, it was absolutely foolhardy to draw urban water supplies from shallow wells, streams and rivers. Great Britain, Rivers Pollution Commission, *Sixth Report of the Commissioners appointed in 1868 to inquire into the best means of preventing the pollution of rivers. The Domestic Water Supply of Great Britain*, H.M.S.O., London, 1874, p. 425.

76 – For the history of Manchester's water supplies see: Aston, Joseph, *A picture of Manchester*, Printed and published by the author, Manchester, 1816; Bateman, John Frederic La Trobe, *History and description of the Manchester Waterworks*, E. and F. N. Spon, London, 1884; Simon, Shena Dorothy (Potter) Lady, *A century of city government, Manchester 1838–1938*, Allen & Unwin, London, 1938.

77 – For the history of Glasgow's water supplies see: Cleland, *Annals of Glasgow*; Bell, Sir James and Paton, James, *Glasgow; its municipal organization and administration*, J. MacLehose, Glasgow, 1896; The Corporation of the City of Glasgow, *Handbook on the municipal enterprise*, [no imprint], Glasgow, 1931.

78 – For the history of Bradford's water supplies see: James, John, *The history and topography of Bradford (in the county of York) with topographical notices of its parish*, Longman etc., London, 1841, p. 118; Cudworth, William, *Historical notes on the Bradford Corporation, with records of the lighting and watching commissioners and Board of highway surveyors*, T. Brear, Bradford, 1881, p. 225.

79 – Butler, Christina Violet, *Social conditions in Oxford*, Sidgwick and Jackson, London, 1912, p. 105.

80 – Smith, Hubert Llewellyn (ed.), *The new survey of London life and labour*, King, London, 1934, vol. 6, chapter 12, p. 318.

81 – Great Britain, Rivers Pollution Commission, *Sixth Report . . . The Domestic Water Supply of Great Britain*, p. 414.

82 – Sayle, Amy, *The Houses of the Workers*, Fisher Unwin, London, 1924, pp. 57–8.

83 – Great Britain, Ministry of Health Advisory Committee on Water, *Report on rural water supplies*, London, 1929, appendix B, p. 26.

84 – Great Britain, Ministry of Health, Ministry of Agriculture and Fisheries, Department of Health for Scotland, *A National Water Policy*, H.M.S.O., London, 1944, pp. 6, 15, 25.

85 – In addition, 46 per cent of the farms in the Cotswolds and 62 per cent in the Vales of Evesham, Gloucester, and Berkeley still lacked internal supplies. See: Payne, Gordon Edgar, *A survey of Gloucestershire: a physical, social and economic survey and plan*, [no imprint], Gloucester, 1946, pp. 183, 196.

86 – Take the Aran Islands off the west coast, for example. When Thomas Mason visited them in the early 1930s he found that: 'Water is brought from the wells, in a small barrel called a tankard, which when full is a considerable weight and it is astonishing how the young girls and women are able to carry

them.' See: Mason, Thomas H., *The islands of Ireland; their scenery, people, life and antiquities,* Batsford, London, 1937, pp. 78–9.

87–Mogey, John M., *Rural Life in Northern Ireland; five regional studies made for the Northern Ireland Council of Social Services, Inc.,* Oxford University Press, London, New York, 1947, p. 208

88–Great Britain, General Register Office, *Census 1951,* chapter 8.

CHAPTER 2 GAS AND ELECTRICITY

1–Fiennes, Celia, *The journeys of Celia Fiennes, Edited and with an Introduction by Christopher Morris,* Cresset Press, London, 1947, p. 186.

2–Cochrane, Thomas, 10th Earl of Dundonald, *The Autobiography of a seaman,* Richard Bentley, London, 1860, vol. 1, pp. 39–40.

3–See: Accum, Frederick, *A practical treatise on gas-light; exhibiting a summary description of the apparatus and machinery best calculated for illuminating streets, houses, and manufactories, with carburetted hydrogen, or coal-gas; with remarks on the utility, safety, and general nature of this new branch of civil economy,* R. Ackermann, London, 1815; Matthews, William, *A historical sketch of the origin, progress, and present state of gas-lighting,* Rowland Hunter, London, 1827; Williams, Trevor I., *A History of the British Gas Industry,* Oxford University Press, 1981.

4–Timmins, Samuel, *William Murdock,* [A biographical sketch], [no imprint], 1894, p. 6.

5–Matthews, *A historical sketch,* p. 23.

6–For a valuable note on Samuel Clegg's career by E. F. Armstrong see *The Journal of the Royal Society of Arts,* Annual Report of Council Session, 1938–39, London, July 7, 1939, pp. 887–90.

7–Falkus, M. E., 'The British Gas Industry before 1850' in *Economic History Review,* 2nd series, vol. XX, no. 3, Dec. 1967.

8–For an excellent summary of the early history of electricity in Britain see: Byatt, Ian Charles Rayner, *The British Electrical Industry 1875–1914. The economic returns to a new technology,* Clarendon Press, Oxford, 1979.

9–London's public electricity supply can be dated to 1889–92. The first provincial power station opened in Bradford in 1889. (Byatt, *The British Electrical Industry,* pp. 96, 105.)

10–Rookes E. B. Crompton lit his house in Dec. 1879/Jan. 1880. Sir Joseph Swan illuminated his in 1880 and in the same year installed a hydro-electric generator to light the library at Cragside, the Northumberland

country house of Sir William Armstrong, a wealthy industrialist and inventor. For details about the slump in gas shares see *A newspaper account of electric lighting taken principally from The Times (1878–1891)* at the British Library.

11–*International Electric and Gas Exhibition at the Crystal Palace, 1882–83,* London, 1883, vols. 1 and 2 contain the Report on Gas.

12–Prepayment or 'penny in the slot' meters were first manufactured in 1887 by Messrs W. Parkinson (*Gas Journal Centenary Volume,* 1949, see article on the Parkinson and Cowan group). By the beginning of this century they were judged to have 'wrought a veritable revolution in the domestic arrangements of that large section of town dwellers who cannot afford to run quarterly bills'. (Webber, William Hosgood Young, *Town gas and its uses for the production of light, heat, and motive power,* A. Constable, London, 1907, p. 155.) In 1945 about 65 per cent of all domestic gas sales took place through prepayment meters. (Great Britain, Ministry of Fuel and Power, *The Gas Industry. Report of the Committee of Enquiry,* H.M.S.O., London, 1945, p. 21.)

13–The Richmond Gas Stove and Meter Company, for example, which was established in Warrington in 1890, opened its first London show rooms in 1895. By 1901 it had show rooms in Plymouth, Bournemouth, Boscombe and Dublin too. (*Gas Journal,* vol. 152, Oct. – Dec. 1920, pp. 391–3.)

14–Chandler, Philip, *The British gas industry: an economic study,* Manchester University Press, Manchester, 1938, pp. 7–8. The gas industry continued to grow between the two world wars, but at a slower rate. Gas sales rose by 27 per cent between 1920 and 1938. (Great Britain, Ministry of Fuel and Power, *Report,* p. 4.)

15–Political and Economic Planning, *Report on the gas industry in Great Britain, a survey of the current trends and problems of the industry, with proposals for its future development,* P.E.P., London, 1939, p. 49. The gas industry had no accurate way of ascertaining the quantities of gas sold for different purposes or the number and types of gas appliance in use.

16–*Ibid.,* p. 50.

17–' "A pioneer" Colonel R. E. Crompton' in *The Electrical Age,* Electrical Association for Women, London, vol. 2, no. 21, July 1935.

18–Much of the electricity used before 1914 was generated by individual consumers.

19–Byatt, *The British Electrical Industry,* pp. 22–3. This was due to the development of the incandescent gas mantle and burner in the 1890s and the gas industry's determination to expand domestic sales. (For further details see chapter 5 on lighting.)

20–Byatt, *The British Electrical Industry*, p. 23. For a detailed description of metal filament lamps and their superiority to incandescent carbon lamps, see Taylor, Frederick Henry, *How to use electric light (with increased economy and efficiency) including a chapter on electric heating*, Percival Marshall, London, 1910, pp. 7–10 and Fleming, John A., *Fifty years of electricity; the memories of an electrical engineer*, The Wireless Press, London, 1921, pp. 162–6.

21–Hannah, Leslie, *Electricity before nationalization. A study of the development of the electricity supply industry in Britain to 1948*, The Johns Hopkins University Press, Baltimore and London, 1979, p. 186.

22–Corley, Thomas Anthony Buchanan, *Domestic electrical appliances*, Cape, London, 1966, p. 19.

23–Political and Economic Planning, *Report on the supply of electricity in Great Britain, a survey of present-day problems of the industry with proposals for reorganization of electricity distribution*, P.E.P., London, 1936.

24 – Hannah, *Electricity before nationalization*, p. 187.

25–*Ibid.*, p. 159.

26–Corley, *Domestic electrical appliances*, p. 19 and Browne, Geoffrey, *Patterns of British Life. A study of certain aspects of the British people at home, at work, and at play, and a compilation of some relevant statistics*, Hulton Research, London, 1950, p. 103.

27–Corley, *Domestic electrical appliances*, p. 16.

28–Lancaster, Mrs, *Electric Cooking, Heating, Cleaning, etc., being a Manual of Electricity in the Service of the Home*, Constable, London, 1914, p. 8.

29–Crompton, Rookes Evelyn Bell, *Reminiscences*, Constable, London, 1928, pp. 108–9, 110–11.

30–Appleyard, Rollo, *The History of the Institution of Electrical Engineers (1871–1931)*, The Institution of Electrical Engineers, London, 1939, p. 167.

31–Crompton, *Reminiscences*, p. 109.

32–For further details of Caroline Haslett's career see: Messenger, R. *The doors of opportunity: a biography of Dame Caroline Haslett, D.B.E., Companion I.E.E.*, Macdonald; Femina, London, 1967.

33–The E.A.W. was originally called the Women's Electrical Association.

34–See for example: Haslett, Caroline (ed.), *The electrical handbook for women*, Electrical Association for Women, London, 1934, and

Household Electricity, The English Universities Press, London, 1942.

35–Randell, Wilfred J., *Electricity and woman; 21 years of progress*, Electrical Association for Women, London, 1945, p. 59.

36 – Messenger, *The doors of opportunity*, pp. 43–5.

37–Scott, Peggy, *An electrical adventure*, J. Truscott and Sons, Electrical Association for Women, London, 1934, p. 32.

38–Edwards, Elsie E., *Report on electricity in working-class homes*, Electrical Association for Women, London, 1935, table 7.

39–Browne, *Patterns of British life*, p. 103.

CHAPTER 3 COOKING

1–Wilson, C. Anne, *Food and Drink in Britain*, Constable, London, 1973.

2–See *Petits Propos Culinaires*, Prospect Books, London.

3–See, for example: Brears, Peter, C. D., *The Kitchen Catalogue*, Castle Museum, York, 1979; Jekyll, Gertrude and Jones, Sydney Roberts, *Old English Household Life*, Batsford, London, 1939; Lindsay, John Seymour, *Iron and brass implements of the English house*, The Medici Society, London and Boston, 1927; Peate, Iowerth Cyfeiliog, *Guide to the Collection of Welsh Bygones*, National Museum of Wales, Cardiff, 1929; *The Welsh house; a study in folk culture*, The Honourable Society of Cymmrodorion, London, 1940; and *Tradition and folk life: a Welsh view*, Faber and Faber, London, 1972.

4–Cash, Margaret (ed.), *Devon Inventories of the sixteenth and seventeenth centuries*, Devon and Cornwall Record Society, new series, vol. 11, 1966.

5–Emmison, F. G., *Jacobean household inventories*, Publications of the Bedfordshire Historical Record Society, vol. 20, 1938.

6–Halliwell-Phillips, James Orchard, *The Yorkshire anthology, a collection of ancient and modern ballads, poems and songs, relating to the county of Yorkshire*, printed for private circulation by C. and J. Adlard, London, 1851, p. 69.

7–Buchanan, John Lanne, *Travels in the western Hebrides: from 1782 to 1790*, printed for G. G. J. and J. Robinson [etc.], London, 1793, pp. 111–12. Similarly primitive pot-hanging arrangements survived in Ireland and Orkney until the mid-nineteenth century.

8–According to a Northumberland clergyman, Hastings M. Neville, the chimney crane was only introduced into the north of England in the nineteenth century. The 'swey' as it was called, consisted of 'a tall iron bracket formed by an upright bar working on a pivot above and below, on one side of the grate', with 'a horizontal arm at right angles to it'. From its arm hung three flat metal crooks of varying lengths. The 'swey' replaced the 'crook' hung from an iron bar in the chimney. (*A corner in the North: yesterday and today with Border folk*, A. Reid, Newcastle-upon-Tyne, 1909, pp. 130–1.)

9–Leadbeater, Mary, *Cottage Dialogues among the Irish peasantry . . . With notes and a preface by Maria Edgeworth*, J. Johnson, London, 1811, vol. I, p. 191.

10–Harris, Mollie, *A kind of magic*, Chatto and Windus, London, 1969, pp. 25–6.

11–N., H., *The Ladies Dictionary, being a general entertainment for the fair sex: a work never attempted before in English*, printed for J. Dunton, London, 1694, p. 420.

12–Baldry, George, *The rabbit skin cap: a tale of a Norfolk countryman's youth written in his old age*, Collins, London, 1939, p. 49.

13–Chomel, Noël, *Dictionnaire Oeconomique; or, the Family Dictionary . . . Done into English from the 2nd ed., lately printed at Paris . . . Revised and recommended by R. Bradley*, D. Midwinter, London, 1725, 2 vols, see entry under *stove*. There is a full description and picture of a stewing stove in Raffald, Elizabeth, *The experienced English house-keeper, for the use and ease of ladies, house-keepers, cooks, etc . . .*, printed by J. Harrap, for the author, and sold by Eliz. Raffald, Confectioner, near the Exchange, Manchester, 1769.

14–See, for example, William Verral's satirical conversation with Hackum about the kitchen equipment available in small country houses. (*A complete system of cookery. In which is set forth a variety of genuine receipts, collected from several years experience under the celebrated Mr de St Clouet, sometime since Cook to his Grace the Duke of Newcastle . . .*, printed for the author and sold by him, London, 1759.) See also Webster, Thomas, *An encyclopaedia of domestic economy*, Longman etc., London, 1844, p. 830.

15–Mitchell, Arthur, *The past in the present: what is civilization?*, D. Douglas, Edinburgh, 1880, pp. 75, 239–41.

16–For the most detailed account of pot-baking in Wales see: Peate, Iorwerth Cyfeiliog, 'The pot-oven in Wales' in *Man*, no. 3, 1943, pp. 9–11.

17–For descriptions of pot-baking in Ireland see: Leadbeater, *Cottage dialogues*, vol. I, p. 174; Cross, Eric, *The tailor and Ansty*, Chapman and Hall, London, 1942, p. 149; O'Donoghue, John, *In a quiet land, With a foreword by Sean O'Faolain*, Coward–McCann, New York, 1958, p. 30; Messenger, John C., *Inis Beag, isle of Ireland*, Holt, Rinehart, and Winston, New York, 1969, pp. 42, 73.

18–Jenkin, Alfred Kenneth Hamilton, *Cornish homes and customs*, Dent, London and Toronto, 1934, pp. 61–2.

19–Scott, Daniel, *Bygone Cumberland and Westmoreland*, W. Andrews, London, 1899, p. 175.

20–Melroe, Eliza, *An economical, and new method of cookery; describing upwards of eighty cheap, wholesome, and nourishing dishes . . .*, printed and published for the author, London, 1798, p. 74.

21–Olivey, Hugh P., *Notes on the parish of Mylor, Cornwall*, Barnicott & Pearce, Taunton, 1907, pp. 52–3.

22–Pococke, Dr Richard, *The travels through England of Dr Richard Pococke, successively Bishop of Meath and of Ossory, during 1750, 1751, and later years, edited by James Joel Cartwright*, Camden Society, Westminster, 1888–9, vol. I, p. 135.

23–See, for example: Woolley, Hannah, *The queen-like closet: Or, Rich cabinet, stored with all manner of rare receipts for preserving, candying, and cookery . . .*, R. Chiswel [etc.], London, 5th edition, 1684; Bailey, Nathaniel, *Dictionarium domesticum, being a new and compleat houshold dictionary, for the use both of city and country*, [etc.], printed for C. Hitch [etc.], London, 1736.

24–Jermy, Louise, *The memories of a working woman*, Goose, Norwich, 1934, pp. 34–5.

25–Marshall, Sybil, *Fenland Chronicle. Recollections of William Henry and Kate Mary Edwards collected and edited by their daughter*, Cambridge University Press, Cambridge, 1967, p. 52.

26–Halliwell-Phillips, *The Yorkshire anthology*, p. 74.

27–Evans, George Ewart, *Ask the fellows who cut the hay*, Faber and Faber, London, 1956, pp. 56–7.

28–Bloom, James Harvey, *Folk lore, old customs and superstitions in Shakespeare land*, Mitchell, Hughes and Clarke, London, 1929, p. 32.

29–Harman, Horace, *Sketches of the Bucks countryside*, Blandford Press, London, 1934, p. 34.

30–Markham, Gervase, *Country Contentments, or the English huswife*, London, 1623, p. 90.

31–Macdonald, John (with an introduction by John Beresford), *Memoirs of an* eighteenth-century footman: travels (1745–79), Routledge, London, 1927, p. 14.

32 – See, for example: Plot, Robert, *The natural history of Staffordshire*, printed at the theatre, Oxford, 1686, p. 337; Aubrey, John, *The natural history and antiquities of the County of Surrey; Begun in the year 1673. Ended 1692*, printed for E. Curll, London, 1718–19, vol. 1, Mr Evelyn's letter to Mr Aubrey; Switzer, Stephen, *An introduction to a general system of hydrostaticks and hydraulicks, philosophical and practical*, T. Astley and L. Gilliver, London, 1729, vol. 2, bk. 3, p. 278.

33 – Mandey, Venterus, and Moxon, J., *Mechanick powers: or, The mistery of nature and art unvail'd, shewing what Great things may be perform'd by mechanick engines, in removing and raising bodies of vast weights with little strength, or force*, printed for the author, London, 1696, p. 72.

34 – Somerville, Thomas, *My own life and times, 1741–1814*, Edmonston and Douglas, Edinburgh, 1861, p. 335.

35 – The smoke jack was described by Girolamo Cardan in *De Variete Rerum* (1557). This book was widely read, both in Latin and translated excerpts. One of the earliest printed English translations of Cardan's description is contained in John Wilkin's *Mathematical Magick*, which first appeared in 1648. (Wilkins, John, *The mathematical and philosophical works of the Right Reverend John Wilkins, late Lord Bishop of Chester*, J. Nicholson, London, 1708, pp. 88–9.)

36 – Aubrey, *The natural history*, vol. 1, Mr Evelyn's letter to Mr Aubrey.

37 – Campbell, R., *The London Tradesman. Being a compendious view of all the trades, professions, arts, both liberal and mechanic, now practiced in the cities of London and Westminster . . .* , T. Gardner, London, 1747, pp. 179–80.

38 – Kalm, Pehr, *Kalm's account of his visit to England on his way to America in 1748*, Macmillan, London and New York, 1892, p. 173.

39 – A Lady, *The New London Cookery, and Complete Domestic Guide*, G. Virtue, London, 1827.

40 – Frederick Accum describes the poor man's spit as follows: 'The meat is suspended by a skin of worsted, a twirling motion being given to the meat, the thread is twisted, and when the force is spent, the string untwists itself two or three times alternatively, till the action being discontinued, the meat must again get a twerl round.' (*Culinary Chemistry, exhibiting the scientific principles of cookery*, R. Ackermann, London, 1821, p. 86.)

41 – Callwell, Josephine M., *Old Irish Life*, Blackwood, Edinburgh and London, 1912, pp. 297–8.

42 – Edwards, Frederick, *On the extravagant use of fuel in cooking operations, with a short account of Benjamin Count of Rumford, and his economical systems, and numerous practical suggestions adapted for domestic use*, Longman, Green, London, 1869, p. 23.

43 – Holland, John, *A treatise on the progressive improvement and present state in the manufactures in metal*, Longman, etc., London, 1831, vol. 2, p. 192.

44 – *Ibid.*, vol. 2, p. 191.

45 – Edwards, Frederick, *A treatise on smoky chimneys, their cure and prevention*, 5th edition revised and enlarged, Longman, Green, London, 1869, pp. 26–30.

46 – Coates, Doris, *Tuppenny rice and treacle. Cottage housekeeping (1900–20)*, David & Charles, Newton Abbot, London, 1975, pp. 17–18.

47 – Rumford, Benjamin, *Collected Works of Count Rumford*, edited by Sanborn C. Brown, vol. 2, *Practical Applications of Heat*, The Belknap Press of Harvard University Press, Cambridge, Massachusetts, 1969.

48 – Although this idea is generally attributed to Rumford, who described it as something which he had invented during his stay in Munich and had then caused to be copied in London in 1795 and 1796, it seems likely that William Strutt of Derby worked out the same idea independently a few years earlier. Strutt was a wealthy cotton manufacturer, to whom many important inventions were attributed by his friend the engineer Charles Sylvester in *The philosophy of domestic economy; as exemplified in the mode of warming, ventilating, washing, drying, and cooking, and in various arrangements contributing to the comfort and convenience of domestic life, adopted in the Derbyshire General Infirmary* (Nottingham, 1819). Among these inventions was a roaster for meat and general baking which 'had the rare advantage of being of the same heat on all sides'. According to Sylvester, it was invented in 1797. The same date is given by John Claudius Loudon in *An Encylopaedia of cottage, farm and villa architecture and furniture* (1833), who cites 1799 as the date of publication of Rumford's design.

49 – See, for example: Skidmore, M. and G., London, *Designs of stoves, ranges, virandas, railings, belconets*, etc. . . . , G. Auld, London, 1811.

50 – Grey, Edwin, *Cottage life in a Hertfordshire village. 'How the agricultural labourer lived and fared in the late '60s and the '70s' . . .* , Fisher,

Knight and Co., St Albans, 1935, pp. 96–108.

51 – Bosanquet, Mrs Helen (Dendy), *Rich and poor*, Macmillan, London, 1896, p. 90.

52 – Fishendon, Margaret White, *House Heating; a general discussion of the relative merits of coal, coke, gas, electricity, [etc.], as alternative means of providing for domestic heating, cooking and hot water requirements, with especial reference to economy and efficiency*, Witherby, London, 1925, p. 127.

53 – Pearson, A., *Economy and other advantages of cooking by gas*, Oxford, 1889, p. 3.

54 – Sugg, Marie Jenny, *The Art of Cooking by Gas*, Cassell, London, 1890.

55 – 'An Experiment concerning the Spirit of Coals inter alia in a Letter to the Honble Mr. Boyle by ye late Revd Jo Clayton DD communicated to the Right Revd Father in God Robert Lord Bishop of Corke to the Right Honble Earl of Egmont F.R.S.', in *Papers relating to the Royal Society*, Birch Collection, British Library, London.

56 – Samuel Clegg, the well known nineteenth-century gas engineer, said that William Murdoch 'frequently cooked chops and steaks over gas jets' in 1792. But this story is probably apocryphal. Clegg often got his facts wrong and there is no mention of gas cooking in Murdoch's own writings or those of his numerous biographers. (See letter from Samuel Clegg, April 10, 1851, in *The Journal of Gas Lighting*, London, vol. 2, 1852.)

57 – *Ibid.*

58 – J. R., 'Economical Application of Gas as a source of heat for culinary and other domestic purposes', in *The Mechanic's Magazine, Museum, Register, Journal and Gazette*, London, vol. 15, 1831.

59 – Letter from James Sharp, May 10, 1851, in *The Journal of Gas Lighting*, London, vol. 2, 1852; Boase, Frederic, *Modern English Biography: containing many thousand concise memoirs of persons who have died since the year 1850*, Netherton and Worth, Truro, 1892–1921.

60 – Loudon, John Claudius, *An Encyclopaedia of cottage, farm, and villa architecture and furniture; containing numerous designs for dwellings, from the cottage to the villa . . .*, Longman etc., London, 1833, pp. 725–6.

61 – Morris, Helen, *Portrait of a Chef. The Life of Alexis Soyer Sometime Chef to the Reform Club*, Cambridge University Press, Cambridge, 1938. Reissued in Oxford Paperbacks, Oxford University Press, Oxford, 1980.

62 – Notably Sidney Leoni and Co., John Wright and Co., H. and C. Davis and Co., and J. C. Stark and Co.

63 – Watts, Frank H., 'Developments in the design of gas appliances and ancillary equipment' in *Gas Engineering and Management*, Dec. 1975.

64 – Smoke abatement committee, London, *Report of the Smoke abatement committee, 1882*, Smith, Elder, London, 1883, p. 17.

65 – The first hiring out scheme was initiated by the Crystal Palace Co., London, in 1869.

66 – Fishendon, *House Heating*, p. 224.

67 – Seabrook, Jeremy, *The unpriviledged*, Longman, London, 1967, p. 42.

68 – Philosophical Society of Glasgow, *Reports relative to exhibition of apparatus for the utilization of gas, electricity, [etc. . . .] held under the auspices of the society, September–October 1880*, Glasgow, 1882, pp. 40–1.

69 – Watts, 'Developments'.

70 – Garlick, D. E., 'The increased consumption of gas that may be obtained by the use of cooking and heating stoves' in *The Gas Engineer's Magazine*, vol. 18, Dec. 10, 1902.

71 – Political and Economic Planning, *Report on the gas industry in Great Britain: a survey of the current trends and problems of the industry, with proposals for its future development*, P.E.P., London, 1939, p. 50.

72 – Mass-observation, *An enquiry into people's homes; a report prepared by Mass-observation for the Advertising Service guild, (the fourth of the 'Change' wartime surveys)*, Murray, London, 1943, p. 88.

73 – Payne, Gordon Edgar, *A survey of Gloucestershire: a physical, social and economic survey and plan*, [no imprint], Gloucester, 1946, p. 197.

74 – Roberts, Robert, *The classic slum: Salford life in the first quarter of the century*, Manchester University Press, Manchester, 1971, p. 83.

75 – Livingstone, F. A. F., 'Household economy and cookery in relation to poverty' in *The new survey of London life and labour* edited by Sir Hubert Llewellyn Smith, P. S. King, London, 1934, vol. 6, p. 319.

76 – Troubridge, Laura (Gurney), Lady, *Memories and reflections*, Heineman, London, 1925, p. 190.

77 – Electricity Council, *Electricity Supply in Great Britain*, Electricity Council, London, 1973, p. 9.

78 – *Ibid.*

79 – *Ibid.*, p. 10.

80 – Bowers, Brian, *R. E. B. Crompton: an account of his electrical work*, H.M.S.O., London, 1969, p. 29.

81 – Gillott, W. A., 'Electric Cooking and Heating in Private Houses' in *The Journal of*

the *Institution of Electrical Engineers*, London, vol. 53, 1915.

82 – Gillott, W. A., 'The 25 year history of domestic electric appliances' in *Electrical Trading*, Royal Jubilee Souvenir Supplement, April 1935.

83 – Scott, Peggy, *An electrical adventure*, Truscott, London, 1934, p. 40.

84 – Sharp, Gladys F., 'Those saucepans. A New Year Resolution' in *The Electrical Age*, Electrical Association for Women, London, vol. 2, no. 17, Jan. 1932.

85 – 'Lessening the Housewife's Dreary Toil' in *The Electrical Age*, Electrical Association for Women, London, vol. 2, no. 17, July 1934.

86 – Political and Economic Planning, *Report on the supply of electricity in Great Britain; a survey of present-day problems of the industry with proposals for reorganization of electricity distribution*, P.E.P., London, 1936, p. 77.

87 – Browne, Geoffrey, *Patterns of British Life; a study of certain aspects of the British people at home, at work, and at play, and a compilation of some relevant statistics*, Hulton Press, London, 1950, p. 104.

88 – Electricity Council, *Background information on electrical domestic appliances, electric heating systems, electric water heating and other domestic uses of electricity*, Electricity Council, London, 1981.

89 – Ray, James, *A compleat history of the rebellion, from its first rise, in 1745, to its total suppression at the glorious battle of Culloden, in April, 1746*, J. Jackson, York, 1749, p. 377.

90 – Burt, Edward, *Letters from a gentleman in the north of Scotland to his friend in London*; . . . S. Birt, London, 1754, vol. 2, p. 279.

91 – Campbell, John, *An exact and authentic account of the greatest white-herring-fishery in Scotland, carried on yearly in the island of Zetland, by the Dutch only . . .*, reprinted from the edition of 1750, W. Brown, Edinburgh, 1885, p. 16.

92 – Mitchell, *The past in the present*, lecture 5.

93 – Morris, H., 'Heating Stones' in *County Louth Archaeological Journal*, Dundalk, 1920, vol. 4, pp. 318–19.

94 – The Albion Lamp Company, self-proclaimed 'pioneer of the oil stove trade', was established in 1872. It produced the Rippingille oil stove for heating and cooking.

95 – Brown, *Patterns of British Life*, p. 106.

96 – In 1912 Dalén won the Nobel prize in physics for his 'automatic gas igniter' that causes lighthouses, lightbuoys, aviation and traffic beacons to light up on the approach of twilight and to switch off at dawn.

CHAPTER 4 HEATING

1 – For further details see Political and Economic Planning, *The market for household appliances*, P.E.P., London, 1945.

2 – O'Donoghue, John, *In a quiet land, With a foreword by Sean O'Faolain*, Coward-McCann, New York, 1958, p. 35.

3 – Plot, Robert, *The natural history of Staffordshire*, printed at the theatre, Oxford, 1686, pp. 115, 125–31.

4 – Martin, Martin, *A description of the Western Islands of Scotland*, A. Bell, London, 1703, p.59.

5 – Thompson, Robert, *Statistical survey of the county of Meath, with observations on the means of improvement; drawn up for the consideration, and under the direction of the Dublin Society*, printed by Graisberry and Campbell, Dublin, 1802, pp. 355–6, 377.

6 – Vancouver, Charles, *General view of the agriculture of the county of Devon; with observations on the means of its improvement. Drawn up for the consideration of the board of agriculture, and internal improvement*, R. Phillips, London, 1808, *passim*.

7 – Robinson, Maude, *A South Down farm in the sixties*, Dent, London, 1938, pp. 4, 26.

8 – Grey, Edwin, *Cottage life in a Hertfordshire village. 'How the agricultural labourer lived and fared in the late '60s and the '70s'*, Fisher, Knight, St. Albans, 1935, pp. 52–4.

9 – Jenkin, Alfred Kenneth Hamilton, *Cornish homes and customs*, Dent, London and Toronto, 1934, pp. 58–9.

10 – Pehr Kalm said that farmers near Carrington, which was a woodless district, used straw as fuel for boiling water and dish-washing. (Kalm, Pehr, *Kalm's account of his visit to England on his way to America in 1748, translated by Joseph Lucas*, Macmillan, London and New York, 1892, p. 276.)

11 – Curwen, John Christian, *Observations on the State of Ireland, principally directed to its agriculture and rural population; in a series of letters, written on a tour through that country*, Baldwin, Cradock, and Joy, London, 1818, vol. 2, p. 161.

12 – O'Sullivan, Humphrey, *The diary of Humphrey O'Sullivan, Edited, with introduction, translation and notes, by Rev. Michael McGrath*, published for the Irish texts society by Simpkin, Marshall, Ltd, London, 1936–7, vol. 2, p. 7.

13 – Bradley, Richard, *A survey of the ancient husbandry and gardening, collected from Cato, Varro, Columella, Virgil, and others . . .*, B. Motte, London, 1725, p. 281.

14 – Meriton, George, *A York-shire dialogue, in its pure natural as it is now commonly spoken in the north parts of York-shire. Being a miscellaneous discourse, or hotch-potch of several country affaires, begun by a daughter, and her mother, and continued by the father, son, uncle, neese, and land-lord*, printed for J. White, York, 1697, p. 70.

15 – Fiennes, Celia, *The journeys of Celia Fiennes, Edited and With an Introduction by Christopher Morris*, The Cresset Press, London, 1947, p. 161.

16 – *A Collection of Welsh Travels and Memoirs of Wales*, printed for and sold by J. Torbruck and E. Rider, Dublin, 1743, p. 64. The first edition of this work appeared in 1738.

17 – Clarke, Edward Daniel, *A tour through the south of England, Wales, and part of Ireland, made during the summer of 1791*, printed at the Minerva press for R. Edwards, London, 1793, p. 116.

18 – Eden, Frederick Morton, Sir, *The State of the Poor: or, An history of the labouring classes in England, from the Conquest to the present period; in which are particularly considered their domestic economy, with respect to diet, dress, fuel, and habitation . . .*, B. & J. White, London, 1797, vol. 2, p. 394.

19 – Jenkin, *Cornish homes and customs*, p. 60.

20 – Mason, Thomas H., *The islands of Ireland. Their scenery, people, life and antiquities*, Batsford, London, 1937, p. 75.

21 – Earl, Derek E., *Forest energy and economic development*, Clarendon Press, Oxford, 1975, p. 22.

22 – King, Gregory, *Two tracts by Gregory King. (a) Natural and political observations and conclusions upon the state and condition of England . . ., Edited with an introduction by George Ernest Barnett*, The Johns Hopkins Press, Baltimore, 1936, p. 35.

23 – Albion, Robert Greenhalgh, *Forests and seapower. The timber problem of the royal navy 1652–1862*, Harvard University Press, Cambridge, 1926.

24 – It is interesting to note B. P. Capper's estimate (1801) that 15 per cent of the land in England and Wales was covered with woods, coppices, commons and waste. A comparable calculation made by W. T. Comber in 1808 suggests that 21 per cent of the land was used in this way. (Darby, Henry Clifford, *A new historical geography of England after 1600*, Cambridge University Press, Cambridge, 1973, table 2.1, p. 103.)

25 – Eden, *The State of the Poor*, vol. 1, pp. 496–501, 547–8.

26 – Great Britain. Forestry Commission, *Report on census of woodlands and census of production of home-grown timber*, H.M.S.O., London, 1928, p. 8.

27 – Great Britain. Ministry of Reconstruction. Reconstruction Committee, Forestry sub-committee, *Final Report*, H.M.S.O., London, 1918, p. 8.

28 – Webster, Angus Duncan, *Firewoods. Their production and fuel values*, Fisher Unwin, London, 1919, p. 13.

29 – See the work of Sydney Robert Jones, for example, and Holme, Charles (ed.), *Old English country cottages*, The Studio, London, Paris, New York, 1906–7; Holme, Charles (ed.), *The village homes of England*, The Studio, London, Paris, New York, 1912; Ditchfield, Peter Hampson, *The cottages and the village life of rural England*, Dent, London, 1912.

30 – Ward, John Dudley Usborne, *A woodman's diary*, Routledge, London, 1952, *passim*.

31 – Eden, *The State of the Poor*, vol. 2, p. 15.

32 – See, for example, Eden, *The State of the Poor*, vol. 1, pp. 104–7 and vol. 2, p. 797 and Grey, *Cottage life in a Hertfordshire village*, p. 53.

33 – Ward, *A woodman's diary*, p. 88.

34 – Sturt, George, *Change in the village*, Duckworth, London, 1959, p. 23.

35 – Albion, *Forests and sea power*, p. 87.

36 – Wordsworth, Dorothy, *Recollections of a tour made in Scotland AD 1803*, edited by J. C. Shairp, Edmonston and Douglas, Edinburgh, 1874, p. 134.

37 – All studies of fuels and fires to date have been concerned with their thermal value and efficiency; the labour required to maintain fires did not concern any of the energy experts writing between 1650 and 1950.

38 – Great Britain. Department of Scientific and Industrial Research. Fuel Research Board, *Special Report No. 2, The peat resources of Ireland. A lecture given before the Royal Dublin Society on 5th March, 1919, by Professor Pierce F. Purcell*, H.M.S.O., London, 1920, p. 5.

39 – *Ibid.*

40 – *Ibid.*, p. 12.

41 – Great Britain. Department of Scientific and Industrial Research. Fuel Research Board, *The winning, harvesting and utilization of peat*, H.M.S.O., London, 1948, p. 1.

42 – Great Britain. Department of Scientific and Industrial Research, *Geological survey of Great Britain; Scotland, Peat deposits of Scotland. Part I. General account by G. K. Fraser*, [no imprint], 1943.

43 – Tighe, William, *Statistical observations relative to the county of Kilkenny, made in the*

years *1800* and *1801*, printed for Graisberry and Campbell, Dublin, 1802, pp. 478–9.

44 – Holland, John, *The history and description of fossil fuel, the collieries, and coal trade of Great Britain*, Whittaker, London, 1841, 2nd edn, p. 52.

45 – Marshall, Sybil, *Fenland Chronicle. Recollections of William Henry and Kate Mary Edwards collected and edited by their daughter*, Cambridge University Press, Cambridge, 1967.

46 – Fairfax–Blakeborough, John and Richard, *The spirit of Yorkshire*, Batsford, London, 1954, p. 167.

47 – Great Britain. Department of Scientific and Industrial Research, *Geological Survey of Great Britain, Scotland, Peat deposits of Scotland*, p. 40.

48 – The description of Irish peat-gathering methods that follows comes from Hall, Samuel Carter, Mr and Mrs, *Ireland: its scenery, character etc. . . .*, How and Parsons, London, 1841–3, vol. 2, pp. 263–5.

49 – Great Britain. Department of Scientific and Industrial Research, *The peat resources of Ireland*, p. 13.

50 – Hely Dutton, writing at the beginning of the nineteenth century, said that 'A labourer will cut as much turf in two days, as will serve his family for a year'. (Dutton, Hely, *Statistical survey of the county of Clare, with observations on the means of improvement; drawn up for the consideration and by the direction of the Dublin Society*, printed by Graisberry and Campbell, Dublin, 1808, p. 175.)

51 – Great Britain. Department of Scientific and Industrial Research. Fuel Research Board. Irish peat inquiry committee, *The winning, preparation and use of peat in Ireland. Reports and other documents*, H.M.S.O., London, 1921, p. 19.

52 – Great Britain. Department of Scientific and Industrial Research, *The peat resources of Ireland*, p. 13.

53 – O'Sullivan, *The Diary of Humphrey O'Sullivan*, vol. 1, p. 89.

54 – Plot, *The natural history of Staffordshire*, p. 115.

55 – Firth, John, *Reminiscences of an Orkney Parish together with old Orkney words, riddles and proverbs*, Orkney natural history society, Stromness, 1974, pp. 107–8.

56 – Jenkin, *Cornish homes and customs*, pp. 59–60.

57 – Great Britain. Department of Scientific and Industrial Research, *The peat resources of Ireland*, pp. 14–15.

58 – Fiennes, *The journeys*, p. 204.

59 – Macaulay, Kenneth, *The history of St.*

Kilda. Containing a description of this remarkable island; the manners and customs of the inhabitants; the religious and pagan antiquities there found; with many other curious and interesting particulars, printed for T. Becket and P. A. De Hondt, London, 1764, p. 128.

60 – Dutton, *Statistical survey of the county of Clare*, p. 175.

61 – Edmonston, Eliza, *Sketches and tales of the Shetland Islands*, Sutherland and Knox, Edinburgh, 1856, p. 13.

62 – Wordsworth, *Recollections of a tour made in Scotland AD 1803*, p. 95.

63 – Burt, Edward, *Letters from a gentleman in the north of Scotland to his friend in London . . .*, S. Birt, London, 1754, vol. 2, p. 279.

64 – Watson, John (ed.), *The annals of a quiet valley*, Dent, London, 1894, p. 88.

65 – Great Britain. Department of Scientific and Industrial Research, *The winning, preparation and use of peat in Ireland*, p. 18.

66 – Fiennes, *The journeys*, p. 258.

67 – Dubourdieu, John, *Statistical survey of the county of Down, with observations on the means of improvement; drawn up for the consideration, and by order of the Dublin Society*, printed by Graisberry and Campbell, Dublin, 1802, p. 216.

68 – The mileage of navigable rivers in England increased during the seventeenth and eighteenth centuries from 685 miles in 1660 to 960 in 1700 and 1, 160 in 1726. (Willan, Thomas Stuart, *River Navigation in England, 1600–1750*, Oxford historical series, London, 1936, p. 133.)

69 – Nef, John U., *The rise of the British coal industry*, Books for Libraries Press, Freeport, New York, 1972, pp. 100–3; Buxton, Neil K., *The economic development of the British coal industry from Industrial Revolution to the present day*, Batsford, London, 1978, p. 33.

70 – They continued to dominate the London coal market until 1845 when the fuel was first borne to the metropolis by rail.

71 – Kalm, *Kalm's account of his visit to England*, pp. 137–8.

72 – Aston, Thomas Southcliffe and Sykes, Joseph, *The Coal Industry of the Eighteenth Century*, Manchester University Press, Manchester, p. 228.

73 – Darby, *A new historical geography of England*, pp. 70–2.

74 – Mitchell, Brian R. with the collaboration of Phyllis Deane, *Abstract of British historical statistics*, Cambridge University Press, Cambridge, 1962, pp. 225–6.

75 – For example, the amount of coal mined in the United Kingdom rose from 64,441,401 tons

in 1854 to 146,969,409 tons in 1880. (Meade, Richard, *The coal and iron industries of the United Kingdom*, Crosby Lockwood and Co., London, 1882, p. 296.) By 1913, 287 million tons were being mined. (Political and Economic Planning, *Report on the British coal industry. A survey of the current problems of the British coal-mining industry and of the distribution of coal, with proposals for reorganization*, P.E.P., London, 1936, p. 1.)

76 – Hawke, Gary Richard, *Railways and economic growth in England and Wales 1840–1870*, Clarendon Press, Oxford, 1970, pp. 87, 173.

77 – Fishendon, Margaret, *House heating; a general discussion of the relative merits of coal, coke, gas, electricity, [etc.], as alternative means of providing for domestic heating, cooking and hot water requirements, with especial reference to economy and efficiency*, Witherby, London, 1925, pp. 190–1.

78 – Anderson, James, *A practical treatise on chimneys, containing full directions for preventing or removing smoke in houses*, printed for C. Elliot, Edinburgh, 1776, p. 3.

79 – Primitive chimneys were extremely common in the poorer cottages of Ireland, Wales and Scotland in the seventeenth, eighteenth, and early nineteenth centuries. When Thomas Garnett visited the Highlands in 1800, he found that most cottages were built out of stones thatched with sods. They consisted of two apartments, one for the cattle and poultry, the other for the family. The latter had a peat fire in the middle of the room, placed on the floor. 'There is frequently a hole in the roof to allow exit to the smoke', he said, 'but this is not directly over the fire, on account of the rain, and very little of the smoke finds its way out of it, the greatest part, after having filled every corner of the room, coming out of the door, so that it is almost impossible for anyone unaccustomed to it, to breathe in the hut.' (Garnett, Thomas, *Observations on a tour through the Highlands and part of the western isles of Scotland . . .*, T. Cadell, jun., and W. Davis, London, 1800, vol. 1, p. 121.)

80 – In 1715, the construction of a chimney for coal fires cost twice as much as a new iron stove-grate. (Gauger, Nicolas, *Fires improv'd: being a new method of building chimneys, so as to prevent their smoaking: in which a small fire, shall warm a room better than a much larger made the common way. With the manner of altering such chimneys as are already built, so that they perform the same effects . . ., Made English and Improved, by J. T. Desaguliers . . .*, J. Senex, London, 1715, pp. 157–61.) Very few rural households had iron stove-grates at this time. Only six are mentioned in farm and cottage inventories dating from 1635 to 1749 of 217 houses in two central Essex parishes, the first reference occurring in 1672 and the second in 1725. (Steer, Francis W. (ed.), *Farm and Cottage inventories of mid-Essex, 1635–1749*, Essex County Council, Chelmsford, 1950.)

81 – Gauger, *Fires improv'd*; *The Fountain of Knowledge: or, British legacy*, London, ca. 1750, pp. 30–3; Anderson, *A practical treatise on chimneys*; Cauty, William, *Natura, Philosophia, and Ars in Concordia; or, nature, philosophy, and art in friendship, an essay in four parts* [no imprint], London, 1772; Walker, A., *A philosophical estimate of the causes, effects, and cure of unwholesome air in large cities . . . To which is prefixed a philosophical dissertation on the causes and cures of smoking chimnies*, [no imprint], 1776; Clavering, Robert, *An essay on the construction and building of chimneys. Including an enquiry into the common causes of their smoking, and the most effectual remedies for removing so intolerable a nuisance: with a table to proportion chimneys to the size of the room*, I. Taylor, London, 1779; Franklin, Benjamin, *Observations on the causes and cure of smoky chimneys in a letter to Dr Ingen-Housz, physician to the emperor, at Vienna*, [no imprint], 1785; Lupton, Thomas, *A thousand notable things, on various subjects; disclosed from the secrets of nature and art; practicable, profitable and of great advantage*, [no imprint], London, 1791; Danforth, Thomas, *The theory of chimnies and fire-places investigated; the principle of those recommended by Count Rumford, fully explained, and their construction improved: and a great improvement, on a principle very little known, and in a manner never practiced . . .*, T. Heptinstall, London, 1796; Rumford, Benjamin, *Chimney fireplaces, with proposals for improving them to save fuel; to render dwelling-houses more comfortable and salubrious, and effectually to prevent chimneys from smoking*, T. Cadell, Jr. and W. Davies, London, 1796; Rumford, Benjamin, *Supplementary observations concerning chimney fireplaces*, T. Cadell, Jr. and W. Davies, London, 1802; Edwards, Frederick, *A treatise on smoky chimneys, their cure and prevention*, 5th edition revised and enlarged, Longman, Green, London, 1869.

82 – Blundell, Nicholas, *The great diurnal of Nicholas Blundell of Little Crosby, Lancashire, transcribed and annotated by Frank Tyrer*, Record Society of Lancashire and Cheshire, Chester, 1968–72, vol. 1, p. 166. For further details of Blundell's problems see vol. 1, pp. 43, 132, 152.

83 – Dickins, Lilian and Stanton, Mary (eds.),

An eighteenth-century correspondence . . ., Murray, London, 1910, p. 429.
84 – Connell, Brian, *Portrait of a Whig Peer. Compiled from the papers of the Second Viscount Palmerston 1739–1802*, Deutsch, London, 1957, p. 347.
85 – See for example *The Frauds and Abuses of the coal-dealers detected and exposed: in a letter to an Alderman of London*, London, 1747, 3rd. ed.
86 – Blundell, *The great diurnal*, vol. 1, pp. 53, 133.
87 – Roberts, Robert, *The classic slum. Salford life in the first quarter of the century*, Manchester University Press, Manchester, 1971, p. 55.
88 – Davies, Margaret Llewelyn (ed.), *Life as we have known it. By Co-operative working women*, The Hogarth Press, London, 1931, p. 56.
89 – Misson, Henri de Valbourg, *M. Misson's Memoirs and observations in his travels over England. With some account of Scotland and Ireland* . . ., translated by Mr Ozell, D. Browne, London, 1719, p. 37.
90 – *Ibid.*
91 – Davies, Walter, *General view of the agriculture and domestic economy of South Wales* . . . *Drawn up for the consideration of the Board of Agriculture and Internal Improvement*, London, 1814, vol. 2, pp. 339–40.
92 – A Society of Gentlemen [Hill, Aaron], *Four essays. 1. On making china ware in England. 2. On a method for furnishing coals at a third of the price they are usually sold at* . . ., printed for J. Roberts, and sold by R. Burleigh and Thomas Corbett, London, 1718, p. 21.
93 – Clarke, *A tour through the south of England*, pp. 217–18.
94 – Eden, *The State of the Poor*, vol. 1, p. 552.
95 – Fishendon, *House heating*, p. 30.
96 – Summers, A. Leonard, *All about anthracite: the world's premier coal*, The Technical Publishing Company, London, 1919, p. 16.
97 – Mayhew, Henry, *London Labour and the London Poor; a cyclopaedia of the condition and earnings of those that will work, those that cannot work, and those that will not work*, [no imprint], London, 1861–2, vol. 2, p. 343.
98 – Phillips, George Lewis, *England's climbing boys. A history of the long struggle to abolish child labour in chimney-sweeping*, Baker Library, Boston, Massachusetts, 1949.
99 – See for example: Fairfax-Blakeborough, John, *Yorkshire village life, humour, and characters*, A. Brown, London, 1955, pp. 165–70; Foakes, Grace, *Between high walls. A London childhood*, Shepheard-Walwyn, London, 1972, p. 5.
100 – Chippendale, Thomas, *The Gentleman and cabinet-maker's director: being a large collection of the most elegant and useful designs of household furniture in the Gothic, Chinese and modern taste*, printed for the author, London, 1754; Welldon, William and John, *The Smith's Right Hand; or, a complete guide to the various branches of all sorts of Iron Work* [no imprint], London, 1765; Skidmore, M. and G., *Designs of stoves, ranges, virandas, railings, belconets, etc.* . . ., G. Auld, London, 1811; Holland, John, *A treatise on the progressive improvement and present state of the manufactures in metal*, Longman etc., London, 1831, vol. 2, ch. 7; Webster, Thomas, *An encyclopaedia of domestic economy*, Longman etc., London, 1844, pp. 73–81; Edwards, Frederick, *Our domestic fireplaces. A new edition, entirely rewritten and enlarged, the additions completing the author's contributions on the domestic use of fuel, and on ventilation*, Longman, Green, London, 1870.
101 – Bryant and May Museum of Fire-making appliances, London, *Catalogue of the exhibits; comp., with an introd. and notes, by Miller Christy*, Bryant and May, London, 1926.
102 – Bryant and May Museum of Fire-making appliances, London, *Catalogue*, p. 9.
103 – Croal, George, *Living Memories of an Octogenarian (chiefly of Edinburgh) from the years 1816 to 1845*, Andrew Elliot, Edinburgh, 1894, pp. 4–5.
104 – See, for example, Jenkin, *Cornish homes and customs*, p. 68.
105 – Evans, Emyr Estyn, *Irish heritage. The landscape, the people and their work*, Dundalgan Press, Dundalk, 1942, pp. 69–70; Ó Danachair, Caoimhín, 'Hearth and chimney in the Irish house' in *Béaloideas. The Journal of the Folklore of Ireland Society*, Dublin, no. 16, 1946, pp. 91–104.
106 – Tighe, *Statistical observations relative to the county of Kilkenny*, p. 482.
107 – Conyers, Dorothea, *Sporting reminiscences*, Methuen, London, 1920, pp. 71–2.
108 – Gauger, *Fires improv'd*.
109 – For details see the first and second editions of *Fires improv'd*. The second was printed by J. Senex, London, in 1731.
110 – Franklin, Benjamin, *An account of the newly invented Pennsylvanian fire-places: wherein their construction and manner of operation is particularly explained* . . ., printed and sold by B. Franklin, Philadelphia, 1744.
111 – See: Durno, J., *A description of a new-invented stove-grate, shewing its uses and advantages over all others; both in point of expence, and every purpose of a chamber fire*, printed by J. Towers in Piccadilly and published by the

inventor, J. Durno, 1753; Sharp, James, *Account of the principle and effects of the Pensilvanian stove-grates, commonly known by the name of American stoves: together with a description of the late additions and improvements made to them by James Sharp* [no imprint], 1781.

112 – Rumford, *Chimney fireplaces* in *Collected Works of Count Rumford, edited by Sanborn C. Brown*, The Belknap Press of Harvard University Press, Cambridge, Massachusetts, 1969, vol. 2, p. 230.

113 – *Ibid.*, pp. 241–3.

114 – Barker, Arthur Henry, *Domestic fuel consumption*, Constable, London, 1920, p. 104; Fishendon, *House heating, passim*.

115 – Virtually every writer on domestic heating in Britain commented on the national prejudice against close-stoves. For a full description of the main types that could have been adopted see *The theory and practice of warming and ventilating public buildings, dwelling houses, and conservatories. Including . . . a description of all the known varieties of stoves, grates, and furnaces; with an examination of their comparative advantages for economising fuel and preventing smoke. By an engineer*, printed for Thomas and George Underwood, London, 1825.

116 – J.W.C., *Our dwellings warmed as they are and as they might be; with a chapter on ventilation*, Lockwood, London, 1875, p. 30.

117 – Although gas heating gained popularity between 1880 and 1950, there are, unfortunately, no statistics for the number of gas heaters in use at any given time. In 1945, however, the Political and Economic Planning Group estimated that gas fires and gas heaters probably only met 5 per cent of the nation's heating requirements. (*The market for household appliances*, P.E.P., London, 1945, p. 79.)

118 – Barker, *Domestic fuel consumption*, p. 104.

119 – Political and Economic Planning, *Report on the gas industry in Great Britain, a survey of the current trends and problems of the industry, with proposals for its future development*, P.E.P., London, 1939, p. 11.

120 – Fishendon, *House heating*, pp. 166–7.

121 – J.W.C., *Our buildings warmed as they are*, pp. v, vi.

122 – Wollstonecraft, Mary, *Letters written during a short residence in Sweden, Norway, and Denmark*, J. Johnson, London, 1797, p. 45.

CHAPTER 5 LIGHTING

1 – Graham, Douglas, *Fun upon fun; or, Leper, the tailor* [no imprint], Glasgow, *c.* 1840.

2 – *The comical tricks of Lothian Tom; with a selection of anecdotes*, [no imprint].

3 – Houghton, John, *Husbandry and Trade improv'd . . .*, [edited by Richard Bradley] Woodman and Lyon, London, 2nd edition, 1728, vol. 2, pp. 48–9.

4 – Thomas Pennant, for example, found that the majority of houses on the isle of Rum lacked windows or chimneys in 1772. (*A tour in Scotland, and voyage to the Hebrides; 1772*, John Monk, Chester, 1774, p. 277.) Arthur Young, who travelled in Ireland between 1776 and 1779, commented that the cottars 'have not always chimneys to their cabbins, the door serving for that and window too'. (*A tour in Ireland; with general observations on the present state of that kingdom: made in the years 1776, 1777, and 1778. And bought down to the end of 1779*, T. Cadell [etc.], London, 1780, p. 21). Mary Leadbeater confirms that this remained true in most parts of Ireland in the early nineteenth century: '. . . many cabins have been built, are building, and ought to be demolished, which have no windows!' she raged, 'all the light that is admitted passes through the door-way and down the hole in the roof, by which the smoke escapes.' (*Cottage dialogues among the Irish peasantry. With notes and a preface by Maria Edgeworth*, Dublin, 1813, vol. 2, p. 225.)

5 – See: Dowell, Stephen, *A history of taxation and taxes in England from the earliest times to the year 1885*, Longman, Green, London, 1888, vols 2 and 3 and Clow, Archibald and Clow, Nan L., *The chemical revolution. A contribution to social technology*, The Batchworth Press, London, 1952.

6 – Swift, Jonathan, *Directions to servants in general; and in particular to the butler, cook, footman, coachman, groom, house-steward . . .*, printed for R. Dodsley . . . M. Cooper, London, 1745, p. 25.

7 – Mayhew, Henry, *London Labour and the London Poor; a cyclopaedia of the condition and earnings of those that will work, those that cannot work, and those that will not work*, [no imprint], London, 1861–2, vol. 2, p. 379.

8 – Rushlights were still being used in: (a) Berkshire in the 1860s and 1870s (Cornish, James George, *James George Cornish: Reminiscences of Country Life, edited by Vaughan Cornish* [no imprint], 1939, p. 29); (b) The Essex/Sussex border in the 1860s and 1870s (Warren, Clarence Henry, *Happy countryman*, G. Bles, London, 1939, pp. 47–8); (c) Hertfordshire in the 1860s (Grey, Edwin, *Cottage life in a Hertfordshire village. 'How the agricultural labourer lived and fared in the late '60s and the '70s'. . .*, Fisher, Knight, St.

Albans, 1935, p. 55); (d) Huntingdonshire in the 1870s and 1880s (Marshall, Sybil, *Fenland Chronicle. Recollections of William Henry and Kate Mary Edwards collected and edited by their daughter*, Cambridge University Press, Cambridge, 1967, p. 51); (e) Country districts in Ireland during the Second World War (Evans, Emyr Estyn, *Irish heritage. The landscape, the people and their work*, Dundalgan Press, Dundalk, 1942, p. 77); (f) The Lake District in the mid-nineteenth century (Watson, John (ed.), *The annals of a quiet valley*, Dent, London, 1894, p. 83); (g) Lancashire farm-houses during the 1870s (Harland, John and Wilkinson, T. T., *Lancashire legends, traditions, pageants, sports*, etc., Routledge, London, 1873, p. 204); (h) Norfolk in the 1870s (Baldry, George, *The rabbit skin cap: a tale of a Norfolk countryman's youth written in his old age*, Collins, London, 1939, p. 39); (i) Sussex in the 1860s (Robinson, Maude, *A South Down farm in the sixties*, Dent, London, 1938, p. 33); (j) Ulster in 1905 (May, Robert, 'Ulster Rushlight, and Candle, holders' in *Journal of the Royal Society of Antiquaries of Ireland*, vol. 35, p. 383); (k) Wales in the 1860s (Evans, Hugh, *The Gorse Glen*, Brython Press, Liverpool, 1948, pp. 138, 150–1); (l) Warwickshire in the 1870s and 1880s (Bloom, James Harvey, *Folklore, old customs and superstitions in Shakespeare land*, Mitchell, Hughes and Clarke, London, 1930, p. 76); (m) Yorkshire in the 1880s and 1890s (Fairfax-Blakeborough, John, *Yorkshire days and Yorkshire ways*, Heath, Cranton, London, 1935, p. 149).

9 – Johnson, Samuel, *A dictionary of the English language . . .*, J. and P. Knapton, London, 1755.
10 – The two classic accounts of rushlight-making are contained in: White, Gilbert, *The natural history of Selborne, in the county of Southampton: with engravings, and an appendix*, B. White, London, 1789, pp. 334–8; Cobbett, William, *Cottage Economy: containing information relating to the brewing of beer, making of bread, keeping of cows* [etc.] . . ., C. Clement, London, 1822, pp. 144–5.
11 – Burton, Alfred, *Rush-bearing: an account of the old custom of strewing rushes; carrying rushes to church; the rush-cart; garlands in churches; morris-dancers; the wakes; the rush*, Brook & Chrystal, Manchester, 1891, pp. 174–5.
12 – Jekyll, Gertrude, *Old West Surrey. Some notes and memories*, Longman, Green, London, New York, 1904, p. 101.
13 – White, *The natural history of Selborne*, p. 337.
14 – This estimate may be slightly optimistic. According to *The Book of English Trades, and*

Library of the Useful Arts (11th edition, London, 1823, p. 383) the average rushlight was 12 inches long and burned for 10 to 15 minutes only.
15 – Jekyll, *Old West Surrey*, pp. 102, 105.
16 – *Ibid.*, p. 105 and Burton, *Rush-bearing*, p. 175.
17 – Ashton, John, *Modern street ballads*, Chatto and Windus, London, 1888, pp. 91–3.
18 – Brontë, Charlotte, *Jane Eyre, an autobiography*, Smith, Elder, London, 1847, ch. 6.
19 – Andrews, Cyril Bruyn (ed.), *The Torrington Diaries, containing the tours through England and Wales of the Hon. John Byng (later fifth viscount Torrington) between the years 1781 and 1794*, Eyre and Spottiswoode, London, 1934–8, vol. 2, pp. 17, 47, 93, 169, 371.
20 – See *The London Songster, for 1838, being one of the finest collections of songs ever published*, [no imprint], 1838, pp. 108–10, the entry under *rushlight* in the *Dictionary based upon Historical Principles*, and the song 'How five and twenty shillings were expended in a week' which refers to 'a three farthing rushlight every night, to catch the bugs and fleas' (Ashton, *Modern street ballads*, pp. 48–51).
21 – For further details see: Dowell, *A history of taxation*, vol. 4, pp. 306–10.
22 – According to Dowell, the tax on a pound of wax and tallow candles was respectively 4d. and $\frac{1}{2}$d. in 1709. In 1711 both duties were doubled and they remained at this level until 1784, when the duty on wax and spermaceti candles was lowered to 3d. the pound. G. R. Porter in *The Progress of the Nation, in its various social and economical relations, from the beginning of the nineteenth century* (Murray, London, 1851, pp. 571–2) shows that the rates of duty between 1800 and 1830 stood at 1d. per pound of tallow candles and 3½d. per pound of wax or spermaceti candles. His tables for tallow, wax and spermaceti candle production in England, Scotland and Great Britain during these 30 years prove that the vast majority of candles were made out of tallow. Candles made from wax or spermaceti were not even produced in Scotland.
23 – Johnson, Samuel, *A journey to the western islands of Scotland*, printed for W. Strahan & T. Cadell, London, 1775, p. 303.
24 – Blundell, Nicholas, *The great diurnal of Nicholas Blundell of Little Crosby, Lancashire, transcribed and annotated by Frank Tyrer*, Record Society of Lancashire and Cheshire, Chester, 1968–72, vol. 2, appendix C, and vol. 1, p. 140.
25 – Callwell, Josephine M., *Old Irish life*, Blackwood, Edinburgh and London, 1912, p. 225.

26 – Neville, Hastings M., *A corner in the north: yesterday and today with Border folk*, A. Reid, Newcastle-upon-Tyne, 1909, p. 83.

27 – Rumford says that his attention first turned to lighting 'in the year 1789, when, being actively engaged in the public service of the late Elector Palatine, reigning Duke of Bavaria, I was employed by His Most Serene Highness in establishing Houses of Industry for the poor, in the cities of Mannheim and Munich. In lighting up these spacious establishments, I first learned to know how much room there was for improvement in the art of illumination; and since that time the subject has frequently been the object of my meditations, and of a variety of experimental researches'; Rumford, Benjamin, 'On the management of light in illumination' in Brown, Sanborn C. (ed.), *Collected Works of Count Rumford*, vol. 4, *Light and Armament*, The Belknap Press of Harvard University Press, Cambridge, Massachusetts, 1970, pp. 97–8.

28 – Rumford, 'Experiments on the relative intensities of the light emitted by luminous bodies' (1794) in Brown, Sanborn C. (ed.), *Collected Works of Count Rumford*, vol. 4, *Light and Armament*, The Belknap Press of Harvard University Press, Cambridge, Massachusetts, 1970, p. 35.

29 – According to the rulings of the 1709 candle tax, people could not use oil lamps in their homes unless they burned fish oil made from fish caught by British fishermen.

30 – Ó Crohan, Tomás, *The Islandman. Translated from the Irish, with a foreword, by Robin Flower*, Chatto and Windus, London, 1934, p. 38. Reissued in Oxford Paperbacks, Oxford University Press, Oxford, 1978.

31 – Edmondston, Eliza, *Sketches and tales of the Shetland Islands*, Sutherland and Knox, Edinburgh, 1856, p. 13.

32 – Mason, Thomas H., *The islands of Ireland. Their scenery, people, life and antiquities*, Batsford, London, 1937, p. 77. Robert May in his article on 'Ulster Rushlight, and Candle, holders', (*op. cit.* p. 389) says that this practice still continued in 1905.

33 – Kermode, P. M. C., 'Rushlights, cruisies, and early candle-holders in the Isle of Man' in *The Antiquary*, London, vol. 38, pp. 233–6.

34 – Jenkins, Alfred Kenneth Hamilton, *Cornish homes and customs*, Dent, London and Toronto, 1934, p. 66.

35 – Ó Crohan, *The Islandman*, p. 39.

36 – The cruisie was variously spelt as crusy, crusie, cruzey, cruzie, croosie; it was also called a crâsset or cruisgean.

37 – Hocart, John S., 'The old Guernsey Lamp, or crâsset' in *Transactions of the Guernsey Society of Natural Science and Local Research*, vol. 5, 1905–8, pp. 452–7.

38 – Firth, John, *Reminiscences of an Orkney parish together with old Orkney words, riddles and proverbs*, Orkney natural history society, Stromness, 1974, pp. 111–12.

39 – Urie, John, *Glasgow and Paisley eighty years ago*, A. Gardner, Paisley, 1919, p. 21.

40 – *The Fifth Year's Transactions of the Carmarthenshire Antiquarian Society and Field Club*, 1911–12, vol. 6, p. 14.

41 – See Bradley, Richard, *A survey of the ancient husbandry and gardening, collected from Cato, Varro, Columella, Virgil, and others . . .*, B. Motte, London, 1725, *passim*, and Webster, Thomas, *An encyclopaedia of domestic economy*, Longman etc., London, 1844, pp. 131–3.

42 – Cannel coal occurred near Whitehaven in Cumberland, Wigan in Lancashire, Broseley in Shropshire, near Sheffield in Yorkshire, and several places in Scotland (Holland, John, *The history and description of fossil fuel, the collieries, and coal trade of Great Britain*, Whitaker, London, 1841, 2nd edn., p. 334).

43 – Fiennes, Celia, *The Journeys of Celia Fiennes, Edited and with an Introduction by Christopher Morris*, The Cresset Press, London, 1947, p. 166.

44 – Quoted in Galloway, Robert L., *Annals of Coal Mining and the Coal Trade. The Invention of the Steam Engine and the Origin of the Railway*, The Colliery Guardian Co., London, 1898, p. 188.

45 – Pennant, Thomas, *A tour in Scotland, and voyage to the Hebrides; 1772*, John Monk, Chester, 1774, pp. 15–16.

46 – Webster, *An encyclopaedia of domestic economy*, p. 98.

47 – Hughes, Joseph, *The history of the township of Meltham, near Huddersfield; in the West Riding of the Country of York; from the earliest time to the present*, J. Crossley, Huddersfield, 1866, p. 2.

48 – Burt, Edward, *Letters from a gentleman in the north of Scotland to his friend in London*, S. Birt, London, 1754, vol. 2, p. 127; Geikie, Archibald, Sir, *A journey through England and Scotland to the Hebrides in 1784, by Barthélemy Faujas de Saint Fond*, H. Hopkins, Glasgow, 1907, pp. 293–4.

49 – This type of holder was often called a 'peer-man' or 'peer-page' and consisted of a block of stone supporting a thin, vertical iron rod which had a moveable arm capable of sliding the splinter up and down into different positions and a clip at the bottom for adjusting

its angle. (See Geikie, Archibald, Sir, *Scottish reminiscences*, Maclehose, Glasgow, 1904, pp. 266–7)

50 – Carr, John, Sir, *Caledonian sketches, or A tour through Scotland in 1807: to which is prefixed an explanatory address to the public upon a recent trial*, Inskeep and Bradford, New York, 1809, p. 409.

51 – Scottish tallow candle production increased by 133 per cent between 1763 and 1791. (Creech, William, *Letters, addressed to Sir John Sinclair, bart., respecting the mode of living, arts, commerce, literature, manners etc. of Edinburgh, in 1763, and since that period. Illustrating the statistical progress of the capital of Scotland*, [no imprint], Edinburgh, 1793, p. 26.) See also note 22.

52 – Hall, James, *Travels in Scotland, by an unusual route: with a trip to the Orkneys and Hebrides*, 1807, vol. 2, p. 440.

53 – Mackenzie, Osgood Hanbury, of Inverewe, *A hundred years in the Highlands*, Edward Arnold, London, 1921, p. 37.

54 – Webster, *An encyclopaedia of domestic economy*, p. 133 and Ó Crohan, *The Islandman*, p. 39.

55 – May, 'Ulster Rushlight, and Candle, holders', *op. cit.*, p. 388.

56 – Buchan, Alexander, *A description of Saint Kilda, giving an account of its situation, extent, soil, product, bays, rocks, adjacent islands, ancient laws and government, religion, customs, and late reformation*, [Glasgow?], 1752, pp. 12–14.

57 – Gray, Robert, *Birds of the west of Scotland including the Outer Hebrides*, Thomas Murray, Glasgow, 1871, p. 502; Mackenzie, *A hundred years in the Highlands*, p. 91.

58 – Gesner, Abraham, *A practical treatise on coal, petroleum and other distilled oils*, Ballière brothers, New York, 1865, 2nd edition, p. 9; Bailey, Edwin M., 'James Young – Founder of the mineral oil industry' in *Institute of Petroleum Review*, vol. 2, 1948, pp. 180–3, 216–21, 249–52, 357–60.

59 – For details see: Robins, Frederick Williams, *The story of the lamp (and the candle)*, Oxford University Press, London, New York [etc.], 1939, ch. 22.

60 – *The Journal of Gas Lighting, Water Supply, and Sanitary Improvement*, vol. 11, 1862, p. 123.

61 – *Chamber's Journal*, June 20, 1891, p. 391.

62 – Nevill, Ralph Henry (ed.), *Leaves from the note-books of Lady Dorothy Nevill*, Macmillan, London, 1907, pp. 272–3.

63 – For 'A dissertation on the instruments that communicate light' that were available in towns and cities in the mid-eighteenth century and for an account of the wax and tallow candle-making industries, see *The Universal Magazine of Knowledge and Pleasure*, John Hinton, London, vol. 4, 1749, pp. 228–32.

64 – There is very little evidence as to what these lamps were like prior to the end of the eighteenth century. Ephraim Chambers in his *Cyclopaedia: or, An universal dictionary of arts and sciences* (D. Midwinter [et al], London, 1741) says that the lamp invented by Girolamo Cardan in the mid-sixteenth century 'was in much use some years ago'. He defined it as consisting of 'a little column of brass, tin, or the like, well closed everywhere, excepting a small aperture at the bottom, in the middle of a little gullet, or canal, where the wick is placed'. It suffered from several grave disadvantages 'as that the air gets into it by starts and gluts; and that when the air in the cavity comes to be much rarified by heat, it drives out too much oil, so as sometimes to extinguish the lamp'.

65 – For details of the whaling trade and how it affected lighting in Britain see: Scoresby, William, *An account of the Arctic Regions, with a history and description of the northern whale-fishery*, Constable, Edinburgh, 1829, vol. 2; Jackson, Gordon, *The British Whaling Trade*, Black, London, 1978; Stackpole, Edouard A., *The Sea-Hunters, The New England Whalemen during the two centuries 1635–1835*, J. P. Lippincott Co., New York, 1953 and *Whales and Destiny. The rivalry between America, France, and Britain for control of the Southern whale fishery, 1785–1825*, University of Massachusetts Press, 1972.

66 – Schrøder, Michael, *The Argand burner. Its origin and development in France and England 1780–1800: an epoch in the history of science illustrated by the life and work of the physicist Ami Argand (1750–1803), Translated from the Danish by Hugh Shepherd*, Odense University Press, Odense, 1969.

67 – Rumford, 'Experiments on the relative intensities of the light emitted by luminous bodies', pp. 33–5.

68 – Webster, *An encyclopaedia of domestic economy*, p. 149.

69 – Chambers, *Cyclopaedia*, see entry under *lamp*.

70 – Rumford, 'On the management of light in illumination', p. 108 onwards.

71 – See note 65. The 1741 edition of Chambers' *Encyclopaedia* is the first to mention spermaceti candles, saying that they are 'of modern manufacture'. It is not clear how soon English chandlers began to make their own spermaceti candles as well as importing them ready-made

from America. However, Sarah Field was describing herself as a 'Maker of the new Sperma Ceti Candles' on a bill-head in 1756, so they were definitely being made in Britain by mid-century. (Groves, Charles Edward and Thorp, William (eds.), *Chemical Technology or chemistry with its applications to arts and manufactures*, P. Blakiston, Philadelphia, 1889–1903, vol. 2, p. 69.)

72–Candles were being made out of palm and cocoa-nut oil by the 1850s. Paraffin candles were first manufactured in 1854 (by J. C. and J. Field) and ozocerite candles in 1870 (by F. Field and G. Siemson).

73–See the article on 'The stearic candle manufacture' in *The Mechanics' Magazine, Museum, Journal, and Gazette*, vol. 56, March 27, 1852, pp. 243–7.

74–Wilson, George F., 'On the manufactures of Price's Patent Candle Company' in *The Journal of the Society of Arts, and the institutions in union*, Bell, London, 1856, pp. 148–56.

75–*Ibid.*

76–Rutter, J. O. N., *Gas-Lighting: its progress and its prospects; with remarks on the ratings of gas-mains, and a note on the electric-light*, John W. Parker, London, 1849, pp. 24–5.

77–Jagger, Mary A., *The history of Honley, and its hamlets from the earliest times to the present*, [no imprint], Honley, 1914, p. 67.

78–Matthews, William, *A compendium of gas-lighting, adapted for the use of those who are unacquainted with chemistry; containing an account of some new apparatus lately introduced*, Rowland Hunter, London, 1827, pp. 103–6.

79–Auer's first mantles consisted of oxides of zirconium, lanthanum and yttrium. In 1886 he patented a mantel containing thorium oxide. But in 1892 he discovered that a mantle containing 99 per cent thorium and 1 per cent cerium gave a much greater intensity of incandescence and it was this type that was most generally adopted.

80–Lewes, Vivian B., 'The future of coal gas and allied illuminants' in *Journal of the Society of Arts*, Bell, London, vol. 51, 1902, p. 107.

81–Chandler, Dean, *Silhouette, Gas Journal Centenary Issue*, London, 1949, p. 113.

82–Political and Economic Planning, *Report on the gas industry in Great Britain*, P.E.P., London, 1939, p. 49.

83–Lewes, Vivian B., 'The incandescent gas mantle and its uses' in *Journal of the Society of Arts*, Bell, London, vol. 48, 1899–1900.

84–*Ibid.*

85–Appleyard, Rollo, *The History of the Institution of Electrical Engineers (1871–1931)*, The Institution of Electrical Engineers, London, 1939, p. 90.

86–Hannah, Leslie, *Electricity before nationalization. A study of the development of the electricity supply industry in Britain to 1948*, The Johns Hopkins University Press, Baltimore and London, 1979, pp. 186, 188.

87–Political and Economic Planning, *Report on the gas industry*, p. 49.

88–Brown, Geoffrey, *Patterns of British Life. A study of certain aspects of the British people at home, at work and at play, and a compilation of some relevant statistics*, Hulton Research, London, 1950, p. 103.

89–Great Britain, Department of Scientific and Industrial Research, *The Lighting of Buildings, by the Lighting Committee of the Building Research Board of the Department of Scientific and Industrial Research*, Post War Building Series no. 12, H.M.S.O., London, 1944.

CHAPTER 6 CLEANING

1–Saussure, César de, *A foreign view of England in the reigns of George I and George II. The letters of Monsieur César de Saussure to his family; tr. and ed. by Madame van Muyden*, Murray, London, 1902, pp. 157, 219–20.

2–Kalm, Pehr, *Kalm's account of his visit to England on his way to America in 1748*, Macmillan, London and New York, 1892, pp. 12–13.

3–*Ibid.*, p. 51.

4–La Rochefoucauld, François Armand Frédéric, duc de, *A Frenchman in England, 1784; being the Mélanges sur l'Angleterre of François de la Rochefoucauld, now edited from the ms. with an introduction by Jean Marchand . . . and translated with notes by S. C. Roberts*, The University Press, Cambridge, 1933, pp. 42–3.

5–Loveday, John, *Diary of a tour in 1732 through parts of England, Wales, Ireland and Scotland, made by John Loveday of Caversham*, privately printed, Edinburgh, 1890, p. 163.

6–Buchanan, John Lanne, *Travels in the western Hebrides: from 1782 to 1790*, printed for G. G. J. and J. Robinson, [etc.], London, 1793, pp. 91–2.

7–Young, Arthur, *A tour in Ireland; with general observations on the present state of the kingdom: made in the years 1776, 1777, and 1778. And brought down to the end of 1779*, T. Cadell [etc.], London, 1780, p. 4.

8–Whitelaw, James, *An essay on the population of Dublin. Being the result of an actual survey taken in 1798, with great care and precision, and*

arranged in a manner entirely new . . .,
Graisberry and Campbell, Dublin, 1805, pp.
50–1, 54–5.
9–See his sermon, 'On Dress'.
10–Kilvert, Francis, *Selections from the diary of
the Rev. Francis Kilvert 1 January 1870 – 19
August 1871 chosen, edited and introduced by
William Plomer*, Cape, London, 1973, vol. 1,
p. 379.
11–The biblical sources showing that it is a
woman's moral duty to uphold high standards
of cleanliness are enumerated by N., H. in *The
Ladies Dictionary, being a General Entertainment
for the fair sex: a work never attempted before in
English*, printed for J. Dunton, London, 1694,
p. 457.
12–For details about the strict sabbatarianism
that made any kind of housework immoral in
god-fearing households, see: Leadbeater, Mary
Shackleton, *Leadbeater Papers*, Bell and Daldy,
London, 1862, vol. 1, *The annals of Ballitore*, pp.
83, 122; Curtis, Mrs Julia, *Mists and monsoons*,
Blackie, London and Glasgow, 1935, p. 44;
Thomas, Maude Morgan, *When I was a girl in
Wales*, Lothrop, Lee and Shepard, New York,
1936, pp. 93–4.
13–François de la Rochefoucauld (*op. cit.* p. 25)
said '*Every Saturday . . . it is customary to wash
the whole house from attic to basement,
outside and in*'. Muriel Sara in *Cornwall
remembered: recollections – Cornish people and
places*, (Hayle, Cornwall, 1970, p. 8) describes
how in her family, which kept two maids, the
house was cleaned from top to bottom on
Saturdays. See also the discussion of step
whitening and floor sanding on pp. 119 and 122
for further evidence of Saturday cleaning.
14–Evangelical Christians always argued that a
clean home was the best way to stop men
spending all their spare time in the pub,
frittering away the family income on alcohol.
See, for example, Marianne Parrott's tract *The
cleanest cottage; or, the influence of home*, [no
imprint], London, 1848, p. 14: 'Where the wife
is quiet and good-humoured, clean and tidy in
her habits, and a good manager, the husband
will love and value even the meanest home,
and generally prefer it to those harvests of vice,
the public-houses.'
   There is some evidence to suggest that
women in rural parts of Ireland believed that
good fairies only visited clean homes. (See
Arensberg, Conrad Maynadier, *The Irish
countryman. An anthropological study*, Macmillan,
New York, 1937, p. 188.)
15–The mediaeval practice of strewing rushes
and sweet-smelling herbs on floors became
increasingly rare during the seventeenth and
eighteenth centuries and had virtually
disappeared by the beginning of the nineteenth
century. Alfred Burton confirms this in his
book *Rush-bearing: an account of the old custom
of strewing rushes; carrying rushes to church; the
rush-cart; garlands in churches; morris-dancers; the
wakes; the rush*, Brook and Chrystal,
Manchester, 1891, p. 11, as does Peter
Thornton in *Seventeenth-Century Interior
Decoration in England, France and Holland*, Yale
University Press, New Haven and London,
1980, pp. 143–4.
16–Williams, Alfred, *A Wiltshire village*,
Duckworth, London, 1912, p. 190.
17–Smith, William, *Morley: ancient and modern*,
Longman, London, Leeds, 1886, p. 98.
18–Bloom, James Harvey, *Folklore, old customs
and superstitions in Shakespeare land*, Mitchell,
Hughes and Clarke, London, 1930, pp. 74–5.
For details of floor decoration patterns in
Scotland (with diagrams of different designs)
see 'Collecteana. Tangled Thread Mazes' in
Folk-Lore, XLVI, 1935, pp. 78–80. For a similar
study of Welsh patterns see William, Eurwyn,
'To keep the devil at bay' in *Country Quest*,
May 1975, pp. 34–6.
19–Barber, Edward (ed.), *Memorials of Old
Cheshire, ed. by the Ven. Edward Barber and the
Rev. P. H. Ditchfield . . .* , Allen, London, 1910,
p. 238.
20–Peate, Iorwerth Cyfeiliog, *The Welsh house;
a study in folk culture*, The Honourable Society
of Cymmrodorion, London, 1940, p. 197.
21–Hanley, Clifford, *Dancing in the streets*,
Hutchinson, London, 1958, p. 15. Thomas
Webster provides the following instructions for
decorating floors with pipe-clay: 'Boil half a
pint of size with the same quantity of whiting
and pipe-clay in two quarts of water; the
stones must be first washed clean with water,
and this mixture afterwards laid smoothly on
them with a flannel; when dry they must be
rubbed with a dry cloth or flannel.' (*An
encyclopaedia of domestic economy*, Longman, etc.,
London, 1844, p. 345.)
22–This was done with chalk or hearthstone, a
soft calcareous sandstone, which in some
places was called firestone.
23–Smith, John Thomas, *The cries of London;
exhibiting several of the itinerant trades of antient
and modern times. Copied from rare engravings, or
drawn from the life . . .* , J. B. Nichols, London,
1839, p. 82.
24–Webster, *An encyclopaedia of domestic
economy*, p. 345.
25–Foakes, Grace, *My part of the river*,

Shepheard-Walwyn, London, 1974, pp. 53–4.

26 – Thomas, *When I was a girl in Wales*, p. 6.

27 – Ridge, William Pett, *London types taken from life*, Methuen, London, 1926, pp. 183, 186–7.

28 – Roberts, Robert, *The classic slum. Salford life in the first quarter of the century*, Manchester University Press, Manchester, 1971, pp. 21–2.

29 – Personal communication from Jennifer Stead.

30 – Jagger, Mary A., *The history of Honley and its hamlets from the earliest times to the present*, [no imprint], Honley, 1914, p. 100. Mrs Jagger implies that these practices had died out before the First World War.

31 – Mackenzie, Osgood Hanbury, of Inverewe, *A hundred years in the Highlands*, Arnold, London, 1921, p. 14.

32 – Titterington, Ellen E., *The domestic life of Thomas Hardy (1921–1928) by Miss E. E. T. (Hardy's parlour-maid), as told to J. Stevens Cox and recorded during three interviews with Miss E. E. T. on the 10th and 24th January, and the 27th February 1963; with an introduction by Richard Curle*, Toucan Press, Beaminster, 1963, p. 14.

33 – *The guide to service. The Housemaid*, [no imprint], London, 1839, p. 6.

34 – *The Book of English Trades, and Library of the Useful Arts, with seventy engravings*, printed for Sir Richard Phillips, London, 1823, p. 66.

35 – The earliest comprehensive cleaning guide is: Glasse, Hannah, *The servant's directory, or house-keeper's companion: wherein the duties of the chamber-maid, nursery-maid, house-maid, landery-maid, scullion, or under-cook . . .*, printed for the author, London, 1760.

36 – For further details see: *A general description of all trades, digested in alphabetical order . . .*, T. Waller, London, 1747, p. 42; Campbell, R., *The London Tradesman. Being a compendious view of all the trades, professions, arts, both liberal and mechanic, now practiced in the cities of London and Westminster . . .*, T. Gardner, London, 1747, pp. 257–8; *The Book of English trades*, pp. 64–8; Jefferies, John Richard, *An English village. A new ed. of Wild life in a southern county . . .*, Little Brown, Boston, 1903, p. 62; Jekyll, Gertrude, *Old West Surrey. Some notes and memories*, Longman, Green, London, New York, 1904, pp. 166–8.

37 – Burt, Edward, *Letters from a gentleman in the north of Scotland to his friend in London*, S. Birt, London, 1754, vol. 1, pp. 105–6.

38 – See, for example: *The compleat family cook*, printed by J. Rawson and son, Hull, 1766. The inside of the titlepage has 'a word of advice to young housemaids', which is to throw wet sand on the floor before sweeping: 'that will gather all the flew and dust, prevent it from rising, cleans the boards, and saves both bedding, pictures and all other furniture from dust and dirt'; Whatman, Susanna, *The housekeeping book of Susanna Whatman 1776–1800 edited by Thomas Balston*, G. Bles, London, 1956. On p. 17 the housemaid is told that 'All the rooms to be dry scrubbed with white sand'.

39 – Swift, Jonathan, *Directions to servants in general; and in particular to the butler, cook, footman, coachman, groom, house-steward . . .*, printed for R. Dodsley . . . and M. Cooper, London, 1745, p. 88.

40 – For a sample of sanding practices see: Smith, *Morley: ancient and modern*, p. 98. In this Yorkshire village 'handfuls of yellow sand were scattered over the bare floor'; Warren, Clarence Henry, *Happy countryman*, G. Bles, London, 1939, pp. 36–7. Mark Thurston, a farm labourer born in 1861 in the village of Larkfield on the Essex/Sussex border, relates that 'sand was all the carpet we ever had at home, and it was the same in most of the cottages . . .'; Grey, Edwin, *Cottage life in a Hertfordshire village, 'How the agricultural labourer lived and fared in the late '60s and the '70s' . . .*, Fisher, Knight and Co., Ltd, St. Albans, 1935, p. 90. 'Some of the people after scrubbing and drying the floors sprinkled sand over the bare boards or bricks. This was supposed to keep the floor clean for a longer time'; Thomas, *When I was a girl in Wales*, pp. 84–5; Evans, Emyr Estyn, *Irish heritage. The landscape, the people and their work*, Dundalgan Press, Dundalk, 1942, p. 152; Jobson, Allan, *A window in Suffolk*, Hale, London, 1962, p. 38. Jobson, in describing what life was like at his grandparents' farmhouse in Middleton-Cum-Fordley village in Suffolk, says: 'When the floor was washed once a week it would be newly sanded, and a whisp of wheat straw placed by the door to wipe one's feet on'; Jenkin, Alfred Kenneth Hamilton, *Cornish homes and customs*, Dent, London and Toronto, 1934, p. 55. 'Over [the moorstone floors] the housewife scattered dry sand, which "took up" the dirt from the men's boots, and could easily be swept away and renewed. Sanding was often done in patterns which gave a pleasing appearance.'

41 – See, for example: Warren, *Happy countryman*, pp. 36–7; Grey, *Cottage life in a Hertfordshire village*, p. 90.

42 – Synge, John Millington, *Collected works edited by Robin Skelton*, Oxford University Press, London, 1966, vol. 2, p. 254.

43 – Jenkin, *Cornish homes and customs*, p. 55.

44 – Plot, Robert, *The natural history of Oxfordshire, being an essay towards a natural history of England*, printed at the theatre, Oxford, 1677, p. 74.

45 – Richard, William, *Wallography; or the Britton describ'd: being a pleasant relation of a journey into Wales; wherein are set down several remarkable passages that occur'd in the way thither*, O. Blagrave, London, 1682, p. 62.

46 – See, for example: *The town and country cook; or, young woman's best guide, in the whole art of cookery*, printed for W. Lane, London, ca. 1760, p. 1.

47 – Jenkin, *Cornish homes and customs*, p. 56.

48 – Price, Rebecca, *The compleat cook; or, the secrets of a seventeenth-century housewife; compiled and introduced by Madelaine Masson*, Routledge and K. Paul, London, 1974, p. 314.

49 – Baillie, Grizell (Hume), Lady, *The household book of Lady Grisell Baillie 1692–1733*, ed., with notes and introduction, by Robert Scott-Moncrieff, T. and A. Constable, Scottish history society, 1911, see under 'memorandums and directions to servants'.

50 – See, for example: Kalm, *Kalm's account*, p. 276; Glasse, *The servant's directory*, pp. 59–60; Mrs Taylor, of Ongar, *The present of a mistress to a young servant: consisting of friendly advice and real histories*, [no imprint], London, 1816, p. 96.

51 – Houghton, John, *Husbandry and Trade improv'd . . ., [edited by Richard Bradley]*, Woodman and Lyon, 2nd edition, London, 1728, vol. 1, pp. 252–3.

52 – This point is made in Forty, Adrian, *The Electric Home. A case study of the domestic revolution of the inter-war years*, The Open University Press, London, 1975, p. 50.

53 – Booth, Cecil H., 'The origins of the vacuum cleaner' in *Transactions of the Newcomen Society for the study of the history of engineering and technology*, vol. 15, 1934–5, pp. 85–98.

54 – Hitchins, Charles F., 'Some early business reminiscences', London, 1923, p. 4 [unpublished typescript at Science Museum, South Kensington, London].

55 – Booth, 'The origins of the vacuum cleaner'.

56 – Browne, Geoffrey, *Patterns of British life. A study of certain aspects of the British people at home, at work and at play, and a compilation of some relevant statistics*, Hulton Research, London, 1950, p. 104.

57 – For an excellent general article on the subject see: Boynton, L. O. J., 'The Bed-bug and the age of elegance' in *Furniture History. The Journal of The Furniture History Society*, vol. 1, 1965, pp. 15–31.

58 – Southall, John, *A treatise of bugs, shewing when and how they were first brought into England. How they are brought into and infect houses. Their nature, several foods, times and manner of spawning and propagating in this climate*, J. Roberts, London, 1730, p. 1.

59 – Hughes, Alfred Weston McKenny, *The Bed-bug. Its habits and life history and how to deal with it*, printed for the Trustees of the British Museum, London, 1949, p. 3.

60 – See, for example: Tryon, Thomas, *A treatise of cleanness in meats and drinks, of the preparation of food, the excellency of good airs, and the benefits of clean sweet beds. Also of the generation of bugs, and their cure*, The author, London, 1682, pp. 7–13 and *England's happiness improved: or, an infallible way to get riches, encrease plenty, and promote pleasure*, R. Clavill, London, 1697, p. 172.

61 – Mayhew, Henry, *London labour and the London Poor; a cyclopaedia of the condition and earnings of those that will work, those that cannot work, and those that will not work*, [no imprint], London, 1861–2, vol. 3, pp. 36–9.

62 – Southall, *A treatise of bugs*, p. 33. It should be noted that Pehr Kalm (*op. cit.* p. 51) also thought that bugs were imported in foreign ships; he dated their rapid spread, however, to the 1720s.

63 – Haselmore, Anthony, *The economist, or new family cookery*, T. and J. Allman, London, 1824, p. 508.

64 – Carlyle, Jane Welsh, *Letters and memorials of Jane Welsh Carlyle. Prepared for publication by Thomas Carlyle, Edited by James Anthony Froude*, George Munro, New York, 1883, letter 7 dated August 1835, p. 7.

65 – *Ibid.*, letter 54 dated August 1843, p. 31.

66 – *Ibid.*, letter 116 dated October 1849, p. 58.

67 – *Ibid.*, letter 147 dated September 1852, pp. 69–70.

68 – Great Britain. Ministry of Health, *Reports on Public Health and Medical Subjects No. 72. Report on the bed-bug*, H.M.S.O., London, 1934, p. 11.

69 – Reeves, Magdalen Stuart, *Round about a pound a week, by Mrs Pember Reeves*, Bell, London, 1913, p. 36.

70 – Roberts, *The classic slum*, p. 58.

71 – Great Britain, Ministry of Health, *Report on the bed-bug*, pp. 4, 16.

72 – See, for example: Godfrey, Boyle, *Miscellanea vere Utilia: or miscellaneous experiments and observations on various subjects*, printed for R. Robinson, London, ca. 1735, pp. 130–6; Bailey, Nathaniel, *Dictionarium domesticum, being a new and compleat houshold dictionary, for the use both of city and country*

[etc.], printed for C. Hitch [etc.], London, 1736, see entry under *bugs*.

73 – Nourse, Timothy, *Campania fœlix. Or, a discourse of the benefits and improvements of husbandry . . . To which are added, two essays: I. Of a country-house II. Of the fuel of London*, printed for T. Bennet, London, 1700, p. 351.

74 – Foakes, *My part of the river*, p. 53.

75 – Pennant, Thomas, *A tour in Wales*, printed by H. Hughes, London, 1778, vol. 2, p. 87.

76 – Young, Arthur, *A tour in Ireland; with general observations on the present state of that kingdom: made in the years 1776, 1777, and 1778. And brought down to the end of 1779*, T. Cadell [etc.], London, 1780, p. 26.

77 – Leadbeater, *Leadbeater Papers*, vol. 1, p. 72.

78 – Kay-Shuttleworth, James Phillips, *The moral and physical condition of the working classes employed in the cotton manufacture in Manchester*, J. Ridgway, London, 1832, p. 23.

79 – Le Fanu, William Richard, *Seventy years of Irish life, being anecdotes and reminiscences*, Macmillan, New York and London, 1893, pp. 106–7.

80 – Morris, Marmaduke Charles Frederick, *Yorkshire reminiscences (with others)*, Oxford University Press, London and New York, 1922, p. 314.

81 – Morris, Marmaduke Charles Frederick, *The British workman, past and present*, Oxford University Press, London, 1928, p. 17.

82 – Carlyle, *Letters and memorials of Jane Welsh Carlyle*, letter dated Oct. 1843, p. 34.

83 – Hudson, Derek, *Munby man of two worlds. The life and diaries of Arthur J. Munby 1828–1910*, Cambridge University Press, Cambridge, 1972.

84 – See, for example, Lawson, John James, *A man's life by Jack Lawson M.P. for Chester-le-Street*, Hodder and Stoughton, London, 1932, p. 47.

85 – Personal communication from Jennifer Stead.

86 – Personal communication from Betty Palmer.

87 – Roberts, *The classic slum*, p. 21.

CHAPTER 7 LAUNDRY

1 – Edwards, George, *From crow-scaring to Westminster; an Autobiography . . .*, The Labour Publishing Company, London, 1922, p. 21.

2 – Great Britain, General Board of Health, *Report by the General Board of Health on the supply of water to the Metropolis (presented to both houses of Parliament)*, H.M.S.O., London, 1850, appendix 3, pp. 220–3.

3 – Smith, John Thomas, *The cries of London; exhibiting several of the itinerant trades of antient and modern times. Copied from rare engravings, or drawn from the life . . .*, J. B. Nichols, London, 1839, p. 81.

4 – *The birth, life, and death of John Franks, with the pranks he played though a meer fool*, [no imprint, c. 1750].

5 – *Simple Simon's Misfortunes: or his wife Margery's outrageous cruelty*, [no imprint, c. 1750].

6 – See *Poets jests, or mirth in abundance*, [no imprint, c. 1775], for a lewd joke to this effect.

7 – Richard, William, *Wallography; or the Britton describ'd: being a pleasant relation of a journey into Wales; wherein are set down several remarkable passages that occur'd in the way thither*, O. Blagrave, London, 1682, p. 52.

8 – Young, Arthur, *A tour in Ireland; with general observations on the present state of that kingdom: made in the years 1776, 1777, and 1778. And brought down to the end of 1779*, T. Cadell [etc.], London, 1780, p. 25.

9 – Dutton, Hely, *Statistical Survey of the County of Clare*, printed by Graisberry and Campbell, Dublin, 1808, pp. 180–1.

10 – Hodgson, John Crawford (ed.), *Six North Country Diaries*, Surtees Society, Durham, 1910, pp. 32, 39.

11 – See, for example: Burt, Edward, *Letters from a gentleman in the north of Scotland to his friend in London; containing the description of a capital town in that northern country; with an account of some uncommon customs of the inhabitants: likewise an account of the Highlands*, S. Birt, London, 1754, vol. 1, p. 52.

12 – *Ibid.*

13 – Hall, Samuel Carter, Mr and Mrs, *Ireland: its scenery, character etc. . . .*, How and Parsons, London, 1841–3, vol. 1, p. 130; Loveday, John, *Diary of a tour in 1732 through parts of England, Wales, Ireland and Scotland, made by John Loveday of Cavesham . . .*, privately printed, Edinburgh, 1890, p. 163.

14 – Synge, John Millington, *Collected Works edited by Robin Skelton*, Oxford University Press, London, 1966, vol. 2, p. 76. Women also washed their clothes in sea-water on the island of St. Kilda in the 1830s. (Seton, George, *St. Kilda, past and present*, W. Blackwood, Edinburgh and London, 1878, p. 243.)

15 – Nodal, J. H. and Milner, G., *A glossary of the Lancashire dialect*, English Dialect Society, London, 1875–82. Stead, Jennifer, 'The uses of urine' in *Old West Riding. A Collection of Original Articles* edited by George Redmonds, vol. 1, no. 2, autumn 1981.

16 – Easther, Alfred, *A glossary of the dialect of Almondbury and Huddersfield*, English Dialect Society, London, 1883.

17 – Great Britain, Health of Towns Commission, *Report on the state of Newcastle-upon-Tyne and other Towns. By David Boswell Reid, Esq., M.D., one of the Commissioners appointed by Her Majesty for inquiring into the state of large towns and populous districts in England and Wales*, H.M.S.O., London, 1845, p. 5.

18 – Taylor, Joseph, *A Journey to Edenborough in Scotland, by Joseph Taylor . . . Now first printed from the original manuscript. With notes by William Cowan*, W. Brown, Edinburgh, 1903, p. 136.

19 – *A Collection of Welsh Travels and Memoirs of Wales*, printed for and sold by J. Torbuck and E. Rider, Dublin, 1743, p. 64. The first edition of this work appeared in 1738. Hall, James of Walthamstow, *Tour through Ireland; particularly the interior and least known parts . . .*, R. P. Moore, London, 1813, vol. 1, p. 233.

20 – Clift, William, *The reminiscences of William Clift of Bramley. Born 1828 and wrote these my reminiscences 1908*, Bird Bros., Basingstoke, 1908, p. 71.

21 – Plot, Robert, *The natural history of Staffordshire*, printed at the theatre, Oxford, 1686, pp. 334–5.

22 – Fiennes, Celia, *The journeys of Celia Fiennes, Edited and with an Introduction by Christopher Morris*, The Cresset Press, London, 1947, pp. 165–6.

23 – Hall, *Tour through Ireland*, vol. 2, pp. 60–1.

24 – Owens, John, *Plain papers relating to the excise branch of the Inland revenue department, from 1621 to 1878; or, A history of the excise* [no imprint], Linlithgow, 1879, pp. 449–51. Dowell, Stephen, *A history of taxation and taxes in England from the earliest times to the year 1885*, Longman, Green, London and New York, 1888, vol. 4, pp. 317–22.

25 – Myddelton, William Martial (ed.), *Chirk Castle accounts, A.D. 1666–1753*, Manchester University Press, Manchester, 1931.

26 – Purefoy, Henry, *Purefoy Letters, 1735–1753, edited by G. Eland*, Sidgwick and Jackson, London, 1931, vol. 1, p. 153.

27 – Susannah Stacey was old-fashioned. From about 1830 most women eked out their soap with soda rather than lye. Woodward, Marcus, *The mistress of Stantons Farm . . .*, Heath Cranton, London, 1938, p. 153.

28 – Stow, John, *The Annales, or Generall Chronicle of England, begun first by maister John Stow, and after him continued . . . unto the ende of this present yeere 1614, by E. Howes*, Imprinted by Thomas Dawson for Thomas Adams, London, 1615. Stubbes, Philip, *The Anatomie of Abuses: containing, A Discoverie or brief Summarie of such notable vices and imperfections, as now raigne in many . . . Countreyes of the worlde: but (especially) in . . . Ailgna (Anglia)*, J. R. Jones, London, 1583.

29 – However, farmers' wives were still making lye from wood ashes in Warwickshire in the 1870s and 1880s (Bloom, James Harvey, *Folk lore, old customs and superstitions in Shakespeare land*, Mitchell, Hughes and Clarke, London, 1930, p. 32) and in Suffolk in the 1910s (Jobson, Allan, *An hour-glass on the run*, Hale, London, 1975, p. 54).

30 – See, for example: Wilson, R. Lucock, *Soap through the ages*, Unilever, 1952; Edward, H. R., *Competition and monopoly in the British soap industry*, Clarendon Press, Oxford, 1962; Musson, Albert Edward, *Enterprise in soap and chemicals: Joseph Crosfield and Sons, Limited, 1815–1965*, A. M. Kelley, New York, 1965; Wilson, Charles, *The history of Unilever. A study in economic growth and change*, Cassell, London, 3 vols, 1970.

31 – For details about the late seventeenth-century soap trade see: Houghton, John, *Husbandry and Trade improv'd . . .*, [edited by Richard Bradley], Woodman and Lyon, 2nd edition, London, 1728, vol. 1, letter dated Feb. 15, 1694/5, pp. 348–54; Houghton said that the London soap-boilers' good soap was usually made out of two parts olive oil and one part tallow. These were boiled for many hours, together with soap-lees (lye made out of pot-ashes slaked with lime). He also described how ball soap was made in Yorkshire and the method of producing Castle soap in Dublin and Lancashire; *Reasons humbly offered by the soap makers of the City of London to the Honourable the House of Commons in Parliament assembled against a Duty to be laid on soap*, London, 1695; Stout, William, *The autobiography of William Stout of Lancaster 1665–1752, edited by J. D. Marshall for the William Stout Tercentary Study Group*, Manchester University Press, Manchester, 1967, pp. 125, 146, 151.

32 – Misson, Henri, de Valbourg, *M. Misson's Memoirs and observations in his travels over England. With some account of Scotland and Ireland, . . . translated by Mr Ozell*, D. Browne, London, 1719, p. 303.

33 – *A general description of all trades, digested in alphabetical order . . .*, T. Waller, London, 1747, p. 196.

34 – Hamilton, Henry (ed.), *Life and labour on*

an *Aberdeenshire estate, 1735–1750, being selections of the Monymusk papers*, [of Sir Archibald Grant, 2nd baronet of Monymusk], Third Spalding Club, Aberdeen, 1946. These were Dantzick soap, soap balls, black soap, Dutch soap, Castile soap, Newcastle soap and London soap.

35 – *The Ladies Advocate; or, An Apology for Matrimony. In answer to the Batchelor's Monitor*, London, 1741.

36 – Davies, David, *The case of labourers in husbandry stated and considered in three parts . . . With an appendix; containing a collection of accounts, shewing the earnings and expences of labouring families in different parts of the kingdom*, P. Byrne, Dublin, 1796. Eden, Frederick Morton, Sir, *The State of the Poor: or, An history of the labouring classes in England, from the Conquest to the present period; in which are particularly considered their domestic economy, with respect to diet, dress, fuel, and habitation . . .*, B. and J. White, London, 1797, 3 vols.

37 – For a typical early soap recipe see: *The Fountain of Knowledge: or, British Legacy*, London, *c.* 1750, p. 4. For examples of farmers' wives who made their own soap see: Woodward, *The mistress of Stantons Farm*, p. 153. Neville, Hastings M., *A corner in the North: yesterday and today with Border folk*, A. Reid, Newcastle-upon-Tyne, 1909, p. 83.

38 – *The Ladies' Library: or, Encyclopaedia of female knowledge, in every branch of domestic economy: comprehending, in alphabetical arrangement, distinct treatises on every practical subject, necessary for servants and mistresses of families . . .*, J. Ridgway, London, 1790, p. 170.

39 – Grey, Edwin, *Cottage life in a Hertfordshire village: 'How the agricultural labourer lived and fared in the late '6os and the '7os'. . .*, Fisher, Knight, St. Albans, 1935, pp. 49–50.

40 – Thresh, John Clough, *Housing of the Agricultural Labourer, With special reference to the County of Essex*, Rural Housing and Sanitation Association, 1919, p. 43.

41 – Jenkin, Alfred Kenneth Hamilton, *Cornish homes and customs*, Dent, London and Toronto, 1934, p. 38.

42 – Davies, Margaret Llewelyn (ed.), *Life as we have known it. By Cooperative working women*, The Hogarth Press, London, 1931, p. 57.

43 – Inglis, James, *Oor ain folk; being memories of manse life in the mearns and a crack aboot auld times*, D. Douglas, Edinburgh, 1894, pp. 104–6.

44 – *Ibid.*, pp. 103–4.

45 – *Merry tales of the wise men of Gotham*,[no imprint].

46 – Houghton, *Husbandry and Trade improv'd . . .*, vol. 1, letter dated Feb. 15, 1694/5, pp. 348–9.

47 – Hardy, Mary, *Mary Hardy's diary, with an introduction by B. Cozens Hardy*, Norfolk Record Society, 1968, vol. 37.

48 – Thompson, Flora, *Lark Rise to Candleford*, Oxford University Press, London, 1945, pp. 512–13.

49 – Baillie, Grizel (Hume), Lady, *The household book of Lady Grisell Baillie 1692–1733, ed., with notes and introduction*, by Robert Scott-Moncrieff, T. and A. Constable, Scottish history society, 1911, p. 279.

50 – See, for example: Thomas, Maude Morgan, *When I was a girl in Wales*, Lothrop, Lee and Shepard, New York, 1936, p. 87.

51 – The main songs about wash-day are: 'Washing Week' originally printed in the *Weekly Magazine or Edinburgh Amusement*, 1771, and reprinted in Logan, William Hugh, *A pedlar's pack of ballads and songs*, W. Paterson, Edinburgh, 1869. 'Driving Away with the Smoothing Iron' or 'Dashing Away with the Smoothing Iron'. Different versions of this are given in Sharp, Cecil James, *One hundred English folksongs*, Oliver Ditson Company, Boston, 1916, and *English folk songs*, Novello, London, 1920. For 'They that wash on Monanday' see note 43.

52 – Eyles, Margaret Leonora, *The woman in the little house . . .*, G. Richards, London, 1922, pp. 31, 46. Flint, Elizabeth, *Hot bread and chips*, Museum Press, London, 1963. Boardman, Stanley R., *1920's boy – recollections of a Yorkshire childhood*, Ridings Publishing Company, Driffield, 1973.

53 – Morris, Marmaduke Charles Frederick, *The British workman, past and present*, Oxford University Press, Oxford, 1928, p. 58.

54 – Smith, *The cries of London*, p. 81. 'They may be seen in the winter time, shivering at the doors, at three or four o'clock in the morning, and are seldom dismissed before ten at night.'

55 – Marshall, Sybil, *Fenland Chronicle. Recollections of William Henry and Kate Mary Edwards collected and edited by their daughter*, Cambridge University Press, Cambridge, 1967, pp. 244–5.

56 – See note 51.

57 – Woodforde, James S., *The diary of a country parson: the Reverend James Woodforde, Edited by John Beresford*, Oxford University Press, London, 1926, vol. 5, p. 198.

58 – Clift, *The reminiscences*, p. 71.

59 – Great Britain, General Board of Health, *Report . . . on the supply of water to the metropolis*, pp. 220–2.

60 – In the mid-eighteenth century, for example, the author of *A Present for a Servant-Maid: or, The sure means of gaining Love and Esteem* laid down the law as follows: 'Muslin, and the very thin old Cambrick and lawn require starching, or they will look like Rags, and not last clean a Moment.' (T. Gardner, London, 1743, p. 75.)

61 – Reckitt, Basil Norman, *The history of Reckitt and Sons, Limited*, A. Brown, London, 1951, p. 18.

62 – For descriptions of the seventeenth-century starch industry see: Plot, Robert, *The natural history of Oxfordshire, being an essay towards the natural history of England*, printed at the theatre, Oxford, 1677, pp. 280–1; Houghton, *Husbandry and Trade improv'd . . .*, vol. I, letter dated May 1694, p. 253. By 1747 starch-making was 'a very considerable as well as profitable Trade, carried on in the Shop-keeping Way; . . . the Starch works are large concerns, and carried on in the country . . .'. (*A General description of all trades digested in alphabetical order*, p. 198.)

63 – Jobson, *An hour-glass on the run*, p. 92.

64 – Cross, Eric, *The tailor and Ansty*, Chapman and Hall, London, 1942, pp. 39–40.

65 – Bell, Florence E. E. (Olliffe) Lady, *At the works, a study of a manufacturing town, by Lady Bell* (Mrs Hugh Bell), Arnold, London, 1907, p. 231.

66 – Steer, Francis W., *Farm and Cottage inventories of mid-Essex, 1635–1749*, Essex County Council, Chelmsford, 1950.

67 – Cash, Margaret (ed.), *Devon Inventories of the sixteenth and seventeenth centuries*, Devon and Cornwall Record Society, new series, vol. II, 1966.

68 – Spence, Elizabeth Isabella, *Sketches of the present manners, customs and scenery of Scotland with incidental remarks on the Scottish character*, 2nd edition, Longman etc., London, 1811, vol. I, pp. 75–6.

69 – Mitchell, Arthur, *The past in the present: what is civilisation?*, D. Douglas, Edinburgh, 1880, lecture 5, p. 122.

70 – Wordsworth, Dorothy, *Recollections of a tour made in Scotland A.D. 1803, edited by J. C. Shairp*, Edmonston and Douglas, Edinburgh, 1874, p. 265. The beetle was used as a substitute mangle in the north of England until the late nineteenth century. (Neville, *A corner in the North*, p. 133.)

71 – Marshall, Rosalind K., *The days of Duchess Anne; life in the household of the Duchess of Hamilton 1656–1716*, Collins, London, 1973, pp. 49–50.

72 – *Transactions of the Society instituted at London, for the encouragement of arts, manufactures, and commerce; with the premiums offered in the year 1798*, vol. XVI, London, 1798. George Jee was not the first inventor of the 'one-way' handle. Ferguson Hardie, for example, patented a similar device in 1791.

73 – Marshall, *Fenland Chronicle*, p. 244.

74 – Mr Baker, of Fore Street, Cripplegate, London, invented a box mangle which combined the advantages of Jee's 'one-way' handle with a fly wheel which equalized the motion of turning the box. See Holland, John, *A treatise on the progressive improvement and present state of the manufactures in metal*, Longman etc., London, 1831–4, vol. 2, pp. 255–9.

75 – Jermy, Louise, *The memories of a working woman*, Goose, Norwich, 1934, pp. 28–9.

76 – Patents for the upright type of mangle first appeared in the late eighteenth century. In 1774, for example, Hugh Oxenham patented 'A mangle of an entirely new construction, made with sliding collars, wood or metal springs, rollers cogged with iron or pinning wheels, to answer all the purposes of mangles without the incumbrance of weight, and will stand in a third part of the room of a common mangle'.

77 – Cutter, B. A. and Town, H. C., 'Some recollections of the domestic wringer and mangle industry' in *The Edgar Allen News*, vol. 45, no. 528, June 1966.

78 – Personal communication from Mr Hugh Kenrick, 1977.

79 – Browne, Geoffrey, *Patterns of British Life. A study of certain aspects of the British people at home, at work and at play, and a compilation of some relevant statistics*, Hulton Research, London, 1950, table 23, p. 104.

80 – Some typical seventeenth- and eighteenth-century examples include: White, John, *A rich cabinet, with variety of inventions: unlock'd and open'd, for the Recreation of Ingenious Sirpits* [*sic*] *at their vacant hours . . .*, London, 1651; *The compleat servant-maid; or, the Young Maidens Tutor*, London, 1677; *The Accomplish'd Female Instructor: or, a very useful companion for Ladies, Gentlewomen, and Others*, London, 1704; Lémery, Nicolas, Apothecary to the French King, *New Curiosities in Arts and Nature: or, a collection of the most valuable secrets in all Arts and Sciences*, London, 1711; *Dictionarium Polygraphicum: or, the whole Body of Arts regularly digested*, London, 1735, vol. 2; *The Fountain of Knowledge: or, British Legacy*, London, c. 1750; Barker, Anne, *The Complete*

servant-maid: or young woman's best companion, London, c. 1770; Lupton, Thomas, *A thousand notable things, on various subjects; disclosed from the secrets of nature and art; practicable, profitable and of great advantage*, London, 1791; *Valuable secrets concerning arts and trades: or approved directions, for the best artists*, London, 1795.

81 – Prince, Ancliffe, *The craft of laundering: a history of fabric cleaning*, Company of Launderers, London, 1970, pp. 22–4.

82 – Glasse, Hannah, *The servant's directory, or housekeeper's companion*, printed for the author, London, 1760, pp. 72, 76–7.

83 – Mascall, L., *A profitable boke declaring dyvers approved remedies, to taking out spottes and staines, in silkes, velvets, linnen, and woolen clothes . . .*, London, 1583.

84 – Tucker, William, *The Family Dyer and Scourer, being a complete treatise on the whole art of cleaning and dying . . .*, Sherwood, Neely and Jones, London, 1817, pp. 24–5.

85 – For details of a late eighteenth-century London dyer's business see: Dagley, D. B., *Mark Thornhill Wade, silk dyer, Soho*, Res. pub. co., London, 1961 and Mansfield, Alan, 'Dyeing and cleaning clothes in the late eighteenth and early nineteenth century' in *Costume, The Journal of the Costume Society*, 1968, no. 2.

86 – The Heating and Ventilation (Reconstruction) Committee of the Building Research Board of the Department of Scientific and Industrial Research, *Heating and Ventilation of dwellings*, Post War buildings series no. 19, 1945, p. 133.

87 – Political and Economic Planning, *The market for household appliances*, P.E.P., London, 1945.

88 – Browne, *Patterns of British Life*, table 23, p. 104.

89 – Needleman, L., *The demand for domestic appliances*, National Institute Economic Review no. 12, Nov. 1960, table 2.

90 – Electricity Council, *Background information on electrical domestic appliances, electric heating systems, electric water heating and other domestic uses of electricity*, Electricity Council, London, 1981.

91 – Montague, M. F. Ashley, 'Notes and Correspondence' in *Isis*, no. 7, 1943.

92 – Bailey, William, *A treatise on the better employment and more comfortable support of the poor in work-houses*, [no imprint], London, 1758, pp. 23–4.

93 – For some early nineteenth-century servants' condemnation of washing machines see *The Servant's guide and family manual: with new and improved receipts, arranged and adapted to the duties of all classes of servants*, printed for John Limbird, London, 1830, p. 134.

94 – William Strutt of Derby was one of the first persons to popularize steam-powered washing and drying machines. The appliances he invented and had installed in the Derbyshire General Infirmary (which opened in 1807) are described in Sylvester, Charles, *The philosophy of domestic economy; as exemplified in the mode of warming, ventilating, washing, drying, and cooking, and in various arrangements contributing to the comfort and convenience of domestic life, adopted in the Derbyshire General Infirmary*, Longman etc., London, 1819.

95 – Mr G. A. Williams of The Hotpoint Electric Appliance Co. Ltd. says that electric washing machines were first introduced into Britain from the United States around 1917. (Williams, G. A., 'Washing Machines: Yesterday and Today' in *Electrical Times*, April 10, 1958.) Foreign firms dominated the electric washing machine market until the 1930s.

96 – Political and Economic Planning, *The market for household appliances*.

97 – For an account of commercial laundry services in London see: The Fabian Society, *Life in the laundry*, The Fabian Society, London, tract no. 112, 1902; Smith, Hubert Llewellyn (ed.), *The new survey of London life and labour*, P. S. King, London, 1933, vol. 5, ch. 8.

98 – Campbell, Agnes, *Report on public baths and wash-houses in the United Kingdom. General report*, printed at the University Press, Edinburgh, 1918, pp. 7, 49, 50.

99 – The Hearing and Ventilation (Reconstruction) Committee, *Heating and Ventilation of Dwellings*, p. 80.

100 – See, for example, Kelsey, W. F. F. and Ginsburg, David, *The Social Survey, Consumer Expenditure Series. Expenditure of Laundries, dyeing and cleaning, mending and alterations and shoe repairing services*, Central Office of Information, London, August 1949. This survey of 1,400-odd U.K. households in Sept. 1948 and April 1949 showed that only 41.5 per cent made use of a laundry or private laundress outside the home, and this was mostly on a limited basis. The percentage of households using laundries varied regionally from 60 per cent in London, 35–50 per cent in the South and East, and 25–35 per cent in Wales, the Midlands, the North and Scotland.

101 – See, for example, Frazer, Lilly Grove, Lady, *First Aid to the Servantless*, Heffer, Cambridge, 1913.

1 – The title of this section comes from a novel by Horace and Augustus Septimus Mayhew, *The greatest plague of life: or, The adventures of a lady in search of a good servant. By one who has been 'almost worried to death'*, D. Bogue, London, 1847.

2 – The following account of Jane Carlyle's experiences with servants is drawn from Holme, Thea Johnston, *The Carlyles at home*, Oxford University Press, London and New York, 1965, appendix, and Carlyle, Jane Welsh, *Letters and memorials of Jane Welsh Carlyle. Prepared for publication by Thomas Carlyle. Edited by James Anthony Froude*, George Munro, New York, 1883, *passim*.

3 – McBride, Theresa M., *The domestic revolution: the modernization of household service in England and France, 1820–1920*, Holmes and Meier, New York, 1976, table 2.6, p. 45.

4 – Adams, Charlotte, *Little servant maids*, S.P.C.K., London, 1851.

5 – Bathgate, Janet, *Aunt Janet's legacy to her nieces; recollections of a humble life in Yarrow in the beginning of the century*, G. Lewis, Selkirk, 1894, p. 65.

6 – Great Britain, Board of Trade, *Report by Miss Collett on the money wages of indoor domestic servants*, Parliamentary accounts and papers, vol. XCII, 1899, p. 25.

7 – The female servant hierarchy hardly changed over the centuries. See, for example: *The Compleat Servant-Maid, or, the Young Maidens tutor, directing how they may fit themselves for any of these employments, viz. waiting-woman, housekeeper, chamber-maid, etc . . .*, [no imprint], London, 1677; N., H., *The Ladies Dictionary; being a general entertainment for the fair sex: a work never attempted before in England*, printed for J. Dunton, London, 1694.

8 – Baillie, Grixel (Hume), Lady, *The household book of Lady Grisell Baillie 1692–1733*, ed., with notes and introduction, by Robert Scott-Moncrieff, T. and A. Constable, Scottish history society, 1911, p. li.

9 – Blundell, Nicholas, *The great diurnal of Nicholas Blundell of Little Crosby, Lancashire*, transcribed and annotated by Frank Tyrer, Record Society of Lancashire and Cheshire, Chester, 1968–72, vol. 1, p. 62.

10 – *Ibid*, vol. 1, pp. 145, 147, 148.

11 – *Life of a licensed victualler's daughter. Written by herself*, Saunders and Otley, London, 1844, p. 23.

12 – Vulliamy, Colwyn Edward, *The Polderoy Papers 1868–1886*, Joseph, London, 1943, p. 273.

13 – Defoe, Daniel, *The behaviour of servants in England inquired into. With a proposal containing such heads of constitutions as would effectually answer this great end, and bring servants of every class to a just regulation*, printed for H. Whitridge, London, 1724. Moreton, Andrew, [i.e. Daniel Defoe] *Every-body's business is no-body's business; or, Private abuses, publick grievances: exemplified in the pride, insolence, and exorbitant wages of our women-servants, foot-men etc.*, [no imprint], London, 1725.

14 – See, for example, Ellis, William, *The country housewife's family companion: or, profitable directions for . . . the management and good economy of the domestic concerns of a country life . . . shewing how great savings may be made in housekeeping*, printed for James Hodges and B. Collins, London, 1750, pp. 180–2.

15 – See, for example, *A treatise on the Use and Abuse of the Second, commonly called, The Steward's Table, in Families of the First Rank*, [no imprint], London, c. 1758. Townley, James, *High life below stairs: a farce of two acts*, [no imprint], London, 1759.

16 – *The parson and the fowls: or, the maid too cunning for her master*, [no imprint].

17 – Purefoy, Henry, *Purefoy Letters, 1735–1753*, edited by G. Eland, Sidgwick and Jackson, London, 1931, vol. 1, pp. 128–32.

18 – Mill, John, *The diary of the Reverend John Mill, minister of the parishes of Dunrossness, Sandwick and Cunningsburgh in Shetland, 1740–1803. With selections from local records and original documents relating to the district. Edited, with introduction and notes, by Gilbert Goudie*, printed at the University press by T. and A. Constable for the Scottish history society, Edinburgh, 1889, p. 18.

19 – Wright, Thomas, *Autobiography of Thomas Wright of Birkenshaw, in the county of York, 1736–1797, Edited by his grandson, Thomas Wright*, J. R. Smith, London, 1864, pp. 142, 144, 146.

20 – Lochhead, Marion, 'Lady Breadalbane's regulations for her servants, 1829' in *Scottish Historical Review*, vol. XXVI, no. 102, Oct. 1947.

21 – There was a disparity between male and female servants' pay through out the period. Male servants received anything from one-half to one-seventh more than females did. There was nothing unusual about this; in every occupation men were paid more than women for similar or identical work.

22 – Beeton, Isabella, *The Book of Household Management*, S. O. Beeton, London, 1861, p. 8.

23 – Johnson, Mary, *Madam Johnson's present: or, the best instructions for young women, in useful and universal knowledge etc . . .*, printed for M.

Cooper and C. Sympson, London, 1754, pp. x, xi.

24 – Ridge, William Pett, *London types taken from life*, Methuen, London, 1926, pp. 186–7. Willis, Frederick, *A book of London yesterdays*, Phoenix House, London, 1960, p. 15. See also Bosanquet, Mrs Helen (Dendy), *Rich and poor*, Macmillan, London, 1896, pp. 83–4. She says that: 'Among the higher class artisans the little nurse-girl, the young slavey or general, and the periodical charwoman are quite frequent.'

25 – For bibliographies of printed cookery books see: Maclean, Virginia Elizabeth, *A short-title catalogue of household and cookery books published in the English tongue: 1701–1800*, Prospect Books, London, 1981 and Schumacher-Voelker, Uta, *Cookery Books published in Britain 1800–1874*, Prospect Books, London, 1983; Driver, Elizabeth, *Cookery Books Published in Britain 1875–1914*, Prospect Books, London, 1983.

26 – S., M., *Domestic Service. By an old servant. Preface by Mrs George Wemyss*, Constable, London, 1917, p. 106.

27 – Great Britain, Ministry of Labour, Committee on present conditions as to supply of female domestic servants, *Report to the Minister of Labour of the Committee appointed to enquire into the present conditions as to the supply of female domestic servants*, H.M.S.O., London, 1923, p. 9.

28 – Pearson, A., *Economy and other advantages of gas*, [no imprint], Oxford, 1889, pp. 1–2.

29 – Great Britain, Ministry of Labour, *Report to the Minister of Labour of the Committee appointed to enquire into the present conditions as to the supply of female domestic servants*, p. 7.

30 – The percentages of servants in the population of England and Wales are derived from the censuses.

31 – Wilkinson, Annie, 'Conversation at Castle Howard – an interview with Miss Annie Wilkinson, laundry maid' in *Costume: the Journal of the Costume Society*, 1969, no. 3.

32 – Fairfax-Blakeborough, John, *Yorkshire village life, humour, and characters*, A. Brown, London, 1955, pp. 148–9.

33 – For advice to the newly servantless household see: Frazer, Lilly Grove, Lady, *First aid to the servantless*, Heffer, Cambridge, 1913; Begbie, Harold, *Life without servants, or the rediscovery of domestic happiness*, Mills and Boon, London, 1916; Peel, Dorothy Constance, *The labour-saving house, by Mrs C. S. Peel*, John Lane, London and New York, 1917; Philips, R. Randal, *The servantless house*, Country Life, London, 1920; Reynolds, N. Clifton, *Easier housework by better equipment*, Country Life, London, 1929; Noble, Mrs Robert, *Labour-saving in the home; a complete guide for the modern housewife*, Macmillan and Eyre and Spottiswoode, London, 1930.

34 – Frazer, *First aid to the servantless*, pp. 90–1, 93–4.

35 – See, for example *The history of Jane Price and Sarah Lightfoot*, [no imprint], London, 1825.

36 – Leadbeater, Mary Shackleton, *Leadbeater Papers*, Bell and Daldy, London, 1862, vol. 1, *The Annals of Ballitore*, p. 194.

37 – Thompson, Flora, *Lark Rise to Candleford*, Oxford University Press, London, 1945, pp. 164–5.

38 – Arch, Joseph, *Joseph Arch, The story of his life, told by himself, and edited with a preface by the Countess of Warwick*, Hutchinson, London, 1898, pp. 9–10.

39 – *A York dialogue between Ned and Harry: or, Ned giving Harry an account of his courtship and marriage state*, [no imprint], p. 15.

40 – Livingstone, Miss F. A. F., 'Household economy and cookery in relation to poverty' in *The new survey of London life and labour edited by Sir Hubert Llewellyn Smith*, King, London, 1934, vol. 6, pp. 332–4.

41 – *A proposal for the due regulating servants, which will be beneficial for the Kingdom in General, and to Private Families in Particular, and no ways obstructive to honest servants, but will furnish a supply of men to recruit the Army*, [no imprint].

42 – Defoe, *The behaviour of servants in England inquired into*, pp. 8–9.

43 – Great Britain, Board of Trade, *Report by Miss Collett*, p. iii.

44 – See, for example, 'Some rules and orders for the government of the house of an earle set downe by Richard Brathwait' (n.d.), printed by R. Triphook, London, 1821, and the bibliography of similar publications contained in *Miscellanea Antiqua Anglicana; or, a select collection of curious tracts, illustrative of the history, literature, manners and biography, of the English nation*, printed for Robert Triphook, London, 1816, and 'A catalogue of the household and family of the Right Honourable Richard Earl of Dorset in the year of our Lord 1613; and so continued until the year 1624, at Knole, in Kent' contained in Sackville-West, Hon. Victoria Mary, *The diary of Lady Anne Clifford with an introductory note by V. Sackville-West*, Heinemann, London, 1923.

45 – Brydges Manuscripts, Huntington Library, Pasadena, California, folio ST44.

46 – Forster, Ann M. C. (ed.), *Selections from The Disbursements Book (1691–1709) of Sir Thomas Haggerston, Bart.*, Surtees Society,

Durham, vol. 180, 1969, p. viii.

47 – Aspinall-Oglander, Cecil Faber, *Admiral's wife. Being the life and letters of the Hon. Mrs Edward Boscawen from 1719 to 1761*, Longman, Green, London, New York, 1940, p. 77.

48 – Macdonald, John (with an introduction by John Beresford), *Memoirs of an eighteenth-century footman: travels (1745–79)*, Routledge, London, 1927, p. 26.

49 – According to J. Huntingford, writing at the end of the eighteenth century, 'The infinite variety of professions, trades and manufactures, joined to the army, navy, and service, leave few men idle, unless from choice: whilst women have ... but few trades, and fewer manufactures to employ them: hence it is, that the general resource of young women is to go to service ...'. (*The Laws of Masters and Servants Considered; with observations on a Bill intended to be offered to Parliament to prevent the forging and counterfeiting of certificates of servants characters ...*, printed for the author, London, 1790, p. 106.)

50 – For further details about the history of the tax, see Dowell, Stephen, *A history of taxation and taxes in England from the earliest times to the year 1885*, Longman, Green, London, 1883, vol. 3, pp. 215–23.

51 – La Rochefoucauld, François Armand Frédéric, duc de, *A Frenchman in England, 1784; being the Mélanges sur l'Angleterre of François de la Rochefoucauld, now edited from the ms. with an introduction by Jean Marchand ... and translated with notes by S. C. Roberts*, The University Press, Cambridge, 1933, p. 25.

52 – Graham, Henry Grey, *Literary and historical essays*, Adam and Charles Black, London, 1908, pp. 40, 143.

53 – Purefoy, *Purefoy Letters, 1735–1753*, vol. 1, pp. 136–7.

54 – Great Britain, Commissioners of Excise, *Appeals relating to the tax on servants; with the opinion of the judges thereon*, printed for Mount and Page, London, 1781, pp. 1–2, 14–15, 22–3.

55 – See, for example: Hannay, James Owen, *The lighter side of Irish life, by George A. Birmingham [pseud.]*, Frederick A. Stokes Company, New York, 1912, p. 230; Callwell, Josephine M., *Old Irish life*, Blackwood, Edinburgh and London, 1912, p. 227.

56 – Conyers, Dorothea, *Sporting reminiscences*, Methuen, London, 1920, p. 131.

57 – McBride, *The domestic revolution*, p. 64.

58 – Butler, Christina Violet, *Domestic Service. An enquiry by the Women's Industrial Council*, Bell, London, 1916, p. 49.

59 – James, A. G. F. Eliot, Mrs, *Our servants. Their duties to us and ours to them*, Ward, Lock, London, 1883.

60 – Buckton, Catherine M., Mrs, *Comfort and cleanliness. The servant and mistress question*, Longman, Green, London, New York and Bombay, 1898, p. 45.

61 – Veritas, Amara, *The Servant Problem: an attempt at its solution by an experienced mistress*, Simpkin, Marshall, London, 1899, p. 178.

62 – Justice, *Solution of the domestic servant problem*, [no imprint], North Shields, 1910.

63 – *The servant problem. Can it be solved? Why not? By an old-established domestic employment agency*, E. R. Alexander and sons, Leyton, 1922.

64 – Ellis, Mrs Havelock, *Democracy in the kitchen*, [no imprint], London, 1894, pp. 5, 13–15.

65 – In 1947, a representative sample of 5,997 British households were asked whether they had any non-resident help (i.e. charwomen) and, if so, the number of hours worked per week. It turned out that 94 per cent had none. Of the 6 per cent that did, 29 per cent had help for 4 hours or less per week, 42 per cent from 5–12 hours per week, and 29 per cent for over 12 hours. A third of households in the highest income bracket had help, compared with 1 per cent in the lowest. More households in the south of England had help than in the Midlands and North. Great Britain, Central Office of Information. Social Survey Division, P. G. Gray, *The British Household. Based on an enquiry carried out in April 1947*, H.M.S.O., London, 1949, appendix II, p. 39.

CHAPTER 9 TIME SPENT ON HOUSEWORK

1 – These are discussed at the end of the chapter, see pp. 191–92.

2 – For some important French investigations of this subject see: Stoetzel, Jean, 'Une etude du Budget-Temps de la femme dans les agglomerations urbaines' in *Population. Revue Trimestrielle*, 1948, pp. 47–62; Girard, Alain, 'Le Budget-Temps de la Femme Mariée dans les agglomerations urbaines' in *Population. Revue Trimestrielle*, 1958, pp. 591–618.

3 – O'Sullivan, Humphrey, *The diary of Humphrey O'Sullivan, Edited, with introduction, translation and notes, by Rev. Michael McGrath*, published for the Irish texts society by Simpkin, Marshall, London, 1936–7, vol. 2, pp. 21–5.

4 – Woodward, Marcus, *The mistress of Stantons Farm ...*, Heath Cranton, London, 1938.

5 – Shaw, Charles, *Manufacturing districts: replies to Lord Ashley, M.P., regarding the education, moral and physical condition of the labouring classes*, J. Ollivier, London, 1842, pp. 19, 26–7;

Gaskell, P., *The manufacturing population of England, its moral, social, and physical conditions, and the changes which have arisen from the use of steam machinery; with an examination of infant labour*, Baldwin and Cradock, London, 1833, p. 109.

6 – Seabrook, Jeremy, *The unprivileged*, Longman, London, 1967, pp. 11–12.

7 – Carlyle, Jane Welsh, *Letters and memorials of Jane Welsh Carlyle. Prepared for publication by Thomas Carlyle, Edited by James Anthony Froude*, George Munro, New York, 1883, *passim*.

8 – Cavendish, Lucy Caroline (Lyttelton), lady, *The diary of Lady Frederick Cavendish, edited by John Bailey* . . . , Frederick A. Stokes Company, New York, 1927, 2 vols.

9 – Evans, Hugh, *The Gorse Glen*, Brython Press, Liverpool, 1948, pp. 14–15.

10 – Shaw, *Manufacturing districts*, pp. 26–7.

11 – Dodd, William, *The factory system illustrated; in a series of letters to the Right Hon. Lord Ashley*, Murray, London, 1842, pp. 63–4.

12 – Blundell, Nicholas, *The great diurnal of Nicholas Blundell of Little Crosby, Lancashire, transcribed and annotated by Frank Tyrer*, Record Society of Lancashire and Cheshire, Chester, 1968–72, vols 1 and 2, *passim*.

13 – Seabrook, *The unprivileged*, pp. 17–18.

14 – Roberts, Robert, *The classic slum. Salford life in the first quarter of the century*, Manchester University Press, Manchester, 1971, p. 36.

15 – Fairfax-Blakeborough, John, *Yorkshire days and Yorkshire ways*, Heath, Cranton, London, 1935, pp. 143–4.

16 – Cross, Eric, *The tailor and Ansty*, Chapman and Hall, London, 1942, pp. 19, 20, 23, 30–2.

17 – Somerville, Mary, *Personal recollections, from early life to old age, of Mary Somerville. With selections from her correspondence. By her daughter, Martha Somerville*, Murray, London, 1873, pp. 17, 21.

18 – Copper, Bob, *A song for every season. A hundred years of a Sussex farming family*, Heinemann, London, 1971, pp. 26–7.

19 – Lawson, John James, *A man's life by Jack Lawson M.P. for Chester-le-Street*, Hodder and Stoughton, London, 1932, pp. 50–1.

20 – Firth, John, *Reminiscences of an Orkney Parish together with old Orkney words, riddles and proverbs*, Orkney natural history society, Stromness, 1974, p. 38.

21 – Marshall, Sybil, *Fenland Chronicle. Recollections of William Henry and Kate Mary Edwards collected and edited by their daughter*, Cambridge University Press, Cambridge, 1967, p. 216.

22 – Andrews, William Linton, *Yorkshire folk: memories of a journalist* . . . , Heath, Cranton, London, 1935, pp. 127–8.

23 – Curtis, Julia, *Mists and monsoons*, Blackie and son limited, London and Glasgow, 1935, p. 44.

24 – Connell, Robert, *St Kilda and the St Kildians*, Hamilton, Adams, London, 1887, pp. 78–80.

25 – Thomas, Maude Morgan, *When I was a girl in Wales*, Lothrop, Lee and Shepard, New York, 1936, pp. 93–4.

26 – *The two wealthy farmers, or, the history of Mr Bragwell*, William Watson and B. Dugdale, Dublin, *c.* 1795, part 3, p. 14.

CHAPTER 10 WOMEN'S ATTITUDES TO HOUSEWORK

1 – Essex, John, *The Young Ladies Conduct: or, Rules for Education under several heads; with instructions upon dress, both before and after marriage. And advice to young wives*, J. Brotherton, London, 1722, pp. xxxiv–xxxv.

2 – The crime of being a scold was unique to women, as were the punishments. (*The Laws respecting women, as they regard their natural rights, or their connections and conduct* . . . , J. Johnson, London, 1777, pp. 21–2.)

3 – For further details about the brank see: Gardiner, Ralph, *Englands Grievance Discovered, in relation to the coal trade; with the map of the River of Tine, and situation of the town and corporation of Newcastle*, originally published in Newcastle in 1655, but reprinted by D. Akenhead and sons, Newcastle, in 1796, p. 117; Plot, Robert, *The natural history of Staffordshire*, printed at the theatre, Oxford, 1686, pp. 389–90; Brand, John, *Observations on the popular antiquities of Great Britain: chiefly illustrating the origin of our vulgar and provincial customs, ceremonies, and superstitions*, F. C. and J. Rivington, London, 1813, p. 108; Dobson, William, *Preston in the olden time; or Illustrations of manners and customs in Preston, in the seventeenth and eighteenth centuries*, Dobson and son, Preston, 1857, p. 25; Harland, John and Wilkinson, T. T., *Lancashire legends, traditions, pageants, sports*, etc., Routledge, London, 1873, p. 166; Guthrie, Ellen Emma, *Old Scottish customs, local and general*, Hamilton, Adams, London, 1885, p. 53; Andrews, William (ed.), *Bygone Cheshire*, Simpkin, Marshall [et al], London, 1895, pp. 242–50; Andrews, William, *Bygone punishments*, Philip Allan, London, 1931, pp. 257–78. (This was first printed in 1899.) Hackwood, Frederick William, *Staffordshire customs, superstitions and folklore*, The "Mercury" Press, Lichfield, 1924, pp. 124–5.

4 – The ducking or cucking-stool is mentioned in the Domesday Survey. According to *The Laws respecting women* (*op. cit.* pp. 21–2), it was also called a trebucket or castigatory. For further details see: Brand, *Observations on the popular antiquities*, pp. 102–8; Dobson, *Preston in the olden time*, pp. 26–7; Harland and Wilkinson, *Lancashire legends*, p. 167; Andrews, *Bygone punishments*, pp. 226–56.

5 – *Simple Simon's Misfortunes: or his wife Margery's outrageous cruelty* [no imprint, *c.* 1750]. For a later version, see: Graham, Douglas, *Comical history of Simple John, and his Twelve Misfortunes* [no imprint, early nineteenth century].

6 – The 1876 Board of Education, for example, identified domestic economy as the most important study for girls.

7 – See, for example: Clarke, Alice, *Working life of women in the seventeenth century*, Routledge, London, 1919; Campbell, R., *The London Tradesman. Being a compendious view of all the trades, professions, arts, both liberal and mechanic, now practiced in the cities of London and Westminster . . .* , T. Gardner, London, 1747; *A general description of all trades, digested in alphabetical order . . .* , T. Waller, London, 1747; *The First Newcastle Directory, 1778, reprinted in facsimile. With an introduction by J. R. Boyle*, Mawson, Swan and Morgan, Newcastle-upon-Tyne, 1889; Roper, John S., *Trades and professions in Wolverhampton, 1802: a directory compiled from the 1802 rate book*, John S. Roper, Wolverhampton, 1969. From 1841, the decennial censuses of England and Wales provide detailed information about the number of men and women in each kind of employment. For a brilliant analysis of women's employment in Victorian times see 'The Adult Woman: Work. Introduction by Leslie Parker Hume and Karen M. Offen' in *Victorian Women. A Documentary Account of Women's Lives in nineteenth-century England, France, and the United States*, edited by Erna Olafson Hellerstein, Leslie Parker Hume, and Karen M. Offen, Stanford University Press, Stanford, 1981.

8 – So far there has not been any comprehensive study of male/female wage differentials, despite the wealth of information on the subject to be found in household and business accounts, local histories, advertisements etc.

9 – Holcombe, Lee 'Victorian wives and property: reform of the married women's property law, 1857–1882' in *A widening sphere. Changing roles of Victorian women* edited by

Martha Vicinus, Indiana University Press, Bloomington and London, 1977.

10 – Layton, David, *Science for the people. The origins of the school science curriculum in England*, Science History Publications, New York, 1973, esp. pp. 29–30.

11 – Russell, Reginald Charles, *Revolution in North Thoresby, Lincolnshire, The enclosure of the parish by Act of Parliament: 1836–1846*, North Thoresby Workers' Association, North Thoresby, 1976, p. 12.

12 – It should also be noted that in the absence of male heirs, women inherited estates in coparcenary. This further reduced their chances of inheriting substantial amounts of capital.

13 – Astell, Mary, *A Serious Proposal to the Ladies For the Advancement of their true and greatest Interest. By a Lover of Her Sex*, printed for R. Wilkin, London, 1694; Wollstonecraft, Mary, *A Vindication of the rights of Women: with strictures on political and moral subjects*, printed for J. Johnson, London, 1792.

14 – One of the best accounts of the struggle for women's suffrage is that by Sylvia Pankhurst. (*The suffragette movement*, Virago Press, London, 1977.)

CONCLUSION

1 – Stoughton Holbourn, Ian Bernard, *The isle of Foula, a series of articles on Britain's loneliest inhabited isle, by the late Professor Ian Bernard Stoughton Holbourn, Laird of Foula for thirty-five years*. Edited, with memoir, by M. C. Stoughton Holbourn, Johnson & Greig, Lerwick, 1938, p. 105; Goodrich-Freer, A., pseud, *Outer Isles*, Constable, Westminster, 1902, p. 199.

2 – Curtis, Julia, *Mists and monsoons*, Blackie, London and Glasgow, 1935, pp. 68–9.

3 – Fairfax-Blakeborough, John, *Yorkshire days and Yorkshire ways*, Heath, Cranton, London, 1935, p. 149.

4 – See introduction to Bradley, Richard, *The Country Housewife and Lady's Director* (1732) by Caroline Davidson, Prospect Books, London, 1980.

5 – Shaw, Charles, *Manufacturing districts: replies to Lord Ashley, M.P., regarding the education, moral and physical condition of the labouring classes*, J. Ollivier, London, 1842, pp. 26–8.

6 – Corley, Thomas Anthony Buchanan, *Domestic electrical appliances*, Cape, London, 1966.

7 – Oakley, Ann, *The sociology of housework*, Martin Robertson, London, 1974 and *Housewife*, Allen Lane, Penguin Books, London, 1974.

List of illustrations

Acknowledgements for the illustrations

British Museum, London: 1, 26, 27, 35, 70, 75, 85, 88, 91, 101, 102, 111, 113. National Gallery of Art, Washington D.C.: 2, 7, 110. Trinity College, Cambridge University: 3. Institute of Agricultural History and Museum of English Rural Life, University of Reading: 4, 8, 14, 52, 53, 93. Library of Congress, Washington D.C.: 5, 6, 13, 25, 31, 32, 33, 34, 36, 46, 49, 58, 74, 80, 83, 84, 86, 92, 112. The Houghton Library, Harvard University (By permission of): 9, 63, 82, 99. Wellcome Institute for the History of Medicine, London (By courtesy of the Wellcome Trustees): 10, 17. Cressida Pemberton-Pigott: 11, 15, 20, 28, 51, 57, 66, 107, 108, 109. Guildhall Library and Art Gallery, London: 12. Colonial Williamsburg Foundation, Colonial Williamsburg: 16, 40, 41, 50, 64, 71, 81, 87, 90, 105, 106. Welsh Folk Museum, St Fagan's, Cardiff: 18, 30. National Library of Medicine, Bethesda: 19. Institution of Electrical Engineers, London: 21. Electrical Association for Women, London: 22, 23, 24, 44, 79. Beamish North of England Open Air Museum, Stanley: 29. John Johnson Collection of Ephemera, Bodleian Library, Oxford: 37, 39, 45, 56, 62, 67, 69, 73, 76, 77, 78, 97, 104. Mrs Edwin Smith: 38. Science Museum, London: 42, 96. British Gas, London: 43. Mary Evans Picture Library, London: 47, 48. Ulster Folk and Transport Museum, Holywood: 54, 55. British Library, London: 59, 60, 95, 98, 103. Mr Emyr Estyn Evans: 61. Schillay & Rehs, Inc, New York: 65. The Milne Museum, Tonbridge: 68. Mr Eurwyn William: 72. The Royal Library, Windsor Castle (Reproduced by gracious permission of Her Majesty the Queen): 89. Tate Gallery, London: 94. The Queen's Picture Collection, St James's Palace, London (Reproduced by gracious permission of Her Majesty the Queen): 100.

Index